Organizational Behaviour in Healthcare

Published in co-operation with the Society for Studies in Organizing Healthcare (SHOC), this series has two strands, the first of which consists of specially selected papers taken from the biennial conferences held by SHOC that present a cohesive and focused insight into issues within the field of organizational behaviour in healthcare.

The series also encourages proposals for monographs and edited collections to address the additional and emergent topics in the field of health policy, organization and management. Books within the series aim to advance scholarship on the application of social science theories, methods and concepts to the study of organizing and managing healthcare services and systems.

Providing a new platform for advanced and engaged scholarship, books in the series will advance the academic community by fostering a deep analysis on the challenges for healthcare organizations and management with an explicitly international and comparative focus.

All book proposals and manuscript submissions are single blind peer reviewed. All chapters in contributed volumes are double blind peer reviewed. For more information on Palgrave Macmillan's peer review policy please visit our website: https://www.palgrave.com/gp/book-authors/your-career/early-career-researcher-hub/peer-review-process

To submit a book proposal for inclusion in this series please contact Liz Barlow for further information: liz.barlow@palgrave.com. For information on the book proposal process please visit this website: https://www.palgrave.com/gp/book-authors/publishing-guidelines/submit-a-proposal

More information about this series at
http://www.palgrave.com/gp/series/14724

Roman Kislov • Diane Burns
Bjørn Erik Mørk • Kathleen Montgomery
Editors

Managing Healthcare Organisations in Challenging Policy Contexts

palgrave
macmillan

Editors
Roman Kislov
Manchester Metropolitan University
Manchester, UK

The University of Manchester
Manchester, UK

Bjørn Erik Mørk
BI Norwegian Business School
Oslo, Norway

Diane Burns
University of Sheffield
Sheffield, UK

Kathleen Montgomery
University of California, Riverside
Riverside, CA, USA

University of Sydney
Camperdown, NSW, Australia

ISSN 2662-1045 ISSN 2662-1053 (electronic)
Organizational Behaviour in Healthcare
ISBN 978-3-030-81092-4 ISBN 978-3-030-81093-1 (eBook)
https://doi.org/10.1007/978-3-030-81093-1

This Palgrave Macmillan imprint is published by the registered company Springer Nature Switzerland AG.
The registered company address is: Gewerbestrasse 11, 6330 Cham, Switzerland

This book is dedicated to all health and social care practitioners, managers and researchers contributing to the global response to the ongoing Covid-19 pandemic.

Preface

This book provides a historical record of the event that never happened.

The 12th Organisational Behaviour in Health Care (OBHC 2020) Conference was scheduled to take place in Manchester, UK, in April 2020. The conference theme—'Managing Healthcare Organisations in Challenging Policy Contexts: Integration or Fragmentation?'—was inspired by the pioneering role of Greater Manchester in implementing devolved arrangements for the provision of health and social care. The aim of the conference was twofold. First, we intended to explore how contemporary policy trends, infused with internal tensions and contradictions, are influencing healthcare systems, organisations, and professions. Second, we aimed to examine the various ways in which policy implementation could be enacted, resisted, and reinvented by healthcare managers and professionals on the ground.

Over 120 delegates from 15 countries had registered for the conference by mid-March 2020. The conference programme had been finalised, and Manchester Art Gallery had been chosen as a conference dinner venue. The Covid-19 pandemic was, however, starting to engulf the world. Employers and national governments were imposing travel restrictions, and many colleagues were no longer able to attend the conference or became increasingly concerned about doing so. The number of people testing positive for the virus in the UK was rising, and the UK government introduced social distancing measures, including restrictions on non-essential travel and social gatherings. The organising committee had no choice but to cancel the conference.

OBHC is a flagship biennial event of the UK-based Society for Studies in Organising Healthcare (SHOC), and there is an established tradition of publishing the best conference contributions in a series of edited volumes. Despite the cancellation of the conference and the global disruption caused by the pandemic—a very challenging context indeed!—we were determined to maintain this tradition. This is how this book came about. It brings together 12 important contributions that were developed from the original submissions accepted for presentation at OBHC 2020. In different ways, these contributions speak to the questions raised by the conference theme, providing a snapshot of cutting-edge research into managing healthcare organisations in challenging policy contexts.

This book would have been impossible without all the preparatory work that went into planning OBHC 2020. We are grateful to Janet Adnams for administrative support; to Aoife McDermott and Mark Exworthy for continuous advice; to Ruth Boaden, Damian Hodgson, and other members of the Organising Committee for contributing to all aspects of conference planning; and to members of the SHOC community for acting as peer reviewers. We would also like to thank Liz Barlow and Md Saif for overseeing the publication process, and all our contributors for their responsiveness and cooperation. Finally, we are greatly indebted to all those health and social care professionals, managers, and service users who acted as research participants for the empirical studies included in this book.

Manchester, UK — Roman Kislov
Sheffield, UK — Diane Burns
Oslo, Norway — Bjørn Erik Mørk
Riverside, CA, USA — Kathleen Montgomery

Contents

Notes on Contributors

Jeffrey Braithwaite is Founding Director of the Australian Institute of Health Innovation, Director of the Centre for Healthcare Resilience and Implementation Science, Professor of Health Systems Research, Macquarie University, Australia, and President of the International Society for Quality in Health Care (ISQua). His research examines the changing nature of health systems. He is particularly interested in healthcare as a complex adaptive system and applying complexity science to healthcare problems.

Jackie Bridges is Professor of Older People's Care at the University of Southampton, UK. Her research focuses on healthcare systems and workforce, particularly nursing, examining the organisational conditions in which health workers are able to deliver responsive, high-quality care to older people with complex needs.

Diane Burns is Senior Lecturer in Organisation Studies at Sheffield University Management School, University of Sheffield, and Deputy Chair of the Society for Studies in Organising Healthcare. She conducts research into organisational processes and outcomes in health and social care, particularly the organisation and management of social care. Her research focuses on issues of job and care quality, commodification of social care, organisational abuse and failure, social care innovation and sustainability. Many of her articles have been published in leading academic journals, and her research has received funding from the Department of Health, the Economic and Social Research Council (ESRC) and the Wellcome Trust. She serves on the Leadership Group of the Sustainable Care Research Programme funded by the ESRC.

Naomi Chambers is Professor of Health Management at Alliance Manchester Business School, University of Manchester. Chambers has a range of teaching, advisory and research interests including healthcare leadership, organisation culture, diversity and inclusion, board governance, healthcare commissioning, health policy and management in Europe, and patient and public involvement.

Kate Churruca is a research fellow in the Complexity Science stream of the Centre for Healthcare Resilience and Implementation Science, within the Australian Institute of Health Innovation at Macquarie University. Her research seeks to assess organisational culture in healthcare and understand its impact on safety and quality of patient care.

Sue Dopson is Professor of Organisational Behaviour, Fellow of Green Templeton College and Deputy Dean of Saïd Business School. Dopson's research lies in the area of innovation, change and healthcare studies. She has led a number of research projects in the health service sector. These include the evaluation of work aimed at improving clinical effectiveness, exploring evidence-based medicine, developing the skills of healthcare managers and investigating the changing role of healthcare assistants within the NHS workforce. More recent research has focused on women's leadership.

Louise A. Ellis is a research fellow in the Centre for Healthcare Resilience and Implementation Science, within the Australian Institute of Health Innovation at Macquarie University. She is part of the Complex Systems Research Stream, using a complexity lens to approach issues of quality and safety in the delivery of healthcare. Her specific areas of expertise are mental health services, organisational culture and systems, and implementation science.

Mark Exworthy is Professor of Health Policy and Management at the Health Services Management Centre, University of Birmingham. His research interests include professional-managerial relations (especially in relation to medical performance), managerialism, NHS commissioning, and policy implementation. Exworthy is also Chair of Society for Studies in Organising Healthcare (SHOC).

Ewan Ferlie is Professor of Public Services Management at King's Business School, King's College London. He has written and published widely on healthcare and higher education organisations and is co-editor of the *Oxford Handbook of Health Care Management*. He was elected as Fellow of the British Academy (FBA) in 2016. He is a founding member, former chairman and former trustee of the Society for Studies in Organising Health Care (SHOC).

Mara Gorli, PhD is Associate Professor of Work and Organisational Psychology at the Faculty of Economics, Catholic University of Milan, Italy. She is also a member of the Leadership and Organisational Cultures Area at CERISMAS, Centre for Research and Studies in Health Care Management, Catholic University of Milan. Her approach in studying organisations is closely linked to reflexive and participative research processes. Her main research focuses on the phenomena of knowing and learning in organisations, with a specific action-oriented and relational approach.

Damian Hodgson is Professor of Organisation Studies at the Management School at the University of Sheffield with broad interests in power, knowledge, identity and control in complex organisations. His recent research has focused on primary care reorganisation, access to care and continuity of care, skill mix and workforce transformation, and the integration of health and care.

Roman Kislov is Reader in Organisation Studies and Director of the Decent Work and Productivity Research Centre in Manchester Metropolitan University, an Honorary Senior Research Fellow at the University of Manchester and a Deputy Lead for Implementation Science in the National Institute for Health Research Applied Research Collaboration (NIHR ARC) Greater Manchester. He conducts qualitative research on the processes and practices of knowledge mobilisation, with a particular interest in communities of practice, intermediary roles, organisational learning and implementation of change. His work crosses disciplinary boundaries between organisation studies, public administration and health services research. It has recently appeared *in Public Administration Review, Organization Studies, Public Administration, Public Management Review, Implementation Science* and *BMJ Quality and Safety*.

Janet C. Long is a senior research fellow in the Centre for Healthcare Resilience and Implementation Science, within the Australian Institute of Health Innovation at Macquarie University. Long is a health systems researcher with interests and expertise in social and professional networks, knowledge translation and implementation science. She has a clinical background as a registered nurse (16 years) and a science background in ecology (7 years). Her passion is studying social interactions and influences within healthcare using social network theory and methodology.

Kristiana Ludlow is Postdoctoral Research Fellow at the Centre for Health Systems and Safety Research, Australian Institute for Health Innovation, Macquarie University, Australia. She is passionate about psychology and aged care research, particularly patient- and family-centred care, care prioritisation and unfinished/missed care. She is experienced in qualitative research methods and Q-methodology.

Russell Mannion, PhD, FRSA, FAcSS holds the chair in Health Systems at the University of Birmingham and is Honorary Professor at the Australian Institute for Health Innovation, Macquarie University. He has over 300 peer-reviewed publications, many in leading journals such as *The Lancet*, *BMJ*, *Social Science and Medicine*, and *The Milbank Quarterly*. He has authored or edited 12 books and was recipient of the Baxter European book award.

Ninna Meier is Associate Professor of Organisational Sociology at Department of Sociology and Social Work at Aalborg University, Denmark. She is a qualitative researcher, who has studied organisation and management of healthcare work in the Danish public healthcare system since 2009. She has published on clinical managerial work, coordination in clinical settings and leadership practices in healthcare, and is the co-editor of a recent book, *Context in Action and How to Study It: Illustrations from Healthcare*, with Sue Dopson. More resent research has focused on relational aspects of work, integrated care across sector boundaries and inter-organisational collaboration.

Claire Mitchell is a senior clinical lecturer on the Speech and Language Therapy degree programme at the University of Manchester. Her clinical health research and Cochrane reviews include working collaboratively with patient and public involvement. This research, as well as her 20 years of clinical experience in the NHS, has led to an interest in healthcare organisation, and she has researched integration of health and social care in the North West of England.

Sassy Molyneux is Professor of Global Health at the University of Oxford, and a senior researcher at the KEMRI-Wellcome Trust Research Programme in Kenya. She is a multidisciplinary researcher with a background in human geography and behavioural studies. Research areas span health policy and systems research (system governance, financing and responsiveness to patients and the public) and empirical ethics, including the everyday ethics of frontline health provision and of conducting studies in resource-poor settings.

Kathleen Montgomery is Professor of the Graduate Division and Emerita Professor of Organisations and Management at the University of California, Riverside; for many years she also has served as Honorary Associate at Sydney Health Ethics. She is a Fellow of the Academy of Social Sciences. She is Past-Chair of the Health Care Management Division at the Academy of Management and is a recipient of the Division's Myron D. Fottler Exceptional Service Award. Her PhD in sociology is from New York University, where she began her research on the medical profession and relationships between professionals and their environment. Her research focuses on trust, conflicts of interest and research integrity. Her work has been published in leading academic journals and books, and she has co-edited several books on healthcare management and healthcare professionals, including Palgrave's 2013 *Patient-Centered Health Care.*

Simon Moralee is Senior Lecturer in Healthcare Management and Deputy Director for MSc Healthcare Leadership (NHS Leadership Academy's Elizabeth Garrett Anderson Programme). He previously worked as a manager in the UK NHS before embarking on an academic career in 2007. He was awarded his PhD in 2016 for a study into institutional change in medical education. His British Academy of Management–funded research is exploring the development of medical leadership in the UK.

Rosemary Morgan is on faculty at the Johns Hopkins Bloomberg School of Public Health in the Department of International Health. She has expertise in gender, gender analysis and intersectionality and works as a gender advisor on multiple global health and health systems projects. She holds a PhD in International Health and Development from the University of Leeds.

Bjørn Erik Mørk is Professor of Innovation at BI Norwegian Business School. He is Research Center Leader for the Centre for Healthcare Management and Program Director for Healthcare Management at BI. The latter role includes responsibility for the National Education in Leadership and Innovation for the Primary Healthcare Services, and for the National Top Management Program for primary and specialist care. Furthermore, he is Honorary Associate Professor at IKON Research Centre, Warwick Business School (UK). When studying healthcare, he draws upon practice-based approaches to innovation, the development and use of new technologies, boundary work, cross-disciplinary collaboration, power and learning. His articles have appeared in journals such as *Academy of Management Annals*, *Human Relations*, *Social Science and Medicine*, *Management Learning* and *Journal of Health Organization and Management*. He has co-authored one methodology book and is co-authoring a book on practice-based perspectives on innovation (both with Cappelen Damm Akademisk).

Kui Muraya is a gender and health systems researcher at the KEMRI-Wellcome Trust Research Programme, Kenya. More recently she was a co-principal investigator in a multi-country study exploring gender and leadership within health systems in Kenya, Nigeria and South Africa. She has expertise in gender, gender analysis, intersectionality and qualitative research and an increasing interest in decolonising global health. She holds a PhD in Health and Social Care.

Marta Piria is a PhD student in Psychology at the Catholic University of Milan, Italy. She collaborates with the Leadership and Organisational Cultures Area at CERISMAS, Centre for Research and Studies in Health Care Management, Catholic University of Milan. Her research interests lie in knowledge sharing and relational processes in multiprofessional and multidisciplinary work groups. She is particularly interested in supporting groups in identifying and dealing with critical issues and differences through co-creating common processes of understanding and learning.

Chiara Pomare is a postdoctoral research fellow in the Centre for Healthcare Resilience and Implementation Science, within the Australian Institute of Health Innovation at Macquarie University. Her research interests include health systems, network science, complexity science and organisational change in healthcare. Pomare's PhD explored the experiences of staff and patients during a large-scale organisational change in an Australian hospital redevelopment.

Catherine Pope is Professor of Medical Sociology at the Nuffield Department of Primary Care Health Sciences, University of Oxford, where she co-directs the Medical Sociology and Health Experiences Research Group. Her research focuses on the organisation and delivery of primary, urgent and emergency care, notably the work and workforce for this care and the impact of digital technologies.

Ronnie Ramlogan is Senior Lecturer at Alliance Manchester Business School, University of Manchester. He is affiliated with the Innovation, Strategy and Sustainability division and Manchester Institute of Innovation Research.

Crispen Sachikonye is a researcher in the Innovation Management and Policy Division at Alliance Manchester Business School, University of Manchester. He is an associate tutor on the Elizabeth Anderson Garrett programme for the NHS Leadership Academy. His research focuses on the governance of non-profit organisations.

Giuseppe Scaratti is Full Professor of Work and Organisational Psychology at the Department of Human and Social Sciences, University of Bergamo, Italy. His research interests include the study of knowing, learning, reflexivity and change in organisations; qualitative methodologies for the study of organisational life and evaluation and assessment of complex and transformative actions. He is also the coordinator of the Leadership and Organisational Cultures Area at CERISMAS, Centre for Research and Studies in Health Care Management, Catholic University of Milan, and a founding member of the TRAILab (Transformative Actions Interdisciplinary Laboratory).

Ewen Speed, PhD is Professor of Medical Sociology in the School of Health and Social Care at the University of Essex. His research is focused on the interface between government and citizens in the provision of health and social care. He has published widely on the role of populism in health policy and on processes of participation and democratic involvement in health and social care.

Abigail Tazzyman is Lecturer in Qualitative Research Methods at the Sheffield Methods Institute at the University of Sheffield. Taking an interdisciplinary approach, her research interests focus on organisation studies, inequalities and medical sociology/health services research and their intersection. Her recent work has focused on gender and organisations, professionalism, power and identity, regulation, workforce transformation, and the integration of health and care.

Johanna Westbrook is Professor and Director, Centre for Health Systems and Safety Research, Australian Institute of Health Innovation, Macquarie University. She is internationally recognised for her research in patient safety and evaluating the effects of information and communication technology in healthcare. This work includes examining how IT systems can be used to integrate older adults' assessments of their quality of life and support the monitoring and delivery of improved aged care services.

Katie Willocks is a research associate at Manchester Metropolitan University working within the Centre for Decent Work and Productivity as part of the Good Employment Learning Lab project. Her research interests lie in the area of theories of practice, leadership learning and leadership development. Willocks has worked extensively with healthcare organisations, and her PhD explored organisational change and learning in the NHS. Subsequent projects have explored leadership development and employee wellbeing as well as medical leadership.

Zahra Zeinali is a medical doctor and public health researcher from Iran. She conducted the research study included in this volume as a Master of Public Health student at the Johns Hopkins Bloomberg School of Public Health. At the time of publication, she is a researcher with Global Health 50/50 and a fellow with the Rockefeller Foundation-Boston University 3D Commission on Health Determinants, Data and Decision-making.

List of Figures

List of Tables

1

Managing Healthcare Organisations in Challenging Policy Contexts: Connections and Contradictions

Roman Kislov, Diane Burns, Bjørn Erik Mørk, and Kathleen Montgomery

Setting the Scene

What makes contemporary policy contexts 'challenging'? How do these challenges play out in the process of policy implementation in healthcare organisations? How do healthcare leaders and other stakeholders respond to the resulting complexities, tensions, and contradictions? Even though these questions seem logically related, they are rarely considered together, with potential answers often scattered across different publications and

R. Kislov (✉)
Manchester Metropolitan University, Manchester, UK

The University of Manchester, Manchester, UK
e-mail: r.kislov@mmu.ac.uk

D. Burns
University of Sheffield, Sheffield, UK
e-mail: d.burns@sheffield.ac.uk

R. Kislov et al. (eds.), *Managing Healthcare Organisations in Challenging Policy Contexts*, Organizational Behaviour in Healthcare,
https://doi.org/10.1007/978-3-030-81093-1_1

scientific disciplines. This volume aspires to contribute to rectifying this omission. Our overarching purpose is to shed light on the complex web of connections that exist between the macro level of policy development, the meso level of policy implementation, and the micro level of interpersonal relationships within organisations, whereby managers and leaders of healthcare organisations are trying their best to make sense of—and succeed in—this complex multi-layered context.

Our introductory chapter starts with articulating the rationale for adopting this approach. This is followed by a brief overview of extant literature aiming to crystallise the three overarching themes: (1) excesses, tensions, and inconsistencies of contemporary policy contexts; (2) translation of policy into practice in complex boundary landscapes; and (3) leadership strategies in challenging policy contexts. The final section briefly summarises the contributions of the twelve chapters constituting this collection, which are divided into three parts broadly corresponding to the themes outlined above. Overall, it would be too ambitious to claim that this introduction provides an exhaustive overview of the literature addressing the questions posed in the very beginning. Instead, our aim here is to selectively illuminate some of the ongoing debates that are of relevance to this edited collection, setting the scene for what follows.

Multi-layered, Dynamic, and Actor-Dependent Nature of Policy Contexts

Why consider policy development, policy implementation, and organisational leadership together? First, macro, meso, and micro levels of context are intertwined, and the resulting influence is exerted through

B. E. Mørk
BI Norwegian Business School, Oslo, Norway
e-mail: bjorn.e.mork@bi.no

K. Montgomery
University of California, Riverside, Riverside, CA, USA

University of Sydney, Camperdown, NSW, Australia
e-mail: kmont@ucr.edu

complex integrated configurations of multiple factors originating at different levels (Dopson et al., 2008; Ferlie & Shortell, 2001). Macro-level factors acting at the policymaking level exercise significant influence both on the broader supra-organisational landscape and on individual organisations, in which policies are supposed to be implemented. Second, translation of policy into practice is iterative rather than linear, with policy formulation, policy adoption, and policy implementation being mutually inter-related, rather than operating as distinct, neatly separated or strictly sequential stages (Campos & Reich, 2019; Candel & Biesbroek, 2016). Finally, organisational leaders do not always act as passive recipients of policies or as silent victims of contextual constraints. They often have a significant influence on policy implementation by choosing which aspects of policy context to bring into organisational discourses and practices and, through adopting a range of strategies, by actively shaping the context (Dopson et al., 2008; Fitzgerald et al., 2002).

Prior to examining these arguments in more detail, it is useful to provide an empirical example from a recent study of policy implementation in English primary care (Checkland, 2018). At the macro level, government sought to reduce resistance to policy reform by setting conditions in which actors were incentivised to behave in ways consonant with policy objectives, whilst perceiving themselves to be acting autonomously. The resulting absence of clear guidelines led meso-level actors to come up with a system of shifting and ambiguous rules which enabled some degree of policy entrepreneurship and situated agency. At the micro level of individual general practices, financial incentives were quite influential in governing behaviour, but they were neither a necessary nor a sufficient condition. Some aspects of policy were still eagerly embraced by general practitioners, even if they were not incentivised directly but offered a promise of elevated professional standing and power. This study vividly illustrates the complex interplay between different levels of context and various groups of actors in an iterative and dynamic policy process.

Excesses, Tensions, and Inconsistencies of Contemporary Policy Contexts

Demographic transitions, changes in demand, global pandemics, and technological progress are external contingencies that find their reflection in healthcare policies. The operation of these forces is accompanied by general tendencies towards codification and formalisation of information in virtually all aspects of our social and working lives, resulting in the proliferation of policies, protocols, and procedures at the international, national, regional, and organisational levels (Kislov et al., 2019; Turner et al., 2014). Different clinical professions, interest groups, and sectors of healthcare are competing for their voices to be heard and translated into policy. In the context of chronically constrained resources, however, not all policies will be implemented as intended (Robinson et al., 2012; Hipgrave et al., 2014). One of the challenges for actors operating in contemporary policy is, therefore, having to deal with multiple policies that, whilst seeking to regulate different aspects of healthcare delivery, are competing for attention, resources, and a top position on the implementation agenda.

To make things even more complicated, the seemingly never-ending nature of public sector reforms, which have been aptly described by some commentators as repeated 'redisorganisation' (Smith et al., 2001), lead to constant shifts in policy priorities (Martin et al., 2012). An initiative that was 'a flavour of the month' yesterday can become 'an old hat' tomorrow. These fads and fashions are often underpinned by shifts in the underlying, ideologically driven governance regimes. An international ideology of *New Public Management* (NPM) has had a profound influence on health policy over four decades. Its main aim is to increase the effectiveness of public services through managerial means, such as introduction of quasi-markets and competition into the public sector, transparent measurement of performance against centrally set targets, and establishment of arm's-length agencies responsible for commissioning, regulating, and monitoring healthcare delivery (Diefenbach, 2009; Ferlie & McGivern, 2014; Ferlie et al., 2009). Since the late 1990s, however, some of the unintended consequences of earlier NPM reforms, such as the fragmentation of the state, have led to the rise of governance networks, also referred to as *New Public Governance* (NPG), promoting the development of collaboration, integration, and horizontal ties between agencies (Dickinson, 2016; Osborne, 2010; Klijn, 2012; Ferlie et al., 2011).

In practice, NPM and NPG are closely intertwined, manifesting in hybrid policy contexts characterised by a complex overlay of different governance arrangements (Dickinson, 2016; Klijn, 2012). In the UK, distinct healthcare policy streams based on networks, hierarchies, and markets have accumulated over time, or 'sedimented', often resulting in 'networked hierarchies', with markets and formal networks being used by the state to conceal and bolster central control (Jones, 2018). It is therefore hardly surprising that these policy contexts are imbued with tensions and ambiguities. Some of them stem from contradictions *within* the (still-dominant) NPM doctrine, such as the tension between gaining control over bureaucracies and achieving managerial empowerment, or the challenge of improving performance and quality while saving costs (Klijn, 2012). There are also incompatibilities *between* the concurrently applied NPM and NPG paradigms, such as market-based competition versus network collaboration, business instruments versus facilitation of interaction and learning, and central steering versus horizontal coordination. These dilemmas are resolved in different ways in different settings (Bevir & Waring, 2018), resulting in a varied landscape that features elements of both fragmentation and integration, which inevitably affects the process of translating policy into practice.

Translation of Policy into Practice in Complex Boundary Landscapes

Policy process unfolds in complex multi-stakeholder contexts, represented by a range of individual and collective actors, such as government agencies, professional associations, commissioners, providers, regulators, service users, and, particularly in low- and middle-income countries, financial donors (Campos & Reich, 2019). Whilst there is a great degree of mutual dependence between actors, they vary in the amount of power and resources; they also may have very diverse views, logics, and interests. These differences are further reinforced by—and themselves contribute to the maintenance of—existing organisational and institutional structures, resulting in persistent silo-working and resistance to cross-boundary collaboration across professions and organisations (Kislov, 2014). In federal states and countries with strong devolved arrangements, regionalisation adds an extra layer of complexity by blurring the lines of accountability and inserting additional levels of decision-making, whilst potentially enabling place-based reconfiguration and integration of services (Checkland et al., 2015; Schuurmans et al., 2021). Boundary work—maintaining, crossing, and reconfiguring multiple types of boundaries described above —therefore forms an essential part of everyday practices performed by healthcare occupations, professions, and organisations (Langley et al., 2019; Bucher et al., 2016).

Policy implementation in such landscapes is iterative, asynchronous, and non-linear. It is fraught with discrepancies, time lags, and compromises as different actors make partial moves towards implementation (Candel & Biesbroek, 2016). Crucially, policies can fail when frontline staff feel that they have limited influence on policy implementation, when policy is meaningless to them or when it provides only the 'recipe' without specifying 'ingredients' or 'skills' required to make things work (Tucker et al., 2021; Gkeredakis et al., 2011). Policy implementation is therefore contingent on active involvement of practitioners, who treat policy as but one of the many sources of knowledge that needs to be adjusted to local concerns. Such policies can succeed only if 'instrumentalised' as a practical resource (Tsoukas & Vladimirou, 2001; Gkeredakis et al., 2011; Gabbay & le May, 2004), often through the discretion of frontline professionals known as 'street-level bureaucrats' (Tucker et al., 2021). Policy implementation and policy development overlap, and implementation can even reshape statutory policy (Campos & Reich, 2019).

As a result, policies rarely, if ever, get implemented as initially intended. First, every system of purposive action has unwanted side effects (Linstead et al., 2014), and even successful policy is no exception. For instance, repackaging original policies into usable protocols, checklists, and other shortcuts enables context-tailored application and integration with other sources of knowledge but may also lead to dilution or distortion of the original message (Kislov et al., 2019). Second, due to inherent policy inconsistencies and ambiguities described in the previous section, some aspects of the policy tend to become more prominent during the process of implementation to the detriment of others. Results-based reforms, for example, usually prioritise formal metrics, tools, and procedures over the development of learning-oriented organisational cultures, which threatens double-loop learning and sustainability of change even if short-term goals are met (Moynihan, 2005; Kislov et al., 2017a). Finally, sometimes the context is 'stronger' than the policy initiative itself. For example, initiatives aiming to improve collaboration across boundaries may, somewhat paradoxically, fall victim to the same formidable institutional forces they were aiming to address, reproducing existing barriers and distinctions and creating new ones (Kislov, 2014; Martin et al., 2009).

Leadership Strategies in Challenging Policy Contexts

So how do managers and leaders of healthcare organisations navigate these complex landscapes? Given the complexity and variability of factors described above, it is perhaps unsurprising that healthcare literature contains examples both of manipulative actors using policy implementation process to advance their own agendas (Greenaway et al., 2007) and of relatively benign post-bureaucratic leadership styles (Ferlie et al., 2011). The latter often takes the form of collective team-based leadership, also referred to as leadership with 'nobody in charge' (Buchanan et al., 2007). This collective, distributed approach is particularly suitable for complex multi-stakeholder contexts following the network principle of organising, where no one party can unilaterally and *a priori* define the nature and quality of public service delivery (Klijn & Koppenjan, 2015). As this mode of organising is based around negotiation and favours soft rules over hard laws (Torfing, 2012), significant political astuteness is vital when dealing with conflicting values espoused by different stakeholders and creating sufficient consensus to achieve goals (Dickinson et al., 2011; Reeleder et al., 2006).

Collective leadership in healthcare normally involves a high degree of engagement from health professionals drawn into managerial roles (Ferlie et al., 2011; Denis et al., 2001), not least due to the fact that shared cultural and institutional structures help clinical leaders enrol colleagues in policy implementation (Oborn et al., 2013). This requires a cadre of clinical-managerial hybrids occupying leadership positions at different levels of healthcare governance who, through their simultaneous membership in different communities of practice, are playing an important boundary spanning role between multiple stakeholder groups (Montgomery, 2001; Llewellyn, 2001; Kislov et al., 2016). Experiences of hybridity, however, vary across professional groups and organisational settings and are not without challenges. Hybrid nurse-managers, for instance, have been shown to experience significant identity conflicts whilst not being seen as 'proper managers' or 'proper nurses' by their peers, which can potentially limit their effectiveness as leaders (Croft et al., 2015). By contrast, some physician managers act as 'willing hybrids' who manage to successfully align and legitimate professionalism with its managerial context, positioning themselves collectively as an influential professional elite (McGivern et al., 2015).

Whilst legitimating and enacting change requires a range of economic, social, and cultural forms of capital (Kislov et al., 2017b), one should not underestimate the importance of rhetorical devices, discursive strategies, narratives, and stories in this process (Sanders & Harrison, 2008; Suddaby & Greenwood, 2005; Bevir & Waring, 2018). Elite policy narratives constructed by policymakers are received, filtered, and negotiated through the sense-making and framing practices of organisational leaders operating in the context of their own local structural and cultural arrangements (Waring et al., 2020). The emergent, pluralistic, and inconsistent nature of policy landscapes can be creatively exploited by local actors, who can choose from a range of sense-making devices (Rowland et al., 2021), justification strategies (Jansson et al., 2021), or evaluative principles (Schuurmans et al., 2021) to form their own local narratives and enact them in their organisations. Different 'parallel frames' may emerge as a result, reflecting diverse interpretations of policy and the localised agendas of stakeholders (Waring et al., 2020). Although these local narratives may end up being internally inconsistent and at odds with one another, they help healthcare managers and leaders exercise their agency, finding ways of surviving—and thriving—in challenging policy contexts.

Structure and Composition of the Edited Volume

Our argument in this introductory chapter has been as follows: multi-layered pluralist healthcare policy contexts are imbued with ambiguities, inconsistencies, and tensions. Translation of policy into practice is iterative, asynchronous, and non-linear. It unfolds in complex multi-stakeholder boundary landscapes which are rife with contestation and which can transform the original policy beyond recognition. Managers and leaders of healthcare organisations, mobilising their hybrid boundary spanning roles and deploying a range of discursive strategies, often manage to use these features of challenging policy contexts to their advantage by playing on multiple contradictions when crafting and enacting their narratives. This may lead to further pluralisation of discourse and significant variation in how different aspects of the policy process are experienced and enacted by different stakeholder groups operating in different settings.

The twelve chapters included in this edited volume showcase this variability. They represent a range of settings, such as hospitals, integrated health and social care initiatives, policy networks, and international charities, located in both high-income (Australia, Italy, and the UK) and low- and middle-income countries. They let us gain an in-depth understanding of some of the narratives and strategies deployed by government policymakers, health and social care professionals, and organisational leaders, as well as learn about the experiences of service users positioned on the receiving end of the policy process. In addition to original empirical research drawing on questionnaires, content analysis, interviews, or observation, the collection includes literature reviews and narrative case studies based on secondary data. A broad range of theoretical approaches are deployed, including theories of governance, literature on boundary work, Laclau's theory of populism, the leadership-as-practice approach, and the intersectionality lens. The twelve contributions illuminate, refine, or problematise different aspects of our overarching argument and are organised in three sections. Their detailed summaries are presented below.

Part I: Analysing Contemporary Policy Contexts

In Chapter 2, which opens this section, Ferlie delves into the long-standing debate in British public policy studies about whether the traditional, centralised model of unitary decision-making (referred to as the 'Westminster and Whitehall' model) is being replaced by a looser and more pluralist model of decision-making with dispersed actors (referred to as 'network governance'). To illustrate the elements of the debate, Ferlie presents some key examples of health policymaking over the past twenty years, drawing on signature pieces of legislation (the 2000 National Health Service Plan and the 2012 Health and Social Care Act). He then focuses on the development of the regional-level Academic Health Science Networks in the English National Health Service (NHS) to analyse the growing involvement of non-civil-service actors, including life scientists, management consultants, charitable foundations, and commercial industries, in developing and implementing health policy and research. Ferlie notes, 'The explicit reframing of the National Health Service here as a driver of national and international industrial investment and growth, and its repositioning as an influential macro purchaser of innovation in an internationally competitive arena, is significant'. Nevertheless, it is difficult to assess the extent to which these non-civil-service actors will continue to influence the Department of Health or the NHS, and there is variation across the four nations of the UK. Ferlie concludes that, while there is evidence of greater pluralisation, this may take the form of a 'relatively narrow opening' to a contained range of knowledge elites.

In Chapter 3, Speed and Mannion tackle a similar question to Ferlie, that of shifts in health policymaking, especially as they can reflect different models of governance and political ideology. These authors pose the question from the perspective of how a move towards more right-wing populism has been co-opted by government to bring about health policy changes. Speed and Mannion frame their chapter with a rich background discussion conceptualising populism as a 'logic of equivalence' (that seeks to join disparate groups against a 'common enemy'—e.g., the professional elite). To illustrate their analysis, the authors present a case study of a proposed change in the working practice of junior doctors, which shifted their working hours to a more onerous seven-day schedule. Questionable data showing a heightened 'weekend mortality effect' were used to justify the proposed policy change. In so doing, this argument created a logic of equivalence between politicians and patients, allied against the excesses of a 'lazy elite', placing their own vested interests above those of patients and contributing to unnecessary deaths. Despite a strong pushback by the medical profession that flawed data were used to justify this policy change, and despite a strike action by junior doctors, the government won the debate. This case demonstrates how a populist approach succeeded in positioning the profession as an 'outgroup' and established a new set of boundaries between doctors, government, and patients. Speed and Mannion argue that populism was successfully used by government actors not necessarily to advance a political ideology, so much as a tactic to achieve a desired policy change.

In Chapter 4, Ludlow, Bridges, Pope, Westbrook, and Braithwaite examine the efficacy of policy recommendations for the integration of older adults' care in Australian and English contexts. Through an investigation of those who formulate policy at the 'blunt end' and those who spend time making the system work at the 'sharp end', these authors compare and contrast the ways in which policymakers advocate for integrated care and the work unpaid carers do to achieve care coordination for older family members. Ludlow and colleagues frame their chapter with a rich background discussion of the discontinuity across services and systems and the various roles of informal carers—typically daughters—in ensuring their family members do not fall between the cracks. The authors use an automated content analysis to map prominent concepts, themes, and their connections within and across health and care policy documents. Next, Ludlow and colleagues contrast these findings with carers' first-hand experiential accounts of integrating care for their older relatives. They highlight that unpaid carers, and the gender imbalance of caregiving, were largely invisible in policy documents, and argue this omission accentuates the disconnect between policymakers' vision for integrated care and the accomplishment of integration on the ground.

Whereas the first three chapters in this section draw on specific policy proposals and changes, Chapter 5 offers innovative approaches to the analysis of healthcare policy. Meier and Dopson encourage researchers to pay more explicit attention to context, which they define as 'a relational construct that specifies what is at any given point considered background for understanding a phenomenon or event. This background/foreground relationship is continually constructed by people as they make sense of their experiences and the social worlds in which they engage'. To illustrate, Meier and Dopson draw insights from the COVID-19 pandemic, arguing that it can be understood as both a radically changed context for health policies and a large-scale change that actors in the healthcare systems need to engage with. The authors discuss different national approaches to COVID-19 in terms of lockdowns, social distancing, mask wearing, and health policies. They conclude by highlighting the message that context is both something you construct as a background for a phenomenon or event and something you enact. Meier and Dopson urge that healthcare managers work to surface their own assumptions and perspectives about context in the policymaking process. They also underscore researchers' responsibility to specify what they analytically bound as context and the consequences for that specific construction of context.

Part II: Translating Healthcare Policy into Practice

This section starts with an exploration of health charities working in Africa. In Chapter 6, Sachikonye, Chambers, and Ramlogan argue that charities operating in complex policy context and exposed to multiple stakeholder influences can experience 'mission drift'. This phenomenon involves gradual adjustment of organisational practices, services, or products to serve purposes that are inconsistent with initially agreed intentions. Using critical realist synthesis methodology, the authors combine evidence from health charities' annual reports with insights from the mission drift and governance literature to understand whether and how charity boards operating in complex and ambiguous environments reconcile the tensions that lead to mission drift. They identify four interconnected political mechanisms activated in response to pressures exercised by different stakeholder groups: 'Maternalism' is used to target the charities' beneficiaries; 'diplomacy' addresses pressures from civil society; 'coaching' is directed at donors; and 'coalitionism' is deployed in charities' dealings with programme partners. Each of these mechanisms can be deployed with variable degrees of strength and have intended and unintended effects. Sachikonye and colleagues conclude that under certain conditions, these mechanisms can reinforce mission drift, rather than reduce or prevent it.

In Chapter 7, Pomare, Churruca, Long, Ellis, and Braithwaite examine the misalignment between policy and staff experiences during hospital redevelopment. These authors use the theoretical lens of 'work-as-imagined' versus 'work-as-done' to identify tensions between what policy recommends and what is possible or feasible for people to implement in the complex reality of healthcare systems. To illustrate their analysis, Pomare and colleagues present a case study of a large metropolitan, public hospital in Australia, undergoing a multimillion-dollar redevelopment project. Analysing exploratory case-study data, the authors identify a relatively high occurrence of stakeholder exclusion from the process; three themes encompassed frequently expressed concerns by staff: 'lack of consultation', 'uncertainty', and 'constant change'. This case demonstrates the nature of the disconnect between the policy (the 'blunt end'), which states that all staff should be involved by way of consultation, and what staff actually experience in practice (the 'sharp end'). While it is clear in the policy documentation that policymakers see the importance of clinician involvement, there is a misalignment among management entities about what the policy actually states and how it is implemented. In addition, whereas hospital redevelopment policy provided one-off infrastructure funding, long-term sustainment of salary expenditure was not taken into account. The authors argue this suggests little consideration for the long-term effects of redevelopment for those at the 'sharp end'.

In Chapter 8, Tazzyman, Mitchell, and Hodgson address some of the challenges related to new 'integrated' models for the provision of health and social care, which are increasingly introduced in many countries. They argue that boundaries related to expertise, remit, budget, and practices represent deep challenges for professional work. The authors therefore ask the following research question: how can work be fully integrated when each sector is funded to do different work, with its workforces being placed on different contracts with different legal obligations, and required to deliver services for geographical areas which do not match up? Empirically, Tazzyman and colleagues draw on a study from an English city where they interviewed twenty-four practitioners across levels that were involved in the integration of health and social care. They find that integration was important for professional identity and boundaries, and that it also had implications for organisational change. Interestingly, the authors also demonstrate that while competitive boundary work was generated due to the top-down reconfiguration, these practitioners were also able to collaborate, create solidarity, and achieve integration by reiterating and acknowledging boundaries rather than downplaying them.

Chapter 9, which concludes this section, is concerned with assessments of organisational cultures in Australian public hospitals. Churruca, Pomare, Ellis, Long, and Braithwaite argue that there is a lack of detailed guidance about how such assessments should be conducted, even though public hospitals are required to do so by national standards. Beginning with a literature review on organisational culture in healthcare and different ways of assessing it, Churruca and colleagues then analyse 597 items used in seven surveys in Australian hospitals. The authors find that these surveys lack a specific healthcare focus, and that different constructs are used even though there are overlapping topics. Furthermore, the use of findings and dissemination vary across different states. According to public policy, the purpose of these surveys is to monitor employee experiences and evaluations of their workplace over time, but the results indicate that there is limited improvement over time. This might be because different actors are responsible for designing, analysing, interpreting, and actioning the surveys. In addition, it may indicate that these surveys are first and foremost regarded as bureaucratic exercises that serve political purposes. The authors argue that if these instruments are to have real practical value, their quality needs to be improved.

Part III: Organisational Leadership in Challenging Policy Contexts

Chapter 10 asks the following questions: what keeps a small minority of NHS Chief Executive Officers (CEOs) in post for much longer than tends to be the norm; and how do they exercise their agency and manage the challenging policy imperatives? Chambers and Exworthy begin with a discussion of the 'CEO paradox' which contrasts the need for stability with the lack of conditions to create it. Stemming from the inconsistencies inherent in the dominant NPM paradigm, this paradox is thought to lead to high turnover among this group of top managers. Drawing on interviews with ten long-serving CEOs, Chambers and Exworthy illuminate the importance of CEO relations (with the Board and externally) in establishing a balance between the interests of their own institution and those of the wider system, and show how CEOs developed and maintained their personal 'staying power' by reinventing themselves as they adapted to changing environments and contexts. Their findings suggest that NHS CEOs with longevity may be able to balance organisational imperatives with personal competencies and motivation. Chambers and Exworthy conclude that the CEO paradox, as applied here, was not so much about the conditions precipitating short-termism or the need for stability, but rather about the intersection of organisational change trajectories and personal career paths. It is also suggested that gradual transformation of the initial NPM-style conditions, which have undermined the likelihood of long-term CEOs, into a more decentred, networked form may make this phenomenon less of a rarity.

In Chapter 11, Willocks and Moralee address the implications of different approaches to conceptualising leadership. The empirical motivation for doing so is that leadership is considered an important way of improving care in the English NHS. Traditionally leadership studies have been concerned with traits and competencies of individual leaders. In contrast, in the last ten years there has been a so-called practice-turn towards 'post-heroic' approaches that understand leadership as a collaborative process, co-constructed by multiple organisational actors. Leadership-as-practice is one of these approaches. In healthcare, there have been relatively few empirical studies using this promising theoretical lens. The authors address this gap by drawing upon a case study focusing on the role of micro-level collective leadership practices in effecting change in UK medical education. They find an intricate connection between the different leadership practices (scanning, signalling, weaving, stabilising, inviting, unleashing, reflecting) described in the oft-cited framework developed by Raelin (2016). Moreover, they demonstrate that there are both tensions and complexities underpinning leadership-as-practice, and that emergent leadership processes are informed by policy context, culture, and history.

Chapter 12 focuses on the lived experiences of healthcare professionals in leading roles. Scaratti, Gorli, and Piria ask the following research question: how do leaders do what they do? The authors present an ethnographic study of narrative accounts from 120 head nurses working in four hospitals in Northern Italy. These nurses participated in five half-day reflexive sessions that focused on the challenges they encountered in their role and organisational position. Through these accounts, Scaratti and colleagues explore the nurses' everyday leadership practices as they are exercised in places, histories, and experiences. The chapter presents three inter-related perspectives: (1) the interpretation of one's leading role, (2) the exercise of authority and power, and (3) the organisational authorship. The authors find that head nurses are constantly confronted by various urgent organisational requests that require them to negotiate boundaries with other organisational members, acting in a hybrid role but without a general recipe for how to enact it.

Chapter 13, which concludes this section, addresses the particular challenges for women's leadership in the healthcare sector. Zeinali, Muraya, Molyneux, and Morgan bring a fresh and more complex approach to reviewing the literature on women's leadership, using an intersectionality lens. They begin by citing World Health Organisation (WHO) statistics that nearly three-quarters of people working in healthcare are women, but that the top levels of leadership and decision-making power remain dominated by men. The authors note that this pattern is seen around the globe, and especially in low- and middle-income countries. The introduction of an intersectionality lens moves the analysis beyond merely an examination of gender inequities; it contributes further insights about the intersection of other social stratifiers, including race, ethnicity, religion, culture, and professional cadre. The authors stress that other intersecting social identities create unique positionalities of privilege and/or disadvantage. They present a list of recommendations for health policymakers and conclude that achieving gender equity in healthcare leadership has been associated with improvements in health systems' governance, functioning, and health benefits more broadly.

Concluding Comments

In our concluding comments (Chapter 14), we synthesise the strands of research presented in the edited volume, finding that 'voice' emerges as a common theme, despite the disparate contexts and research questions posed by the authors of the twelve chapters. Notably, we discern instances of suppression of voice, mobilisation of voice, and skilful management of voice. This framing allows us to identify dysfunctional effects when voice is suppressed, either explicitly or implicitly through oversight, as well as to highlight positive outcomes when voice is effectively mobilised and skilfully managed. We then use the framework of voice for a discussion of implications for practice and directions for future research. We conclude by urging the scholars of healthcare organisations to listen—and respond—to the plurality of voices, aiming to represent the diversity of perspectives, amplify those views that are unjustly suppressed, and facilitate dialogues among multiple stakeholders operating in challenging policy contexts.

References

Bevir, M., & Waring, J. (2018). *Decentring health policy: Learning from British experiences in healthcare governance*. Routledge.

Buchanan, D. A., Addicott, R., Fitzgerald, L., Ferlie, E., & Baeza, J. I. (2007). Nobody in charge: Distributed change agency in healthcare. *Human Relations, 60*(7), 1065–1090. https://doi.org/10.1177/0018726707081158

Bucher, S. V., Chreim, S., Langley, A., & Reay, T. (2016). Contestation about collaboration: Discursive boundary work among professions. *Organization Studies, 37*(4), 497–522. https://doi.org/10.1177/0170840615622067

Campos, P. A., & Reich, M. R. (2019). Political analysis for health policy implementation. *Health Systems & Reform, 5*(3), 224–235. https://doi.org/10.1080/23288604.2019.1625251

Candel, J. J., & Biesbroek, R. (2016). Toward a processual understanding of policy integration. *Policy Sciences, 49*(3), 211–231. https://doi.org/10.1007/s11077-016-9248-y

Checkland, K. (2018). Governing primary care: Manipulated emergence, ambiguous rules and shifting incentives. In M. Bevir & J. Waring (Eds.), *Decentring health policy: Learning from British experiences in healthcare governance* (pp. 52–69). Routledge.

Checkland, K., Segar, J., Voorhees, J., & Coleman, A. (2015). 'Like a circle in a spiral, like a wheel within a wheel': The layers of complexity and challenge for devolution of health and social care in Greater Manchester. *Representations, 51*(4), 453–469. https://doi.org/10.1080/00344893.2016.1165514

Croft, C., Currie, G., & Lockett, A. (2015). Broken 'two-way windows'? An exploration of professional hybrids. *Public Administration, 93*(2), 380–394. https://doi.org/10.1111/padm.12115

Denis, J.-L., Lamothe, L., & Langley, A. (2001). The dynamics of collective leadership and strategic change in pluralistic organizations. *Academy of Management Journal, 44*(4), 809–837. https://doi.org/10.5465/3069417

Dickinson, H. (2016). From new public management to new public governance: The implications for a 'new public service'. In J. R. Butcher & D. J. Gilchrist (Eds.), *The three sector solution: Delivering public policy in collaboration with not-for-profits and business* (pp. 41–60). ANU Press.

Dickinson, H., Freeman, T., Robinson, S., & Williams, I. (2011). Resource scarcity and priority-setting: From management to leadership in the rationing of health care? *Public Money & Management, 31*(5), 363–370. https://doi.org/10.1080/09540962.2011.598352

Diefenbach, T. (2009). New public management in public sector organizations: The dark sides of managerialistic 'enlightenment'. *Public Administration, 87*(4), 892–909. https://doi.org/10.1111/j.1467-9299.2009.01766.x

Dopson, S., Fitzgerald, L., & Ferlie, E. (2008). Understanding change and innovation in healthcare settings: Reconceptualizing the active role of context. *Journal of Change Management, 8*(3–4), 213–231. https://doi.org/10.1080/14697010802133577

Ferlie, E., Dopson, S., Fitzgerald, L., & Locock, L. (2009). Renewing policy to support evidence-based health care. *Public Administration, 87*(4), 837–852. https://doi.org/10.1111/j.1467-9299.2009.01796.x

Ferlie, E., Fitzgerald, L., McGivern, G., Dopson, S., & Bennett, C. (2011). Public policy networks and 'wicked problems': A nascent solution? *Public Administration, 89*(2), 307–324. https://doi.org/10.1111/j.1467-9299.2010.01896.x

Ferlie, E., & McGivern, G. (2014). Bringing Anglo-governmentality into public management scholarship: The case of evidence-based medicine in UK health care. *Journal of Public Administration Research and Theory, 24*(1), 59–83. https://doi.org/10.1093/jopart/mut002

Ferlie, E. B., & Shortell, S. M. (2001). Improving the quality of health care in the United Kingdom and the United States: A framework for change. *Milbank Quarterly, 79*(2). https://doi.org/10.1111/1468-0009.00206

Fitzgerald, L., Ferlie, E., Wood, M., & Hawkins, C. (2002). Interlocking interactions: The diffusion of innovations in health care. *Human Relations, 55*(12), 1429–1449. https://doi.org/10.1177/0018726702128782213

Gabbay, J., & le May, A. (2004). Evidence based guidelines or collectively constructed "mindlines?" Ethnographic study of knowledge management in primary care. *British Medical Journal, 329*, 1013. https://doi.org/10.1136/bmj.329.7473.1013

Gkeredakis, E., Swan, J., Powell, J., Nicolini, D., Scarbrough, H., Roginski, C., et al. (2011). Mind the gap: Understanding utilisation of evidence and policy in health care management practice. *Journal of Health Organization and Management, 25*(3), 298–314. https://doi.org/10.1108/14777261111143545

Greenaway, J., Salter, B., & Hart, S. (2007). How policy networks can damage democratic health: A case study in the government of governance. *Public Administration, 85*(3), 717–738. https://doi.org/10.1111/j.1467-9299.2007.00661.x

Hipgrave, D. B., Alderman, K. B., Anderson, I., & Soto, E. J. (2014). Health sector priority setting at meso-level in lower and middle income countries: Lessons learned, available options and suggested steps. *Social Science and Medicine, 102*, 190–200. https://doi.org/10.1016/j.socscimed.2013.11.056

Jansson, K., Tuunainen, J., & Mainela, T. (2021). Concealing paradoxes in decision-making during hospital hybridization—A systems theoretical analysis. *Journal of Health Organization and Management, 35*(2), 195–211. https://doi.org/10.1108/JHOM-08-2020-0334

Jones, L. (2018). Sedimented governance in the English National Health Service. In M. Bevir & J. Waring (Eds.), *Decentring health policy: Learning from British experiences in healthcare governance* (pp. 17–33). Routledge.

Kislov, R. (2014). Boundary discontinuity in a constellation of interconnected practices. *Public Administration, 92*(2), 307–323. https://doi.org/10.1111/padm.12065

Kislov, R., Hodgson, D., & Boaden, R. (2016). Professionals as knowledge brokers: The limits of authority in healthcare collaboration. *Public Administration, 94*(2), 472–489. https://doi.org/10.1111/padm.12227

Kislov, R., Humphreys, J., & Harvey, G. (2017a). How do managerial techniques evolve over time? The distortion of "facilitation" in healthcare service improvement. *Public Management Review, 19*(8), 1165–1183. https://doi.org/10.1080/14719037.2016.1266022

Kislov, R., Hyde, P., & McDonald, R. (2017b). New game, old rules? Mechanisms and consequences of legitimation in boundary spanning activities. *Organization Studies, 38*(10), 1421–1444. https://doi.org/10.1177/0170840616679455

Kislov, R., Wilson, P., Cummings, G., Ehrenberg, A., Gifford, W., Kelly, J., et al. (2019). From research evidence to "evidence by proxy"? Organizational enactment of evidence-based health care in four high-income countries. *Public Administration Review, 79*(5), 684–698. https://doi.org/10.1111/puar.13056

Klijn, E. H. (2012). New public management and governance: A comparison. In D. Levi-Faur (Ed.), *The Oxford handbook of governance* (pp. 201–214). Oxford University Press.

Klijn, E. H., & Koppenjan, J. (2015). *Governance networks in the public sector*. Taylor & Francis Group.

Langley, A., Lindberg, K., Mørk, B. E., Nicolini, D., Raviola, E., & Walter, L. (2019). Boundary work among groups, occupations, and organizations: From cartography to process. *Academy of Management Annals, 13*(2), 704–736. https://doi.org/10.5465/annals.2017.0089

Linstead, S., Maréchal, G., & Griffin, R. W. (2014). Theorizing and researching the dark side of organization. *Organization Studies, 35*(2), 165–188. https://doi.org/10.1177/0170840613515402

Llewellyn, S. (2001). 'Two-way windows': Clinicians as medical managers. *Organization Studies, 22*(4), 593–623. https://doi.org/10.1177/0170840601224003

Martin, G. P., Currie, G., & Finn, R. (2009). Reconfiguring or reproducing intra-professional boundaries? Specialist expertise, generalist knowledge and the 'modernization' of the medical workforce. *Social Science and Medicine, 68*(7), 1191–1198. https://doi.org/10.1016/j.socscimed.2009.01.006

Martin, G. P., Weaver, S., Currie, G., Finn, R., & McDonald, R. (2012). Innovation sustainability in challenging health-care contexts: Embedding clinically led change in routine practice. *Health Services Management Research, 25*(4), 190–199. https://doi.org/10.1177/0951484812474246

McGivern, G., Currie, G., Ferlie, E., Fitzgerald, L., & Waring, J. (2015). Hybrid manager-professionals' identity work: The maintenance and hybridization of medical professionalism in managerial contexts. *Public Administration, 93*(2), 412–432. https://doi.org/10.1111/padm.12119

Montgomery, K. (2001). Physician executives: The evolution and impact of a hybrid profession. *Advances in Health Care Management, 2*, 215–241. https://doi.org/10.1016/S1474-8231(01)02028-6

Moynihan, D. P. (2005). Goal-based learning and the future of performance management. *Public Administration Review, 65*(2), 203–216. https://doi.org/10.1111/j.1540-6210.2005.00445.x

Oborn, E., Barrett, M., & Dawson, S. (2013). Distributed leadership in policy formulation: A sociomaterial perspective. *Organization Studies, 34*(2), 253–276. https://doi.org/10.1177/0170840612473552

Osborne, S. P. (2010). The (new) public governance: a suitable case for treatment? In S. P. Osborne (Ed.), *The new public governance? Emerging perspectives on the theory and practice of public governance* (pp. 1–16). Routledge.

Raelin, J. A. (2016). *Leadership-as-practice: Theory and application*. Routledge.

Reeleder, D., Goel, V., Singer, P. A., & Martin, D. K. (2006). Leadership and priority setting: The perspective of hospital CEOs. *Health Policy, 79*, 24–34. https://doi.org/10.1016/j.healthpol.2005.11.009

Robinson, S., Williams, I., Dickinson, H., Freeman, T., & Rumbold, B. (2012). Priority-setting and rationing in healthcare: Evidence from the English experience. *Social Science and Medicine, 75*(12), 2386–2393. https://doi.org/10.1016/j.socscimed.2012.09.014

Rowland, P., Fancott, C., & Abelson, J. (2021). Metaphors of organisations in patient involvement programs: Connections and contradictions. *Journal of Health Organization and Management, 35*(2), 177–194. https://doi.org/10.1108/JHOM-07-2020-0292

Sanders, T., & Harrison, S. (2008). Professional legitimacy claims in the multidisciplinary workplace: The case of heart failure care. *Sociology of Health & Illness, 30*(2), 289–308. https://doi.org/10.1111/j.1467-9566.2007.01052.x

Schuurmans, J. J., van Pijkeren, N., Bal, R., & Wallenburg, I. (2021). Regionalization in elderly care: What makes up a healthcare region? *Journal of Health Organization and Management, 35*(2), 229–243. https://doi.org/10.1108/jhom-08-2020-0333

Smith, J., Walshe, K., & Hunter, D. J. (2001). The "redisorganisation" of the NHS: Another reorganisation involving unhappy managers can only worsen the service. *British Medical Journal, 323*(1262). https://doi.org/10.1136/bmj.323.7324.1262

Suddaby, R., & Greenwood, R. (2005). Rhetorical strategies of legitimacy. *Administrative Science Quarterly, 50*(1), 35–67. https://doi.org/10.2189/asqu.2005.50.1.35

Torfing, J. (2012). Governance networks. In D. Levi-Faur (Ed.), *The Oxford handbook of governance* (pp. 99–112). Oxford University Press.

Tsoukas, H., & Vladimirou, E. (2001). What is organizational knowledge? *Journal of Management Studies, 38*(7), 973–993. https://doi.org/10.1111/1467-6486.00268

Tucker, D., Hendy, J., & Chrysanthaki, T. (2021). How does policy alienation develop? Exploring street-level bureaucrats' agency in policy context shift in UK telehealthcare. *Human Relations*. Published online before print. https://doi.org/10.1177/00187267211003633

Turner, S., Higginson, J., Oborne, C. A., Thomas, R. E., Ramsay, A. I. G., & Fulop, N. J. (2014). Codifying knowledge to improve patient safety: A qualitative study of practice-based interventions. *Social Science and Medicine, 113*, 169–176. https://doi.org/10.1016/j.socscimed.2014.05.031

Waring, J., Crompton, A., Overton, C., & Roe, B. (2020). Decentering health research networks: Framing collaboration in the context of narrative incompatibility and regional geo-politics. *Public Policy and Administration*. Published online before print. https://doi.org/10.1177/0952076720911686

Part I

Analysing Contemporary Policy Contexts

2

The Pluralisation of the UK Health Policy Process?

Ewan Ferlie

Introduction

This chapter addresses the long-standing debate in British public policy studies about whether there is a move from the traditional 'Westminster and Whitehall' model of decision making within what has historically been a centralised unitary state.[1] The question raised is whether government in the United Kingdom has been moving towards a looser and more pluralist model involving more and more dispersed actors, sometimes characterised as the 'network governance' paradigm (Rhodes, 2007).

These general arguments will be explored here specifically in relation to changing modes of health policy making in the United Kingdom which have been under-explored in this debate in the past (but see

[1] This chapter is a revised version of the OBHC 2020 keynote address delivered as a webinar in April 2020.

E. Ferlie (✉)
King's College London, London, UK
e-mail: ewan.ferlie@kcl.ac.uk

R. Kislov et al. (eds.), *Managing Healthcare Organisations in Challenging Policy Contexts*, Organizational Behaviour in Healthcare,
https://doi.org/10.1007/978-3-030-81093-1_2

Alvarez-Rosete & Mays, 2008, 2014). But perhaps the doctrine of health care and health policy exceptionalism has been taken too far?

The chapter will firstly review some academic literature and debate in relation to changing modes of governance in the United Kingdom's health care sector. It will then adduce and review some key examples of policy making. It is finally concluded that there is evidence of a shift to a more pluralist system, but as yet in a bounded and provisional way.

Some Academic Literature and Debate

The Classic Westminster and Whitehall Model of Public Policy Making in the United Kingdom

Within political science literature on the United Kingdom State, the conventional 'Westminster and Whitehall' model (Marsh, 2008; Ham, 2009) draws attention to the role of basic political institutions and conventions, strongly centralised in London, in shaping policy making. These features include a majoritarian electoral system which normally leads to single-party control and prevents the formation of multi-party coalitions; collective Cabinet-based government headed by a Prime Minister as first among equals; individual departments (e.g. Department of Health and Social Care) relating to their distinct policy fields; ministerial leadership (from the relevant Secretary of State and then junior ministers) of 'their department', supported by an expert, permanent, and neutral civil service as the key source of policy advice.

Alvarez-Rosete and Mays (2008, p. 184) suggest this pattern leads to a policy process displaying 'relatively centralised, veto free, political decision making where big legislative breakthroughs and reverses can happen on a regular basis'. So public or health management reforms introduced by one government can then be easily reversed by its successor.

Or: From Government to Governance?

Rhodes (2007) developed an alternative 'Differentiated Polity' model of UK government, arguing there has been a move 'from government to governance'. 'Governance' is portrayed as a looser and broader term than 'government'. There had also been a shift in underlying governance mode in his view from hierarchy and/or markets towards networks used to coordinate the many autonomous partners. There were many more actors now involved in policy and delivery, including private and third sector actors, as a result of sustained privatisation and outsourcing, so that government now 'steered' rather than simply directed. It had indeed given away its old ownership rights in various sectors.

The old centralised nation state apparent in the United Kingdom had also lost functions upwards (to the European Union, at least until 2020 when the pattern dramatically changed) and other international bodies; sideways (to the new generation of executive agencies); and downwards (through devolution to Scotland and Wales). While the core executive (Prime Minister's Units; Treasury; Cabinet Office) launches hyperactive initiatives, they are (in Rhodes' view) pulling 'rubber levers' to no real effect. The implication is that the Departmental Barons (such as the Secretary of State for Health and Social Care) retain pre-eminence and that cross Whitehall initiatives will not generate traction.

Or: The Asymmetric Power Model?

Marsh et al. (2003) and Marsh (2008) contest this account, putting forward an alternative 'asymmetric power' model. The differentiated polity account is seen as underestimating the strong structural inequalities apparent in British society, then reflected in a relatively closed public policy process. High degrees of participation may be evident in 'low politics' arenas (e.g. local government) but not those of 'high politics' at the centre. While they concede some move away from the old Westminster and Whitehall model, they still argue that central government retains substantial power resources that it can deploy when it wants to. There is an embedded top-down and centralised British political tradition which privileges a decisive form of central government which is difficult to disturb at any fundamental level.

Characterising the Health Policy Process in the United Kingdom

Policy sectors often exhibit distinctive policy fields and an associated policy community, within which actors may well possess differential levels of power. A classic American account of health care decision making argues for strong professional (medical) dominance (Alford, 1977), potentially evident at a macro policy level as well as a micro clinical level or meso organisational level.

Some accounts of the United Kingdom's health policy process suggest a traditional and narrow pattern of domination by ministers and civil servants in the Department of Health and a small number of elite clinical groupings (notably the Royal Colleges) (Ham, 2009), with users, health-orientated pressure groups and also economic interests present but seen as more secondary. The British Medical Association is seen as losing influence in the 1980s under anti–trade union and anti-corporatist governments led by Mrs Thatcher, and there were also attempts in this period to increase the role and power base of the health management community as a challenge to medical domination. The United Kingdom's health policy field also displays a dense system of technical advisory machinery, often populated by research leading and senior clinical academics who can be seen as composing a knowledge elite (Freidson, 1985). The advisory power of such clinical academics remains considerable and may even have increased with the growing volume of research funding, research-based knowledge and of randomised control trials. Institutionally, this advisory apparatus benefitted from the formation and growth of National Institute of Health Research (founded in 2006) and is well embedded in its advisory machinery.

Alvarez-Rosete and Mays (2008) suggest that the United Kingdom's health policy domain has been less affected than other public policy sectors by the move to network governance–style policy making from the 1990s, with relatively weak emergence of new actors and new institutional arenas. Rather, significant micromanagement, strong upwards accountability lines, and vertical performance management have continued, given the high political and media salience of National Health Service 'delivery' to ministers. So there has been no transformation to what are 'longstanding, relatively closed and centralised policy networks' (p. 197).

Some Key Examples of Health Policy Making in the United Kingdom

We now benchmark this academic debate against recent major examples of the UK health policy process, following Ham's call (2009) for empirically informed studies to test alternative health policy theories.

The Devolution of Health Care Competences

The Westminster and Whitehall model assumes a centralised and unitary nation state, with a strong notion of a UK rather than separate devolved jurisdictions. Yet a significant constitutional reform in the New Labour period (1997–2010) was the devolution of various competences (including in health care) to the newly created parliaments and assemblies in Scotland, Wales, and Northern Ireland in the late 1990s. There are now, for example, four health ministers in the United Kingdom, drawn from four different political parties and the best-known minister (Matt Hancock) is technically the Secretary of State for Health and Social Care in England and has no UK-wide role.

Moreover, such devolution has had real consequences as health care policy has developed on different lines in the four jurisdictions, reflecting different political preferences (broadly speaking, Wales and Scotland can be seen as politically to the left of England) and also distinct health policy communities. Greer (2004) characterised this variation as a 'four-way bet': Scotland bet on clinical professionalism and managed clinical networks; England bet on markets and management; Wales on localism and Northern Ireland on 'permissive managerialism'.

So Scotland seems closer to retaining elite professional dominance, reflecting the presence there of a group of research-intensive universities as an important element of a small and cohesive health policy community. Clinical networks are favoured over markets as a mode of governance. England seems closer to the more recent but equally well-known pattern of the New Public Management, espousing more of a markets/management mix.

Northern Ireland presents a different pattern of 'permissive managerialism'. Greer (2004) here refers to the problem of overcoming a tradition of sectarianism and a low expectation of creative health policy ideas coming from politicians essentially elected to defend their communities' interests. The medical profession is seen as less dominant there than in Scotland. The resulting vacuum has created an opportunity for health managers to step forward and take on a more dominant role than elsewhere. In addition, health care organisations are under less top-down political pressure than elsewhere in the United Kingdom (perhaps because sectarian rather than performance logic is dominant in the political domain), so that health care managers have more of an opportunity to create a local management and organisational style.

Wales presents perhaps the most interesting example of a distinctive approach to health policy making in the United Kingdom. Drakeford (2006) (ex-Minister of Health in Wales, currently first Minster there and originally a Professor of Social Policy at Cardiff University) argues that the Welsh ten-year plan (National Assembly for Wales, 2001) was deliberately and distinctively based on ideas from the so-called New Public Health Movement (Hunter, 2003). This movement aimed at tacking the basic social and economic determinants of health rather than promoting an acute sector and beds led strategy. The subtitle of the plan is itself significant: 'a plan for the NHS with its partners' in signalling a commitment to network governance modes of working: 'the Welsh Document puts the National Health Service near the centre of a network of policy and delivery actors whose shared ambition is to produce an impact upon the social and economic determinants of health' (Drakeford, 2006, pp. 549–550).

Local Health Boards were set up as powerful and integrated commissioners to help drive population-level health improvement forward, drawing in broad membership from professional groups, local authorities, the voluntary sector and the public and patients (Drakeford, 2006, p. 551). The attempt to construct a commissioner-led service contrasted with the pattern of provider-led dominance in England, with a weakly developed commissioning function there.

Overall, the devolution of health policy competences to Scotland, Wales, and Northern Ireland suggests a substantial shift to a more pluralistic model.

The 'High Politics' of Health Policy

Perhaps the best two examples of 'high policy making' in UK health policy over the last twenty or so years are the 2000 National Health Service Plan (under New Labour) and the 2012 Health and Social Care Act (under the Conservative and Liberal Democrat coalition). Here we consider both in turn specifically in terms of their decision-making processes. There has been no new legislation for NHS reorganisation since 2012 (perhaps reflecting the difficult experience of the 2012 Act), so there is no later exercise to analyse.

The Policy Process Around the National Health Service Plan 2000: A Hybrid with Some Network Governance?

Alvarez-Rosete and Mays (2014) suggest that the preparation of the 2000 National Health Service Plan took place in ideal conditions for a network governance–influenced policy process as not only were these ideas in the ascendancy (and favoured by the then New Labour government) but finances were buoyant, so that it was possible to use such growing resources to form larger coalitions of the willing and hence 'buy change'. Health care lobbies and interest groups were unlikely to oppose plans for extensive growth, after years of tight finances.

At first glance, they argue there were some network governance–like elements in the early stages of the process, including a broadly based consultation exercise, the setting up of inclusive 'Modernisation Action

Teams', and a deliberate strategy of 'Big Tent' coalition building which led to many key stakeholders signing the preface of the Plan in highly visible support. On the other hand, Alvarez-Rosete and Mays (2014) still find 'a strong element of hierarchy, dominating other modes of governance' (p. 639). The subsequent writing of the plan was to a considerable extent still dominated by the Prime Minister, the Secretary of State for Health, and a few close advisers, especially politically appointed Special Advisers. This small circle at the centre was more influential than the 'partial and controlled' erosion of traditional boundaries by the Modernisation Action Teams. So influence from network governance–style ideas on the health policy process was apparent but also subordinated to elements of continuing hierarchical domination, and the degree of centralisation increased as the process moved from consultation to the later stage of writing the text.

2012 Health and Social Care Act: Reverting to the Westminster Model

Timmins (2012) provides the best account of the policy and legislative process around the 2012 Health and Social Care Act. After the 2010 election, a Conservative Secretary of State for Health (Andrew Lansley) took up post. He had been a long-standing Shadow Secretary of Health and had made many speeches on health policy, so he felt he had laid out a clear prospectus. The Conservative party's proposals for health care had not been intensively scrutinised either during the election campaign or during the negotiations around the formation of the Conservative Liberal Democrat coalition that created the new government, so that intense scrutiny was to happen later. More broadly, the new government was keen to get on with public service reform early, drawing a lesson from New Labour administrations that it had been left too late.

A health care White Paper was produced in just sixty days outlining future overall direction but was short and thin (for the text, see Department of Health, 2010), proceeding therefore without any sustained or meaningful consultation at that stage. It proposed a reorganisation of primary care to increase the influence of family doctors on commissioning, along with an extension of competition reflecting the doctrine of 'any willing provider'. A semi-independent National Health Service Commissioning Board was to be set up. There was also to be managerial delayering, removal of management tiers, and a substantial reduction in management costs. The White Paper further coincided with the beginning of Treasury-led austerity so the injection of considerable new resource or the old 'buying change' approach was no longer an option. Indeed, this was the beginning of the age of 'austerity' and what was to prove a decade of tight finances for the public services, including the NHS.

With the benefit of hindsight, there was a failure to spot and cultivate some key interest groups, both professional (e.g. the Royal College of Nursing and Royal College of General Practitioners) and political (e.g. the well-respected Baroness Shirley Williams later came out to lead the markets-averse rank-and-file of the left of the Liberal Democrats) against marketisation.

In the United Kingdom, the legislative process conventionally starts with the government introducing a Bill in the House of Commons which is debated, if need be amended, and then eventually accepted or rejected by a vote in the House. The government had achieved a working majority so would have hoped that its Bills would be passed, although there were some internal tensions between the two political parties in the coalition in relation to the role of the market in health care. If passed by the Commons and then the other house, the House of Lords, and it gains the Queen's consent, a Bill then becomes an Act and is official legislation.

In this case, the initial and lengthy Bill had no fewer than 550 pages with the result that there was something potentially offensive in it for almost everyone. The Bill got into increasing political and parliamentary difficulties as it went through the Commons and was 'called in' by the Prime and Deputy Prime Minister. At this point, a belated consultation exercise (the so-called Future Forum) took place but at a very late stage. The Bill was eventually passed as an Act but the process was tortuous in the extreme. The Secretary of State for Health was replaced shortly afterwards.

Timmins' lesson drawing (p. 143) from the process includes the dictum: 'build a consensus or at least some support'. The lessons of 2000 (e.g. the collectively signed preface) were curiously either forgotten or ignored: Timmins suggests that the latter is the case as departmental officials suggested more consultation but were overruled politically. Another lesson for the civil service (pp. 136–137) was: 'recognise the weakness of the civil service in the face of a determined minister'. The Department of Health felt itself in a weak position, especially in the formulation phase. It appears that it suggested the options of less or no legislation, but that was overruled politically.

Overall, it is here concluded that the health policy process in 2000 exhibited a mixed mode with some contained presence from network governance ideas, but by 2012 there had been a reversion to a Westminster-led model, more than a Whitehall-led model. This distinction is here drawn as there was a pattern in this case of individualised political leadership from a newly appointed, experienced, and determined Secretary of State for Health and a more marginal role than usual for civil service advice, at least until the point at which the policy process started to unravel.

Health *and* Wealth

This section draws on a recent report on the creation, impact, and development of regional-level Academic Health Science Networks in the English NHS (Ferlie et al., 2017, specifically the work package on national policy development). These networks are part of a developing regional infrastructure created through successive national initiatives to progress knowledge mobilisation and the diffusion of evidence-based innovations, including also Academic Health Science Centres and Applied Research Collaborations.

The Academic Health Science Networks have a distinctive role within this wider infrastructure in progressing the commercialisation as well as the faster diffusion of evidence-based innovations and should contribute to wealth and job creation as well as better health care outcomes. They sought to draw in prominent personnel from the private sector as well as National Health Service personnel. We were especially interested in this study in exploring the broadening of the health care innovation landscape to include the stimulating of economic growth and how the rising economic growth agenda led to policy attempts to bring the National Health Service with other key actors in the health and life sciences sectors and other important actors, including universities, small and medium enterprises, and large firms.

The report's analysis of national policy development noted an interesting long-term development which was the increasing involvement of central economic departments (notably the Treasury and also the Department of Business, Energy and Industrial Strategy, previously known as the Department of Business, Innovation and Skills) in constructing a policy agenda and a novel policy community around economic growth and wealth creation in health care (especially in relation to the life sciences, bio pharma and medical devices). This novel prism counterbalances the traditional perspective of the Department of Health and also traditional clinician and academic dominance more orientated to clinically orientated and health outcome–related goals in treatment and research.

Why might this broadening of health policy into health and wealth policy have happened? The 2008 Global Financial crisis revealed the economic overdependence of the United Kingdom on an overblown and risky financial sector which then went into deep recession. The question arose: which other industrial sectors might step up to provide alternative sources of global economic competitiveness, economic growth, and high value jobs? The bio pharma, life sciences, and medical device industries were seen as among relatively few credible candidates.

There was an important political context. The British Chancellor of the Exchequer and the Treasury had earlier secured a powerful position across the whole of economic and social policy in the 2000s as part of a wider political bargain within the New Labour government. Jockeying for position between the Prime Minister (Tony Blair) and the Chancellor of the Exchequer (Gordon Brown who went on to become the next Prime Minister) may be part of the political context. Marsh et al. 2008 note that the Treasury had expanded its role beyond the detailed control of public expenditure to launch much broader social policy initiatives, such as welfare to work in social security policy. Interventions by such parts of the core executive (as the Treasury clearly is)—if sustained over time—might reshape traditional and departmentally based policy communities by bringing in new actors.

The Treasury took an intense interest in aspects of health policy with implications for public expenditure or wealth generation. It sponsored significant policy reviews from senior and economically credible outside figures (e.g. a banker; a venture capitalist but usually not health care sector leaders) of health and social policy (e.g. Wanless Report, 2002). Cooksey Report (2006) (see below; it is important to state this report was Treasury led but with Department of Trade and Industry and Department of Health involvement) represents an important review of health research funding. The review was chaired by David Cooksey, a senior businessman, venture capitalist, and public policy adviser, rather than by a clinician or health care manager. Alvarez-Rosete and Mays (2008, p. 190) argue: 'the Cooksey review and its recommendations reflect the increased power of the Treasury as well as that of the Department of Trade and Industry and the health care industries (especially the pharmaceutical industry) over health research as opposed to the Department of Health. In future, health research is to be justified more explicitly for its contribution to the economy'. There appeared, in other words, to be an important shift in departmental leadership of health research from the Department of Health to the Treasury and its repositioning as a driver of economic growth.

Shaw and Greenhalgh's (2008) systematic review of a corpus of health research policy texts similarly suggests a colonisation of the research agenda in primary care, as evident in the statement of research policy of the Department of Health (2006), which the authors see as dominated by the business needs of bio pharma to enrol more patients in trials.

The Business Department's rediscovery of an industrial strategy, after a long period of policy-level laissez-faire, led it towards an analysis of promising sectors. This focus soon led it to spot the strong economic growth potential of the life sciences sector (BIS, 2011). The (re)positioning of domestic health policy to ensure the United Kingdom remains competitive in global life sciences markets was a key theme. BIS (2011), for instance, wants the United Kingdom to become 'the global hub for life sciences' (p. 6). It argues (p. 5): 'the industry is changing and the UK must adapt so we can compete in this challenging environment. The UK must capitalise on its strengths: its world class science and clinical research, talent base if pioneering life sciences researchers and the NHS, where discovery can be translated into results for patients. The race is on and we need to move quickly to ensure the UK is where innovation happens'.

This strategy document produced by the Business Department (BIS, 2011) should be seen as an emblematic example of a policy text focused on the life sciences sector and one written from an economic perspective. Perhaps its core proposals lay in attempts to create a globally competitive innovation 'eco system' including but going well beyond the traditional health care sector, arguing: 'new ways of working between universities, hospitals and businesses need to be developed to place the UK at the forefront of medical research now and in the future' (2011, p. 8).

The explicit reframing of the National Health Service here as a driver of national and international industrial investment and growth and its repositioning as an influential macro purchaser of innovation in an internationally competitive arena are significant. There is thus evidence of a continued focus on National Health Service Research and Development and its connection and contribution to economic growth in the life sciences sector over a decade of policy making and over successive governments of different political colours.

In addition, the creation of the Office of the Life Sciences (circa 2012) was an important new body (unusually) set up jointly between the Business Department and the Department of Health to promote the life sciences sector. It even had its own junior joint minister for a period and the Office continues today. The current minister is based in the Business Department but also has a junior ministerial post at Health in respect of COVID vaccine policy.

Overall, it is concluded that a long and consistent policy stream around knowledge mobilisation and the economic growth potential of the health care sector, led by the central economic departments, has significantly broadened the policy community at least in this knowledge mobilisation domain from one traditionally led by health policy communities to a novel and hybrid one which emphasised wealth creation at least as much as health.

A More Diverse Eco System for Health Policy and Management Knowledge

National governments vary to the extent to which they face—and may indeed shape—an open or a closed market for public policy advice (Pollitt & Bouckaert, 2017). In a closed system, civil service insiders possess a near monopoly. In an open system, by contrast, alternative knowledge producers emerge as significant sources. Pollitt and Bouckaert (2017, p. 67), for instance, compare and contrast France, where ideas for reform tended to come from internal 'usual suspects' and the United Kingdom in the 1980s, where Mrs Thatcher's suspicion of civil service domination led her to turn to less statist right-wing think tanks (and business advisers) for alternative advice. So the post-1980s United Kingdom is here cast as a relatively open policy system interested in searching for sources of advice beyond the civil service.

What does this analysis imply for the health care policy process? In the traditional model, advice would come narrowly from the civil servants at the Department of Health and also from a well-elaborated and specialist clinical and scientific advisory machinery, reflecting strong influence from the academic clinical elite embedded in technical and scientific domains. Currently (2020) and in the response to the coronavirus epidemic, the Scientific Advisory Group for Emergencies (https://www.gov.uk/government/organisations/scientific-advisory-group-for-emergencies) is a good example of such insider and expert-based machinery. There have, however, been concerns expressed by some as to its independence from political influence so it is interesting to note that an independent scientific grouping (https://www.independentsage.org/) has recently been set up under a former Government Chief Scientific Adviser as an alternative source of advice. This development is in itself a worked example of the pluralisation of advice in the scientific as well as policy domain.

A complex, London-based, knowledge eco system for health policy advice has been previously characterised by Ferlie et al. (2019) as a co-located 'quadruple helix' of knowledge production (Carayannis & Campbell, 2009). This model adds to the more conventional 'triple helix' (as populated by government, industry, and universities as the three helices) to suggest an additional role for non-profit and civil society–based organisations.

London houses not only the central departments of government (including the Department of Health and Social Care) but also a clustering of different think tanks. Think tanks may be party politically orientated (such as the Fabians which have long been affiliated to the Labour Party), non-party political but more generic (such as the Institute for Government) and/or sectorally based (including the King's Fund, the Nuffield Trust, and the Health Foundation in the case of health care). The number and variety of think tanks seem to be increasing over time. Think tanks may provide broad animating ideas, such as the work of Blond (2010) at the *Res Publica* think tank on developing the so-called Big Society narrative of public management reform (rather briefly) influential around 2010 which advocated the greater use of social enterprises and staff-owned mutuals as providers. These ideas have perhaps had more impact on the social care than the health care sector.

Think tanks may also undertake applied and policy-orientated work for the Department of Health or government more widely or publish pamphlets or accessible books (e.g. Blond, 2010) on rising policy issues which act as a potential bridge into the policy worlds. Key staff may rotate between think tanks and government departments, and move back again.

In addition, London houses many management consultancies, both globalised consultancies with major London offices which work across sectors (but including a health care practice) and some smaller consultancies which are more specifically public services and third sector focused (e.g. Office for Public Management, now renamed as Traverse). It has not always been easy to explore concretely the influence of such consultancies inside the Department of Health but there are glimpses.

Kirkpatrick's et al. (2016) analysis (on the basis of such evidence as exists) suggests (pp. 524–525) an upward trend in spending on management consulting in the UK health care sector. They estimate consulting work in the health care sector now accounts for about 5 per cent of the total turnover of the fees earned by the United Kingdom's management consulting sector. They also argue that the major consulting firms have all had involvement in the health care sector, most notably McKinsey. There indeed appears to be an interchange of personnel between McKinsey and senior levels of the National Health Service (p. 529) and its influence survives changes in political control. Service redesign and strategic reviews have been important area for management consulting activity historically, while areas of current growth include 'lean' systems, and new information technologies. We comment that 'lean' draws on a distinct and well-developed body of management knowledge in its own right.

There are few empirical studies of management consulting activity in action in the UK health care sector and we need more. McGivern et al. (2018) is an exception as they explored in case study work the key role for one major consultancy in devising an implementation strategy for the important productivity enhancing Quality, Innovation, Productivity and Prevention Programme, designed to support the Department of Health in meeting ambitious post-2010 financial targets without (hopefully) sacrificing quality.

In addition, some major and very-well-funded charitable foundations (such as Wellcome) are located in London which can represent a strong a civil society voice. Some of the think tanks (Health Foundation; National Endowment for Science, Technology and the Arts) also have substantial endowments which give them more autonomy in agenda setting. The Young Foundation has a special expertise and interest in applied social research, community development, bottom-up change, and social innovation, with a specific programme of work in social innovation.

Finally, London contains a number of university-based public or health policy departments within a grouping of well-known and research-intensive universities. Some leading public policy academics from these departments may bridge into the world of government by taking on formal or informal advisory roles or may be seconded on a short-term basis to the Department of Health or even the Prime Minister's Office.

Of course, this 'geo knowledge'–based view of London is partial as London is also a global city, exposed to international currents of management and policy knowledge. The operation of a global nexus of business school and management consulting knowledge has already been described by Thrift (2005) and Engwall (2010). These knowledge sources and flows now appear to be influential in British health policy and management as well as the private corporate world. Ferlie et al. (2019) previously suggested that high-prestige American health care organisations, management consulting firms, and academic faculty who have written well-known books may be influential sources, as the flow of management knowledge appears often to be from such high-status sources in the United States of America to the United Kingdom.

Concretely, it appears that the work of Michael Porter (Harvard Business School) on value-based health care (Porter & Teisberg, 2006) has attracted serious interest in elements of the NHS (including in London) as it was seen by some as a framework which could possibly lead to a more creative response to austerity than 'salami slicing' cost savings (Van Elk et al., 2020). In addition, the writing of Michael Moore (Kennedy School of Government, Harvard) on public value (Moore, 1995) has also attracted some interest in national agencies in the National Health Service which went on to commission literature review work (Williams & Shearer, 2011) in this area.

It is thus concluded that a diverse and indeed growing range of non–civil service sources of health policy and management knowledge exist within the London public and health policy space. It is not always easy to trace empirically the extent to which they influence the Department of Health or the National Health Service (or the route by which such influence is exercised) but we have a few glimpses. More work in this important area is indicated.

Concluding Discussion

What is the overall pattern across the examples that have been reviewed?

Some but Limited Pluralisation and No Strong Trend as Yet

There is some but limited evidence of a move to greater pluralisation. Devolution can be seen as a strong example of a move to multi-level governance, but is also a rare and an early one. The Welsh case is interesting for its development of an explicitly alternative approach to policy and governance of the health care sector.

The two cases examined of 'high policy making' showed, if anything, a move back to ministerially (rather than Whitehall or civil service) driven policy making between the National Health Services Plan (2000) and the 2012 Health and Social Care Act, with a retreat from the 'big tent' approaches evident in 2000, albeit that opening was combined with tighter central control later on in the policy process. But are there special circumstances in 2010–2012 in terms of political personalities and the rapid formation of a coalition government which are unlikely to be repeated in future exercises?

Health and Wealth: The Rise of Economic Actors

The continuing (and evident under different political parties) health and wealth stream of policy offers an important policy making opening to central economic departments and a range of economic and business interests from the life sciences sector going beyond the Department of Health and the usual clinical/academic apparatus and health care interest groups. The attempt here to construct a novel and mixed health/wealth policy community is an interesting development.

A New Knowledge Economy in London

Finally, the various dimensions identified of a new knowledge economy of health policy and management advice, clustering in central London, appear as rather broader than a traditional civil service–dominated advisory process.

Narrow Opening to Alternative Policy Elites?

Pluralisation in the UK health policy system, as a whole, seems then to take the form of a relatively narrow opening to a contained range of alternative elites (notably, business or knowledge elites) so it is clearly bounded.

There is little evidence of enhanced democratic involvement or influence from subregional or elected local government, with the possible exception of the interesting New Public Health–orientated model in Wales. More empirical research into health policy making processes there and the extent to which these ideas are enacted in practice (e.g. in the response to COVID) would be most interesting.

Need to Track Future Developments

It will be interesting to see how the next big English health policy exercise plays out in terms of the policy process. It will then be important and possible to assess, on the one hand, whether network governance principles are revived with the 2010–2012 process now being seen as a negative role model. On the other hand, it is also possible that what appears to be an instinctively centralising post-2019 government with its power base lying in the Prime Minister's office rather than the individual departments' acts to recentralise the policy process, including in the health domain as a highly politically sensitive field.

A recentralising centre might (for instance) simply act to abolish agencies deemed to have failed (as may recently have been apparent in the case of Public Health England) or restrict the current substantial independence of the National Health Service Commissioning Board, thereby signalling some reversion to the old Westminster and Whitehall model.

There has not been much high-level health policy making recently in the United Kingdom which might be used to test these arguments further and no legislation at all (perhaps learning from the difficult lessons of the 2012 experience). So where are possible candidates for future examples? The papers from any enquiry into the handling of the 2020 coronavirus epidemic in the United Kingdom should be analysed in terms of the decision-making processes revealed and the role of different actors.

It is also just possible that a much promised but also much delayed policy document ('White Paper') on the future of social care may materialise as it has recently been signalled as a major priority for the Prime Minister, as well as for the Department of Health and Social Care. What type of policy process might be revealed in any such exercise? One argument is that it might be expected to be highly 'network governance' like, given the distinctive set of conditions in the sector: the highly multisectoral nature of the field (with large private and voluntary sectors); substantial private funding from 'self-payers'; the service commissioning role of local authorities; and the presence of active elements of civil society and NGOs with new ideas about a 'wellness'- rather than the old dependence-based paradigm. In addition, 'evidence' here takes a broader form than in conventional acute medicine and may include user-driven and experiential elements and forms of knowledge more than randomised control trials. So the policy process around any social care White Paper could well be a good future test of the 'from government to governance' argument.

Implications for Reflective Policy Makers and Health Care Managers

What are the implications of this analysis for reflective policy makers and managers working in the UK health care sector? If the provisional conclusion of a move to bounded pluralism is confirmed in later empirical work, then it will be important for these practitioners to consider how to develop ways of working effectively with some novel groups from outside the traditional health care sector which are now assuming enhanced importance.

This chapter suggests these groups notably include the business community and its leaders within increasing commercialisation and 'from bench to bedside' exercises in attempts to accelerate the diffusion of innovations and also alternative knowledge providers, notably in the acquisition and effective use of novel management and policy knowledges. This task of developing effective working may require in the first instance the establishment and management of effective relationships with these 'outside' groups. Reflection on the importing of policy and organisational models from outside the sector and how they may require adaptation to the NHS may be important in the knowledge domain.

Finally, health policy making processes and the stakeholders involved may well vary across the four nations of the United Kingdom, so reflection on whether Greer's (2004) useful analysis suggesting substantial variation is still accurate would be important. If it is, what are the implications for designing an appropriate policy process at national level and building associated health policy communities?

References

Alford, R. R. (1977). *Health care politics: Ideological and interest group barriers to reform*. University of Chicago Press.

Alvarez-Rosete, A., & Mays, N. (2008). Reconciling two conflicting tales of the English health policy process since 1997. *British Politics, 3*(2), 183–203.

Alvarez-Rosete, A., & Mays, N. (2014). Understanding NHS policy making in England: The formulation of the NHS plan, 2000. *British Journal of Politics and International Relations, 16*(4), 624–644.

Blond, P. (2010). *Red tory*. Faber and Faber.

Business Innovation and Skills, Department of. (2011). *Strategy for UK life sciences*. Department of Business, Innovation and Skills.

Carayannis, E. G., & Campbell, D. F. (2009). Mode 3 and 'Quadruple Helix': Toward a 21st century fractal innovation ecosystem. *International Journal of Technology Management, 46*(3–4), 201–234.

Cooksey Report. (2006). *A review of UK health funding*. HM Treasury.

Department of Health. (2006). *Best research for best health*. Department of Health.

Department of Health. (2010). *Equity and excellence: Liberating the NHS*. HMSO, Cm7881.

Drakeford, M. (2006). Health policy in Wales: Making a difference in conditions of difficulty. *Critical Social Policy, 26*(3), 543–561.

Engwall, L. (2010). Business schools and consultancies. In M. Kipping & T. Clark (Eds.), *The Oxford handbook of management consulting* (pp. 364–385). Oxford University Press.

Ferlie, E., Nicolini, D., Ledger, J., D'Andreta, D., Kravcenko, D., & de Pury, J., (2017). NHS top managers, knowledge exchange and leadership: The early development of academic health science networks—A mixed-methods study. King's College London: Final Report, see https://www.ncbi.nlm.nih.gov/books/NBK436464/

Ferlie, E., Dopson, S., Bennett, C., Fischer, M., Ledger, J., & McGivern, G. (2019). *The politics of management knowledge in times of austerity*. Oxford University Press.
Freidson, E. (1985). The reorganization of the medical profession. *Medical Care Review, 42*, 11–35.
Greer, S., (2004). *Four way bet: How devolution has led to four different models for the NHS*. Constitution Unit.
Ham, C. (2009). *Health policy in Britain* (6th ed.). Palgrave Macmillan.
Hunter, D. (2003). *Public health policy*. Polity Press.
Kirkpatrick, I., Lonsdale, C., & Neogy, I. (2016). Management consulting in health. In E. Ferlie, K. Montgomery, & A. R. Pedersen (Eds.), *The Oxford handbook of health care management* (Chap. 25, pp. 517–538). Oxford University Press.
Marsh, D. (2008). Understanding British government: Analysing competing models. *The British Journal of Politics and International Relations, 10*(2), 251–268.
Marsh, D., Richards, D., & Smith, M. (2003). Unequal plurality: Towards an asymmetric power model of British politics. *Government and Opposition, 38*(3), 306–332.
McGivern, G., Dopson, S., Ferlie, E., Fischer, M., Fitzgerald, L., Ledger, J., & Bennett, C. (2018). The silent politics of temporal work: A case study of a management consultancy project to redesign public health care. *Organization Studies, 39*(8), 1007–1030.
Moore, M. H. (1995). *Creating public value: Strategic management in government*. Harvard University Press.
National Assembly for Wales. (2001). *Improving health in Wales—A plan for the NHS with its partners*. National Assembly for Wales.
Pollitt, C., & Bouckaert, G. (2017). *Public management reform* (4th ed.). Oxford University Press.
Porter, M. E., & Teisberg, E. O. (2006). *Redefining health care: Creating value-based competition on results*. Harvard Business Press.
Rhodes, R. A. (2007). Understanding governance: Ten years on. *Organization Studies, 28*(8), 1243–1264.
Shaw, S. E., & Greenhalgh, T. (2008). Best research—For what? Best health—For whom? A critical exploration of primary care research using discourse analysis. *Social Science & Medicine, 66*(12), 2506–2519.
Thrift, N. (2005). *Knowing capitalism*. Sage.

Timmins, N. (2012). *Never again?: The story of the health and social care act 2012: A study in coalition government and policy making*. Institute for Government and the King's Fund.

Van Elk, S., Trenholm, S., Lee, R., & Ferlie, E. (2020). *Adopting management philosophies: Management gurus, justification and the economies of worth*. Internal Working Paper: London: King's Business School.

Wanless Report. (2002). *Securing our future health: Taking a long term view*. HM Treasury.

Williams, I., & Shearer, H. (2011). Appraising public value: Past, present and futures. *Public Administration, 89*(4), 1367–1384.

3

Performing Populist Health Policy: The Case of the English National Health Service

Ewen Speed and Russell Mannion

Introduction: The Rising Tide of Populism

There can be little doubt that many western liberal democracies are witnessing a revival in right-wing populist movements and leaders. However, explaining this shift in the global political landscape is far from straightforward. As an analytical concept, populism is fraught with ambiguity and there is a lack of consensus as to how best to understand the current populist moment (see Laclau 2005b; Mudde & Rovira Kaltwasser, 2018). Two competing explanations have been put forward for the global rise of populism (Inglehart & Norris, 2016). One view is that it is the result of

E. Speed (✉)
School of Health and Social Care, University of Essex, Essex, UK
e-mail: esspeed@essex.ac.uk

R. Mannion
Health Service Management Centre, University of Birmingham, Birmingham, UK
e-mail: r.mannion@bham.ac.uk

R. Kislov et al. (eds.), *Managing Healthcare Organisations in Challenging Policy Contexts*, Organizational Behaviour in Healthcare,
https://doi.org/10.1007/978-3-030-81093-1_3

increased economic inequality and growing social exclusion associated with post-industrial societies which have helped fuel popular resentment against traditional political institutions, particularly among the so-called left-behinds. An alternative reading is based on the cultural backlash thesis, which views populism as a retro-backlash against successive waves of progressive cultural change which since the 1970s has sought to foster greater social tolerance of diverse lifestyles and cultures. From this perspective, large segments of the population, particularly older people, white men, and those with less formal qualifications, are said to resent the displacement of their traditional social values. This, it is argued, has created a dissatisfied pool of potential voters who are susceptible to populist appeals that offer a return to a purported 'golden age' of national identity and traditional social values. Our view is that both economic and cultural explanations are behind the rise of populism, but the relative influence of each depends on the context of each country.

Despite conflicting explanations for the rise of populism, what is clear is that recent years have seen the rise to prominence of right-wing populist politicians, including Trump in the United States, Bolsonaro in Brazil, Duterte in the Philippines, Erdoğan in Turkey and Orban in Hungary. In this chapter we focus on specific practices involved in the performance of populism, in order to better understand what the exercise of populist politics might be shown to do.

We consider the implications of this upsurge in right-wing populism for health policy and health professionals. It is presented through an analysis of a particular health policy in the UK (the so-called seven-day NHS; see Conservative Party, 2015). The seven-day policy relates to alleged unwarranted variation in the quality of treatment and care, with typically poorer patient outcomes over the weekend. Our analysis relates specifically to industrial action undertaken in 2015/2016 by junior doctors in the UK, in which the seven-day NHS was a central focal point. We present our analysis over four sections. First, we review recent academic literature to outline the contours of right-wing populist health policy making. Then drawing on Laclau's work on the theory of logics of equivalence and difference we elucidate how a specific political dispute involving the medical profession played out in a particular performative context. By identifying the influence of common populist practices on mainstream contemporary policy context, we demonstrate the ways in which right-wing populist politics serves to prioritise (or marginalise) specific approaches to health policy, often by seeking explicitly to undermine the role or authority of different actors (e.g. by challenging the legitimacy of specific social groups by undermining their claims to expertise).

Populism, Policy and Healthcare

There is a small but growing body of literature situated at the intersection of populism and health policy (see Greer et al., 2017; Speed & Mannion, 2017, 2020; Pavolini et al., 2018; Lasco & Curato, 2019; Lasco, 2020; De Cleen & Speed, 2020). We contend that consideration of political ideology is central to making sense of how health policies are framed (Herwartz & Theilen, 2014) and that the study of populism in the context of health policy is central to this ideological framing. However, it is important to note that we are not necessarily interested in ideology as it plays out in terms of populist policy. Rather, we argue that the performance of populism, by a politician of any persuasion, is a process which facilitates discreet political ends. Populism enables politicians to express specific social rationalities (and to disavow others) in ways which can be seen to facilitate their favoured ideological projects and to denigrate those of their rivals. Our analysis demonstrates how the performance of populism can be used as a vehicle for the enactment of ideology in the context of health policy.

In addressing similar political processes, Lasco and Curato (2019) define medical populism as 'a political style that constructs antagonistic relations between 'the people' whose lives have been put at risk by 'the establishment'. This political spirit of antagonism is predicated on characterisations of who 'the people' are, and by implication othering whole classes of society as *not* being of their people. This process trades on notions of nativism (De Cleen & Speed, 2020) to create in-groups and out-groups. Similarly, Greer et al. (2017) link populism with nativism, authoritarianism and a preference for 'the common sense of the people' over elite or expert and professional knowledge (see also Mudde, 2010).

These populist practices raise very immediate and direct concerns for public health in a time of COVID, when processes around infection control, quarantine and potential vaccination need the involvement of the entire population, not specific in-groups. Lasco and Curato also identify the notion of crisis, and how healthcare issues are typically played out in a context of a moral panic, predicated upon the mobilisation of real and immediate threats to collective (nativist) values, often using inflammatory rhetoric to invoke 'folk devils' (Mannion & Small, 2019). Such moral panic/crises then function as a means of justifying actions to counter this 'immediate' threat. This is a useful outline of these processes, but it is important to note that we are not suggesting this as a model of populist policy making, rather that these are populist techniques or practices which have been shown to be effective in furthering particular political agendas. This again is to return to the point that populism is a set of practices that allow particular forms of politics to get done, rather than being a form of politics in and of itself.

There are other clear links between populism, politics, healthcare professions and the framing of health policy. Pavolini et al. (2018) identify three key components that are critical to an understanding of the complex relationship between healthcare governance and the professions. Their analysis shows two types of healthcare system based on different approaches to governance and how this relates to populist politics. Type one healthcare systems are well-resourced, with a well-developed network-based model of governance and with central involvement of the professions in the policy process. Type one systems tend to be more resistant to populist politics. Conversely, type two healthcare systems are poorly resourced, combined with neo-liberal New Public Management (NPM) forms of governance, and lower levels of trust in authority (e.g. healthcare providers and professionals). Type two systems tend to be more susceptible to populist politics. The UK NHS corresponds with Pavolini et al.'s second type of health system (e.g. poorly resourced, low-trust, NPM-style governance).

Whilst this analysis is useful, in this chapter we are interested in building upon these previous studies to analyse populism as a set of rules (or grammars) which play out across forms of policy, regardless of whether they are expressly populist or not (De Cleen et al., 2018). Similarly, we do not regard populist policies as distinct examples of a right-wing political strategy (De Cleen & Speed, 2020). Rather they are a set of strategies that enable political actors to accomplish specific ends across a range of settings. In taking this type of approach, it becomes necessary to direct an analytical focus onto the performative components of populist politics (that is to say, what it accomplishes, and how).

Conceptualising Populism as Logics of Equivalence and Difference

Our approach to the study of populism is informed by the work of Laclau (2005a, 2005b). In relation to the performance of populism, Laclau sets out two central components, structured around logics of equivalence and difference.

A logic of equivalence is premised on the idea that different groups of actors may have an equivalence in terms of facing the same common enemy. The notion of equivalence in this logic is more negatively construed around a shared common enemy, rather than a more positive shared interest. Shared opposition to an expert professional elite would be an example of a logic of equivalence. For example, take the political rhetoric on mask wearing in relation to COVID-19. Those on the political right have mobilised against mask wearing, regarding it as an infringement on civil liberties, whereas the political left has embraced mask wearing as a necessary public health intervention that will prevent the spread of infection. The performance of a logic of equivalence in this context might be that right-wing logic which portrays the act of wearing masks as a matter of individual choice, rather than government-mandated behaviour, and seeks to oppose mandatory mask wearing as a policy. This then offers a direct connection between a whole host of like-minded actors (libertarians, anti-science lobby and so forth, who have aligned with anti-mask rhetoric) (Rosenbaum, 2020). This could be seen as drawing a line of equivalence (against mask wearing), railed against common enemies—the pro-mask lobby and public health professionals, painted as a scientific, liberal elite.

In contrast, a logic of difference is concerned with practices which seek to maintain existing social structures (Glynos & Howarth, 2007). In this context social demands and identities are managed in 'ways that do not disturb or modify a dominant practice or regime in a fundamental way' (Howarth, 2010, p.321). Again, in the context of the UK response to COVID-19, this might be seen in the promotion of the view that the economic impact of a full-scale national lockdown would be worse than the impact of the pandemic on public health (bringing it down to a question of livelihoods or lives). This difference between the economic and the public health contexts would tend to be mobilised around concerns about population mental health and so forth (e.g. the impact of a lockdown on population mental health will be worse than the impact of not imposing a lockdown). If the imposition of a national lockdown were resisted, this could in part be due to the vested interests of specific economic actors, at the expense of other public health actors, such that the status quo of the vested economic interests is protected against further lockdown. The 'difference' operates at the level where it is difficult for any meaningful equivalences to be drawn, such that it becomes difficult to act against the status quo, for example for public health and economic interests to align against government—public health interests and economic interests have been cast as antithetical to each other, when this is not necessarily the case. Logics of difference operate on a principle of 'divide and conquer', and it is here that the value of populist politics becomes apparent. Such populist tropes enable the mobilisation of particular logics of difference, and the disavowal of other counter logics, to protect the status quo.

In terms of the consequence of this framing, Laclau (2005a) argues that 'populism's relative ideological simplicity and emptiness should be approached in terms of what those processes of simplification and emptying attempt to perform, that is to say, the social rationality they express' (p.14). Logics of equivalence and difference are central in the expression of specific social rationalities. In the analysis that follows in seeking to surface how these populist performances are enacted we consider an illustrative case drawn from the UK.

The Seven-Day NHS and Junior Doctors

Our case is the political debate led by the then Secretary of State for Health, Jeremy Hunt, that commenced in the UK in 2015 around proposals for a seven-day NHS. The seven-day issue was a policy first proposed in the party political election manifesto of 2015 (Conservative Party, 2015). It claimed that there was a need 'to increase spending on the NHS, provide seven-day-a-week access to your GP and deliver a truly seven-day NHS'. We chose this example for a number of reasons. First, it is an apposite case study of populist performativity. It would be difficult to characterise the then Secretary of State for Health Jeremy Hunt as either a popular or a populist politician, but this example demonstrates how the government used a form of performative populism to frame and legitimise a particular set of changes in UK health policy. The ways in which Hunt articulated healthcare reform, very much in a mainstream political context (i.e. not framed on a marginal or extreme form of right-wing populism), highlight the analytical utility of a performative characterisation of populism. In turn this demonstrates a very clear need to assess the role of populism in the context of mainstream politics, to enable us to regard populism as a practice of all politics, not as a marginal property of the political or policy extremes.

The particular case was played out during an extended and acrimonious ten-month dispute between junior doctors and the government regarding the introduction of new working practices. Central to these changes was the deployment of a new employment contract for junior doctors, which altered their core working hours from 7am to 7pm Monday–Friday, to 7am to 10pm Monday–Saturday (i.e. a change that resulted in a total of thirty hours now counting as core contracted hours that previously would have qualified as overtime). The public and parliamentary discussion of these changes coincided with widespread reports in the scientific literature and mainstream media that there was excess mortality within the UK health system, and that this mortality was largely attributable to differing staffing levels in hospitals between weekdays and weekends. In July 2015, in a speech in the UK legislature about the NHS, Hunt stated:

> about 6,000 people lose their lives every year because we do not have a proper seven-day service in hospitals. Someone is 15% more likely to die if they are admitted on a Sunday than if they are admitted on a Wednesday. That is unacceptable to doctors as well as patients. In 2003–04, the then government gave GPs and consultants the right to opt out of out-of-hours and weekend work, at the same time as offering significant pay increases. The result was a Monday-to-Friday culture in many parts of the NHS, with catastrophic consequences for patient safety. (HC Deb 2015)

These are very serious claims and could clearly cause alarm to potential patients admitted at the weekend. According to Hunt's statement, weekend patients were 15% more likely to die. Furthermore, he quickly attributed the blame for this 15% anomaly at the door of the medical profession and an established Monday-to-Friday working culture. The clear implication is that the 15% difference in mortality rates is because GPs and hospital consultants do not work on weekends. However, this interpretation of the research evidence is at odds with much of the published research (Craven, 2015). Hunt's claim of excess mortality levels in the NHS was apparently drawn from what was (at the time of the debate) a pending publication in the *British Medical Journal* (see Freemantle et al., 2015), which claimed an estimated figure of 11,000 excess deaths in NHS hospitals at weekends.

The profession was vocal in its opposition to this representation of the data, but Hunt doubled down, claiming there were eight published papers which demonstrated a weekend effect (Dearden, 2016). The author of one of those eight cited papers stated that his analysis could never have shown that higher staffing on weekends reduced mortality (ibid.). Another of the cited 'eight' was the report by Freemantle, from which Hunt had drawn his initial 6000 claim. It is true that Freemantle's study reported that 11,000 more people died on a weekend than on a weekday. However, as Craven (2015) asserts, the report authors did not make any claims regarding the cause of these deaths, nor did they take a view on what proportion of those deaths may have been avoidable. In other words, and somewhat crucially, the authors did not say that any patients had died *because* they were admitted on a weekend. Godlee, the editor in chief of the *British Medical Journal*, went on the public record accusing Hunt of blatantly misrepresenting an academic article published in the journal. In his reply to Godlee, Hunt stated that his 'comments ... while giving a rough estimation of the *BMJ* article, [are] also drawn on ... other evidence' (Kmietowicz, 2015). Given the high stakes of the debate, for Hunt to admit this emotive figure was derived using a 'rough estimate' would seem to be ill-advised at the very least.

In a telling analysis, Taylor (2016) highlights that what the Freemantle paper actually shows is that people are less likely to die in hospital at the weekend. This is because the analysis presented by Freemantle et al. related to the risk of death for patients *admitted* to hospital at the weekend, not to patients being treated in hospital at the weekend. This is a crucial difference. For Taylor, a plausible explanation for this pattern might relate to out-of-hours care in nursing homes or at GP surgeries on Saturday mornings. Excess deaths may have nothing to do with junior doctors' working practices, at the weekend or any other time. Relatedly, Aldridge et al. (2017) in a paper in the *Lancet* warn that 'policy makers should exercise caution before attributing the weekend effect mainly to differences in specialist staffing' (178). At the time (nor indeed since) this element of doubt about the robustness of the evidence did not appear important to the government.

This claim of excess deaths can be read as a populist appeal, deployed to create a logic of equivalence between politicians and patients, simultaneously aligned them against the excesses of a lazy elite unsympathetically inured in their Monday-to-Friday working culture. It functions to undermine the standing and status of junior doctors; that is, to portray the profession and their working practices, as contributing to the unnecessary deaths of 11,000 people. This enabled the government to portray doctors as placing their own vested interests (pay and conditions) above those of patients.

Hunt continued to talk up excess weekend mortality in the NHS and proposed the solution to this issue was the development of the seven-day NHS initiative—whereby the objective of the policy is very much couched in its name. It would appear that the fact that the policy prejudges any assessment of the available evidence is not a problem. This is perhaps a textbook example of policy-based evidence (PBE; see Cairney, 2019), whereby a policy maker is clearly decided upon their relevant policy and then seeks to identify relevant information to support that policy. There is a clear lack of consensus in the literature about the quality of the information cited by government to justify the introduction of this policy. In terms of the social rationality that the government view expressed, this specific performance of the problem functioned to identify the medical profession as the common 'enemy of the people'.

This line of equivalence was, as would be expected, rejected and countered by the medical profession (see Rimmer & Kmietowicz, 2015; Craven, 2015). The profession sought to create and maintain a logic of difference between themselves and government, claiming that Hunt had misrepresented the weekend mortality data. This strategy on the part of the profession functioned to seek to protect existing relations with the public and presented the junior doctors as the wronged party. By implication they are also claiming to be those with the public interest at heart, that is, more so than government. An early review of hospital admissions immediately after Hunt's speeches by a team of medical researchers (Gan & Kanaris, 2015) suggested that Hunt's rhetoric (which they labelled 'the Hunt effect') was leading to excess mortality amongst a group of patients who were too afraid to attend hospital at the weekend. However, this profession's logic of difference proved largely ineffective in countering the equivalences drawn by government. The medical profession's populist appeals to the official misuse of data proved insufficient against the government's populist characterisation of indolent professionals unwilling to work at the weekend.

Within this populist performance on the part of government, the facts of the matter are downplayed, such that the relative quality or representation of the evidence is backgrounded by emotive appeals which castigate 'self-serving professional elites'. These appeals functioned to undermine the claims of 'objective evidence' and credentialed expertise. In turn, the vilification of 'uncaring' doctors served to align with the interests of a broader neo-liberal political movement seeking to limit the power of the profession (Speed & Gabe, 2013, 2019) based on a poorly resourced, NPM-style, low-trust model of healthcare governance (Pavolini et al., 2018). The issue of public debate becomes one where political representations of self-serving professional elites are contrasted against the profession's representations of untruthful politicians, and the facts of the matter become difficult to establish, never mind discuss. Furthermore, this populist rhetoric which painted a picture of self-serving and incompetent managers and clinicians was used to double down on a pre-existing narrative of 'value for money' and inefficiency in the use taxpayer's money (Lansley, 2010) coupled to socio-political demands for more private provision of healthcare services (see Letwin & Redwood, 1988; Speed, 2018). This speaks to the wider political ideology which might be seen to underpin these moves.

To return to the seven-day NHS, the net outcome of this populist performance was that the government won the debate. This was despite the fact that junior doctors undertook unprecedented strike action across England against the imposition of the new contract in April 2016. These strikes had high levels of initial public support (Spooner et al., 2017). However, subsequent strike action in September 2016 was suspended amid reported declining public support for industrial action. Behind the glare of publicity, the junior doctors, following arbitration talks, took a decision to suspend their industrial action. Then, in the autumn of 2016, the government imposed the new contract, without the consent of junior doctors, in what could be interpreted as an act of bad faith. More bad faith was demonstrated when the day after the unilateral imposition of the junior doctor contract, a letter signed by NHS leaders was published in a national newspaper. It claimed that they supported the imposition of the contract and that they backed the government to do 'whatever it deems necessary' to break the deadlock (Lintern, 2016). Following initial publication of the letter, fourteen NHS leaders who were named as signatories on the letter subsequently claimed that they did not support any such imposition. One chief executive claimed that she had not known her name was even on the letter, whilst one Chief Executive said that the letter they had signed did not advise the government to do 'whatever it deems necessary' (Elgot, 2016).

Additionally, the junior doctor contract was simply one amongst many new contractual agreements for the medical profession being developed by the central government at this time. Perhaps, in a move indicative of the power of populist appeals (but also in part a reflection of differential power relationships across hospital consultants and government *and* junior doctors and government) in March 2017, NHS consultants voted against an automatic ballot of members with regard to the new consultants' contract, preferring to opt for individual choice over contractual terms in discussion with government, rather than a collective ballot (Rimmer, 2017).

The junior doctors' example demonstrates quite clearly the effectiveness for government of a populist strategy in the context of mainstream politics. Our case study demonstrates how, in this context, the populist performance cannot be described as a form of extreme or marginal politics that so often characterises populist rhetoric. Rather, and far more straightforwardly, the expression of this specific populist social rationality functioned to make the out-group (in this case the junior doctors, but by extension all members of the medical profession) marginal to a precarious unity (or equivalence) of government and people, who in turn were unified against that self-serving professional elite. The success of these practices would appear to be in the strength of the logic of equivalence. The Secretary of State for Health, by invoking this conflict, successfully developed a new set of boundaries between doctors, government and patients. By invoking the death of parents, partners, sons and daughters (e.g. of friends and family), the government draws a very powerful logic of equivalence, seeking to pit patients and their families against the profession. Furthermore, the government identified itself as best placed to legislate (through implementation of a seven-day NHS) to sort this problem out, to assert the general will of the people because the problem has, successfully, been attributed to professional truculence. The assertion of needless deaths due to weekend understaffing functioned to articulate a set of socio-political demands. In turn, junior doctors were largely powerless to resist these demands (and importantly), regardless of the erroneous reading of the data upon which such assertions were made.

Conclusion: Populism and Policy Success

Across this case we have sought to highlight the analytical utility of conceiving of populism as a form of political logics. This approach enables an analysis of the ways in which the performance of populist politics can express very specific and particular social rationalities. In this sense, populism is not in itself ideological, but rather operates as a vehicle for the mobilisation of political strategy. Our approach facilitates an analysis which focuses on mobilisation of these specific social rationalities, in pursuit of political *and* policy ends; that is, a primary and overarching intention of the seven-day NHS policy was to impose a new contract on all NHS doctors in a way that fundamentally altered their terms of employment. This issue was a completely separate issue that was successfully backgrounded by government through the performance of the seven-day NHS debacle.

As such, in this chapter, we have interpreted populism as a performative act which serves to mobilise public opinion, political action and policy formulation and implementation towards particular ends. We reject the notion that populism is simply an ideological characteristic of extremist or marginal politics. There is a clear need to critique what populism does, rather than point to what it is.

To accomplish this, we need to consider the ways in which populist politics can be seen to coalesce around particular sets of political or structural moments (as sets of political demands or practices). In turn these demands or practices may be organised to buttress (or resist) new or existing political boundaries or frontiers. In this sense, populism in relation to the seven-day NHS serves as a logic of equivalence behind which a disparate alignment of groups is achieved against a perceived common enemy.

The net effect is that several consequences of these political demands may be backgrounded or concealed. For example, the fundamental change to core contracted hours of employment is lost amidst claims of excess weekend mortality. The alignment of mutual equivalence against the perceived vested interest of the profession functions to rob the profession of any consequent legitimacy, with the moral concerns of excess mortality trumping any other counter claims of unfairness. That is to say, the logic of equivalence about an indolent profession functioned to create a far more robust alliance across government and the public, than any logic of difference that the medical profession was able to mobilise around the veracity of the government analysis. The descriptions by the Secretary of State for Health of excess mortality expressed a far more gripping social rationality than claims of problematic industrial relations between the profession and the state.

It is important to note that the two key players in our analysis were the government and the medical profession. This is not to say that there were no other vested interests involved. Our analysis is intended to demonstrate the way in which government was able to express a particular social rationality, and to then use this to countervail the profession, rendering them largely ineffectual. Our example shows very clearly how these populist practices undermined credible claims against the legitimacy of that government. It also suggests the motivation for these policies may have been driven more by political ideology (policy-based evidence) rather than being evidence-based policy making.

This brings us back to the need to understand the political performance of populism in terms of what it does, what actions it accomplishes and in whose interests these actions might be taken. It is insufficient simply to highlight the problems with the veracity (or lack thereof) of populist rhetoric—that is, whether claims are fake news or real news. Rather, right-wing populist practices need to be considered as performative vehicles and understood in terms of the wider political interests they serve.

It is in this context that the evidence and expertise might retain some standing and credibility in the face of a post-truth populist politics (Speed & Mannion, 2017). In the context of health policy and public health, similar populist practices to those we outline here can be seen to be fostering social, political and economic inequality in population health (see Speed & Mannion, 2020), particularly around issues in reproductive and sexual health, but also in the context of vaccination programmes. It will also have a very real effect on health, medicine and social care professions.

By focussing on what populism does, we can shed light on the direct consequences of these types of tactics. The case we have selected illustrates a tendency to perform populism around logics of equivalence, which function to identify in-groups and out-groups and mobilise public and political actions with (or against) those groups. In this context performative populist practices can be understood as attempts to forge new political alignments through processes of contestation and change, and this raises very real concerns in relation to the form and function of policy making. Questions of evidence-based policy versus policy-based evidence are not new; where the novelty lies is in the use of populist performative practices to enact the work of policy making. This is accomplished by policy makers seeking to use populist performances to constrain and limit the terms of the debate, not at the margins of extreme politics, but very much in the political mainstream. It is to this development that we need to pay the most attention, if we are to ensure that health policy continues to serve the interests of all stakeholders rather than shore up partisan interests. A populist politics driven by division and promoting health inequalities can only be bad for all of our health.

References

Aldridge, C., Bion, J., Boyal, A., Chen, Y.-F., Clancy, M., Evans, T., et al. (2017). Weekend specialist intensity and admission mortality in acute hospital trusts in England: A cross-sectional study. *The Lancet, 388*(10040), 178–186. https://doi.org/10.1016/S0140-6736(16)30442-1

Cairney, P. (2019). The UK government's imaginative use of evidence to make policy. *British Politics*. https://doi.org/10.1057/s41293-017-0068-2

Conservative Party. (2015). *The Conservative Party manifesto 2015*. Conservative Party.

Craven, D. (2015). The statistical sins of Jeremy Hunt. *British Medical Journal, 351*(6358). https://doi.org/10.1136/bmj.h6358

De Cleen, B., Glynos, J., & Mondon, A. (2018). Critical research on populism: Nine rules of engagement. *Organization, 25*(5), 649–661.

De Cleen, B., & Speed, E. (2020). Getting the problem definition right: The radical right, populism, nativism and public health comment on "A scoping review of populist radical right parties' influence on welfare policy and its implications for population health in Europe". *International Journal of Health Policy and Management*.

Dearden, L. (2016). Jeremy Hunt 'misrepresenting' data on weekend death rates at NHS hospitals, says research surgeon, *The Independent*, 13 February, https://www.independent.co.uk/news/uk/home-news/jeremy-hunt-misrepresenting-data-on-mortality-at-nhs-hospitals-doctor-who-conducted-study-saysa6872281.html (accessed 23 August 2021).

Elgot, J. (2016). Health chief: Letter backing 'whatever is necessary' on contracts was not agreed, *The Guardian*, 12 February, https://www.theguardian.com/society/2016/feb/12/health-chief-letter-whatever-necessary-contracts-not-agreed (accessed 23 August 2021).

Freemantle, N., Ray, D., McNulty, D., Rosser, D., Bennett, S., Keogh, B. E., & Pagano, D. (2015). Increased mortality associated with weekend hospital admission: A case for expanded seven day services? *British Medical Journal, 351*. https://doi.org/10.1136/bmj.h4596

Gan, H. W., & Kanaris, C. (2015). Increased mortality associated with weekend hospital admission: a case for expanded seven day services? *British Medical Journal, 351*, h4596.

Glynos, J., & Howarth, D. (2007). *Logics of critical explanation in social and political theory. Logics of critical explanation in social and political theory.* Routledge.

Greer, S. L., Bekker, M., De Leeuw, E., Wismar, M., Helderman, J.-K., Ribeiro, S., & Stuckler, D. (2017). Policy, politics and public health. *European Journal of Public Health, 27*(suppl_4), 40–43.

Herwartz, H., & Theilen, B. (2014). Health care and ideology: A reconsideration of political determinants of public healthcare funding in the OECD. *Health Economics, 23*(2), 225–240. https://doi.org/10.1002/hec.2917

Howarth, D. (2010). Power, discourse, and policy: Articulating a hegemony approach to critical policy studies. *Critical Policy Studies, 3*(3–4), 309–335. https://doi.org/10.1080/19460171003619725

Inglehart, R., & Norris, P. (2016). Trump, Brexit, and the rise of populism: Economic have-nots and cultural backlash.

Kmietowicz, Z. (2015). Hunt dismisses BMJ editor's claims that he misused weekend mortality data. *BMJ, 351*, h6789. https://doi.org/10.1136/bmj.h6789

Laclau, E. (2005a). Populism: What's in a name? In F. Panizza (Ed.), *Populism and the mirror of democracy* (pp. 32–49). Verso.

Laclau, E. (2005b). *On populist reason.* Verso.

Lansley, A. (2010). *Equity and excellence: Liberating the NHS.* Department of Health.

Lasco, G. (2020). Medical populism and the COVID-19 pandemic. *Global Public Health*, 1–13.

Lasco, G., & Curato, N. (2019). Medical populism. *Social Science & Medicine, 221*, 1–8. https://doi.org/10.1016/j.socscimed.2018.12.006

Letwin, O., & Redwood, J. (1988). *Britain's biggest enterprise.* Centre for Policy Studies.

Lintern, S. (2016). Dalton tells Hunt to "do what is necessary" on junior doctors' contract. *Health Service Journal.* https://www.google.co.uk/url?sa=t&rct=j&q=&esrc=s&source=web&cd=&cad=rja&uact=8&ved=2ahUKEwjvytPC25jtAhXVilwKHboqBHgQFjAAegQIBBAC&url=https%3A%2F%2Fwww.

hsj.co.uk%2Fworkforce%2Fdalton-tells-hunt-to-do-what-is-necessary-on-junior-doctors-contract%2F7002346

Mannion, R., & Small, N. (2019). On folk devils, moral panics and new wave public health. *International Journal of Health Policy and Management, 8*(12), 678.

Mudde, C. (2010). The populist radical right: A pathological normalcy. *West European Politics, 33*(6), 1167–1186. https://doi.org/10.1080/01402382.2010.508901

Mudde, C., & Rovira Kaltwasser, C. (2018). Studying populism in comparative perspective: Reflections on the contemporary and future research agenda. *Comparative Political Studies, 51*(13), 1667–1693. https://doi.org/10.1177/0010414018789490

Pavolini, E., Kuhlmann, E., Agartan, T. I., Burau, V., Mannion, R., & Speed, E. (2018). Healthcare governance, professions and populism: Is there a relationship? An explorative comparison of five European countries. *Health Policy, 122*(10), 1140–1148.

Rimmer, A. (2017). Consultants vote against automatic ballot on new contract. *British Medical Journal, 356.*

Rimmer, A., & Kmietowicz, Z. (2015). BMJ editor writes to Hunt over misuse of weekend mortality data. *British Medical Journal, 351.*

Rosenbaum, L. (2020). Tribal Truce—How can we bridge the partisan divide and conquer Covid? *New England Journal of Medicine, 383*(17), 1682–1685. https://doi.org/10.1056/NEJMms2027985

Speed, E., & Gabe, J. (2013). The Health and Social Care Act for England 2012: The extension of "new professionalism". *Critical Social Policy, 33*(3). https://doi.org/10.1177/0261018313479010

Speed, E., & Mannion, R. (2017). The rise of post-truth populism in pluralist liberal democracies: Challenges for health policy. *International Journal of Health Policy and Management, 6*(5). https://doi.org/10.15171/ijhpm.2017.80

Speed, E. (2018). Transforming a public good into a private bad: Political legitimacy, wilful deceit and the reform of the NHS in England. In M. Bevir & J. Waring (Eds.), *Decentring health policy* (pp. 187–204). Routledge. https://doi.org/10.4324/9781315310817

Speed, E., & Gabe, J. (2019). The reform of the English National Health Service: Professional dominance, countervailing powers and the buyers' revolt. *Social Theory & Health*. https://doi.org/10.1057/s41285-019-00116-x

Speed, E., & Mannion, R. (2020). Populism and health policy: Three international case studies of right-wing populist policy frames. *Sociology of Health & Illness*.

Spooner, S., Gibson, J., Rigby, D., Sutton, M., Pearson, E., & Checkland, K. (2017). Stick or twist? Career decision-making during contractual uncertainty for NHS junior doctors. *BMJ Open, 7*(1), e013756.

Taylor, P. (2016). Jeremy Hunt's way with statistics, *London Review of Books LRB Blog*, 10 February, https://www.lrb.co.uk/blog/2016/february/jeremyhunt-s-way-with-statistics (accessed 23 August 2021).

4

Policy Delusions and Dutiful Daughters: Imagined Versus Real Care Integration for Older People

Kristiana Ludlow, Jackie Bridges, Catherine Pope, Johanna Westbrook, and Jeffrey Braithwaite

Introduction

Care systems for older adults have many stakeholders, but in this chapter, we focus on two groups: those who formulate policy at the blunt-end and those who spend time making the system work at the sharp-end (Braithwaite et al., 2017; Hollnagel, 2004). By examining care integration at these policy-making and frontline-doing ends of care systems, we compare and contrast the ways in which policymakers advocate for integrated care and the work unpaid carers (often daughters) do to achieve

K. Ludlow (✉) • J. Westbrook • J. Braithwaite
Australian Institute of Health Innovation, Macquarie University, North Ryde, NSW, Australia
e-mail: kristiana.ludlow@mq.edu.au; johanna.westbrook@mq.edu.au; jeffrey.braithwaite@mq.edu.au

J. Bridges
School of Health Sciences, University of Southampton, Southampton, UK
e-mail: jackie.bridges@soton.ac.uk

R. Kislov et al. (eds.), *Managing Healthcare Organisations in Challenging Policy Contexts*, Organizational Behaviour in Healthcare,
https://doi.org/10.1007/978-3-030-81093-1_4

care coordination for older family members. We are particularly interested in attempts to create integrated care for older adults in England and Australia. In these two countries, formal care is provided to older adults by the healthcare system (e.g., hospitals, primary care), aged and/or social care systems (e.g., home care, residential care), and those service providers who work across the two systems (e.g., general practitioners, nurses and allied health professionals).

In this chapter we consider integrated care (also called 'streamlined', 'seamless', 'coordinated' and 'joined up' care) across care settings, services, specialities or systems. Care integration is a recurrent policy ambition, attempting to address discontinuities and fragmentation in caring systems (Coleman, 2003; Rajan & McKee, 2019). Various policy documents that intend to shape, structure, or influence care systems—White Papers, five-year plans, and other authoritative, instrumental reports—speak of the need for integrated services; but we understand little about how integration is achieved via policy, in contrast to how it is achieved on the frontlines of the system.

Policymakers do not make a system work on the ground so much as they indicate how they would like it to be. Managers are one candidate group for making care systems operate smoothly, but they tend to work in silos (e.g., health regions, hospitals, care homes), and are often unable to integrate services across the care continuum due to a focus on their own responsibilities. Clinicians look after patients episodically; one person, condition, or group of patients at a time, so they too are not a ready solution to integration (Hajek, 2013). Aged care and social care workforces face systemic problems including staffing shortages, rigid routines, and inadequate skill-mix that hinder care delivery (Ludlow, Churruca, Mumford, et al., 2020a). This is not to say these professional groups do not have an important role to play in care coordination, but rather the fragmented and siloed nature of formal care systems impedes professionals' capacity to integrate care for older adults.

C. Pope
Nuffield Department of Primary Care Health Sciences, University of Oxford, Oxford, UK
e-mail: catherine.pope@phc.ox.ac.uk

Turning the care system on its head, service users (i.e., patients, aged care clients or residents) may be better placed to ensure integration. This often requires a personal capacity that may not be available, especially for older people and those living with chronic conditions, functional limitations, or diminished resources. Who looks after and integrates the care of those who have many needs, but less capacity to manage their condition or circumstances? The answer, resoundingly, is family members, who disproportionately do the work of looking after people in these categories.

The Role of Family Members in Caregiving and Care Integration

Family members 'bridge the gaps' in care when an older person's care needs are unmet (Ludlow, Churruca, Ellis, et al., 2020b; Puurveen et al., 2018). Bookman and Harrington (2007) referred to family caregivers as the 'shadow workforce', providing care in the home, healthcare institutions and the community, whilst being untrained, unpaid, and unrecognised members of the care workforce. They interviewed 50 US family caregivers, two-thirds of whom were women. Families spoke about inadequate coordination and communication within and across healthcare institutions, a lack of continuity of care, a disconnect between community services, problems accessing information, and the difficulties dealing with the complexity of different systems. In a system described as 'uncoordinated, fragmented, bureaucratic, and often depersonalised' (p. 1011), caregivers coordinated care, ensuring that their loved ones did not fall through the cracks. They did this by occupying various roles:

- Case manager: coordinating care and managing relationships across siloed providers
- Patient advocate: arguing for and supporting patients when necessary care was not provided or when quality was poor
- Medical record keeper: documenting and conveying important medical information and personal histories
- Paramedic: providing medical and personal care, monitoring diets and nutritional intake, and managing medications

In related work, Wong-Cornall et al. (2017) conducted interviews with 13 family caregivers in New Zealand, the majority of whom were Maori women caring for older family members. Caregivers were found to promote continuity of care in three key ways: extending chronic care into the home through engagement and relationship building across a range of healthcare professionals, facilitating the transfer of information between providers, and managing care consistently and flexibly. Both Bookman and Harrington (2007) and Wong-Cornall et al. (2017) discussed a lack of acknowledgement from healthcare services and policymakers regarding the pivotal role family play in the care of older persons. They called for updated policy to better support caregivers, and a greater recognition of family caregivers as 'partners in an integrated model of care' (Wong-Cornall et al., 2017, p. 2).

The Gender Imbalance in Caregiving and Other Unpaid Work

Global evidence shows that women do the majority of unpaid work in society, including caregiving (Ferrant & Thim, 2019; International Labour Organization, 2019). In England, Anne Oakley's pioneering studies of domestic labour found that few men in heterosexual partnerships contributed to housework (Oakley, 1974). Subsequent surveys have confirmed that these gender imbalances in domestic labour persist (Adjei & Brand, 2018; Allan & Crow, 2001). In the workplace there is ample global evidence that women are more likely to 'put their work life on hold' to raise children and care for relatives, friends, and neighbours (Boniol et al., 2019; PwC, 2019; United Nations General Assembly, 2019). Compared to men, they forgo promotions to a greater extent, need to take greater leaves of absence, and ask for flexibility with work arrangements more frequently.

For 40 years, researchers have written about the 'sandwich generation' (Miller, 1981), and the 'women in the middle' phenomenon (Boyd & Treas, 1989) to describe how women bear most of the responsibility for the generation above them and the generation below. This literature (see also Bridges & Lynam, 1993; Chisholm, 1999; DeRigne & Ferrante, 2012; Do et al., 2014; Doress-Worters, 1994; Evans et al., 2016, 2019;

Gillett & Crisp, 2017; Huvent-Grelle et al., 2015; Raphael & Schlesinger, 1994; Riley & Bowen, 2005; Solberg et al., 2014; Steiner & Fletcher, 2017; Stephens et al., 1994) points out that women in their mid-years do more than their share of looking after ageing parents and children, regardless of family composition or living arrangement. Metaphors such as *juggling all the balls*, *herding cats*, and *being on a hamster wheel* are often used.

In seminal, highly cited work, Montgomery, Gonyea, and Hooyman (Hooyman & Gonyea, 1995, 1999; Montgomery et al., 1985) developed and articulated a feminist perspective on family care. They saw caring as a feminist issue, reinforced the fact that women were primary caregivers of older adults and children, noted the social context of caregiving, and critiqued long-term care policy. They did this at a time of markedly changing trends in the workforce, policy, and population demographics. Against the context of the 1980s and 1990s and the rise of dual-income families, women were much more likely to be working and studying compared to past eras, while simultaneously caregiving and running the family home.

In Australia, 2018, females made up 71.8% of unpaid primary carers of older adults or people with a disability (Australian Bureau of Statistics, 2019) and in the UK, 59% of people caring for a parent or older relative are women (Petrie & Kirkup, 2018). Close female relatives, typically daughters, are disproportionately likely to be primary caregivers of older people (Grigoryeva, 2017; Patterson & Margolis, 2019; Szinovacz & Davey, 2013), and so we focus here on the daughter's role as integrator-in-chief of care. Specifically, this chapter examines and contrasts how the care integration role of 'dutiful daughters' is reflected in policy and experienced in practice. We use the term 'dutiful' as recognition that the act of caregiving is often undertaken out of necessity (because of gaps in formal care) or expectation (societal norms). Care organisation can be challenging in a complex political context, due in part to multiple and competing narratives and the co-existence of a variety of mechanisms of governance, each influencing care in multiple and sometimes contradictory ways. Our chapter demonstrates significant tensions between policymakers' vision for integrated care and the actions of family members in integrating care for older adults. We reveal disparities in how unpaid carers and caring are valued, considered, and understood at the sharp- and blunt-ends of care systems.

Methods

Policy documents were sourced from government websites in 2019 to understand how policymakers framed integration as a solution to fragmented care systems and how they considered the role of unpaid carers and families in care integration. Selected policy documents included the more recent plans and strategies from each country: England's Five Year Forward View (NHS, 2014), Next Steps on the NHS Five Year Forward View (NHS, 2017), The NHS Long Term Plan (NHS, 2019a), and Australia's Long Term National Health Plan (Australian Government, Department of Health, 2019a). We also included national policy focused on integrated care (Australian Government, Department of Health, 2019b; Health and Social Care Committee, House of Commons, 2018; NHS, 2019b, 2019c; Productivity Commission, 2017). As each Australian State and Territory has its own Department of Health with responsibility for governing public health systems, we also included the most recent plans and strategies from each State and Territory as well as documents targeting integrated care (ACT Health, 2018; Australian Government, Department of Health, 2019c; Government of South Australia, 2017; Government of Western Australia, Department of Health, 2015; Northern Territory Government, 2018; NSW Health, 2014, 2016, 2018; Queensland Government, The Department of Health, 2019; Safer Care Victoria, 2018; Victorian Government, 2016). These policy documents are not exhaustive but were purposively selected to represent current strategic plans and targeted integrated care policy.

Automated content analysis was performed on the policy documents using Leximancer 4.5 (Smith & Humphreys, 2006) to mine the text (of Australian and English documents separately) and create concept maps representing prominent concepts (smaller dots, or nodes), themes (larger circles), and their connections (lines between the nodes). Names of organisations, people, and countries; function words such as 'the' and 'it'; and numbers were excluded from the analysis. While Leximancer summarises the core components of a body of text, it does not provide context or nuanced meaning (e.g., negative and positive connotations). We therefore scrutinised the documents to understand how family, specifically daughters, were (or were not) implicated in integrated care policy or the strategic plan documents. We also looked at carer-specific policy for England and Australia to understand how these documents reflected and addressed gender in caregiving.

To explore how integrated care is experienced in practice, we examined four case accounts of informal care provided by daughters. These cases are illustrative, highlighting the kinds of work done, on the frontline, to integrate care. Two of the accounts were developed by two members of the author team through their engagement in a deliberative reflective writing task using auto-ethnography methods (Ellis et al., 2011). Each author wrote diary entries about the care of their parents which they shared in team meetings to compare experiences and identify themes of interest. The other two accounts were developed through discussions with a convenience sample of daughters that shared their stories of caring for their parents. We reviewed these stories in team meetings to identify common threads. The stories shared similar features, centred around two prominent characteristics: multi-generational caregiving and the guilt of seeking formal care support. These accounts were developed into two 'composite narratives' (Willis, 2019). Composite narratives acknowledge the complexities of individuals' experiences while delivering a cohesive account of a phenomenon. Names and identifying details have been changed throughout. As a team we discussed the four case accounts, focussing on the role and contribution of the daughter in each, and comparing and contrasting the reported experiences with the findings from our policy analysis. These cases provide experiential narratives of everyday care integration challenges: we recognise that they are partial, and unique, but they are each, we contend, credible and illustrative of the matters at hand.[1]

[1] The four case accounts were derived from discussions with a convenience sample of chapter authors and their contacts who gave permission for anonymised composite narratives to be reproduced. This part of the chapter was unfunded and was not a formal research study, so ethical approval was not sought; however, the authors followed the guidance on ethics in autoethnographic research (Sikes, 2015).

Results

Policy

How Policy Frames Integration as a Solution to Fragmented Systems of Care

The concept maps resulting from the Leximancer analysis of England's and Australia's documentation on care integration policy and strategic plans are presented as Figs. 4.1 and 4.2, respectively. These maps indicate recurring concepts and themes in policymakers' intentions for integrated care systems.

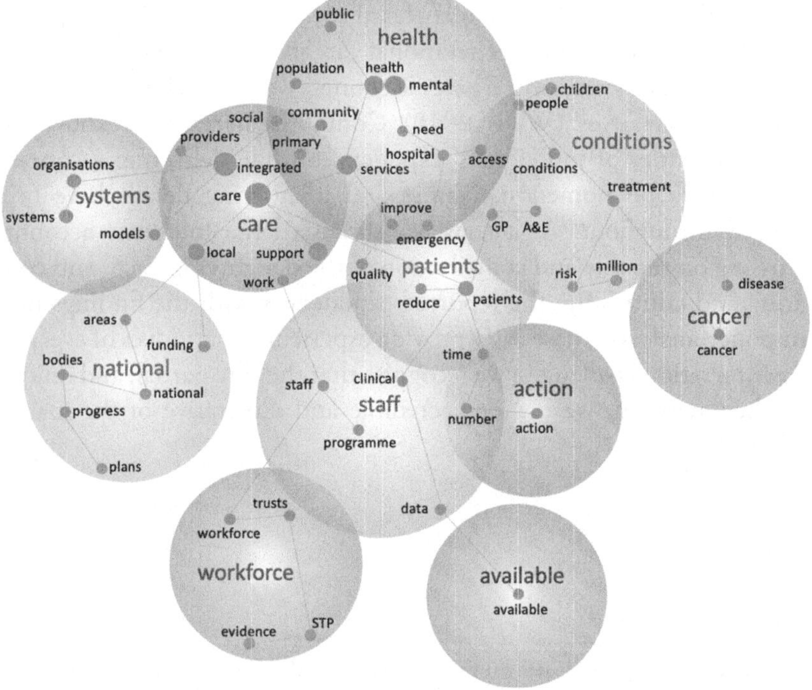

Fig. 4.1 England's policy documentation. (Source: Authors' conceptualization, developed using Leximancer [Smith & Humphreys, 2006]; Note: A&E = Accident and Emergency; GP = General Practitioner; STP = Sustainability and Transformation)

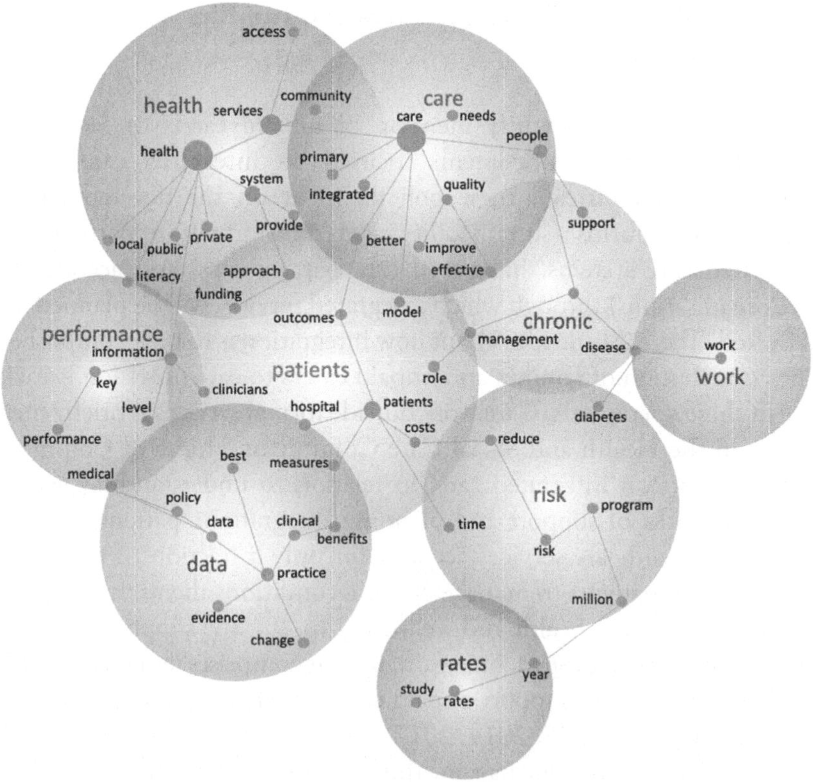

Fig. 4.2 Australia's policy documentation. (Source: Authors' conceptualization, developed using Leximancer [Smith & Humphreys, 2006])

Figures 4.1 and 4.2 demonstrate considerable overlap in England's and Australia's policy documents. Key foci include stakeholders (e.g., patients, staff), common conditions (e.g., cancer, diabetes), care services (e.g., community, primary), the use of data (e.g., evidence), support (e.g., funding), and organisation of care (e.g., private, public, local, national). Within both countries, integration is a key concept falling under the 'care' theme. Family members and unpaid carers are absent in the concept maps.

The Consideration of Unpaid Carers and Families in England's Policy

We were unable to identify mention of unpaid carers or families in national government documents focused on integrated care (NHS, 2019b, 2019c). Instead, these policies focus on the development of organisational forms (sustainability and transformation partnerships, integrated care systems, integrated care partnerships, and accountable care organisations) through which integrated services will be planned and delivered. There is little idea about how integration is to be accomplished. The contribution of families and unpaid carers to care provision is invisible in these documents. Care work outside formal services is briefly mentioned in the Health and Social Care Committee, House of Commons' (2018) report on integrated care, in relation to understanding personalised networks of support and planning integration: 'patients' interactions with healthcare services account for only a fraction of their lives. The ability of patients to manage chronic conditions themselves is therefore critical to their health and wellbeing' (p. 9). The supporting role of unpaid carers is mentioned, but again, what it comprises remains invisible.

The need to better support unpaid carers is reflected in the NHS strategic policy plans (NHS, 2014, 2017, 2019a), but the work that they do is not well specified. Once again, this renders the work invisible. These NHS documents focus on identifying who performs caring roles, so that they can be signposted to advise and support, paying attention to their health needs, educating them in the management of long-term conditions, providing help with crisis management, recognising their expertise and their carer role, and including them in planning care and partnership working. It is interesting to note that these interventions all serve to keep people in their caring role, with no alternatives on offer or an acknowledgement that unpaid carers might prefer not to care at all.

The 2014 Care Act assigns the wider responsibility of promoting unpaid carer wellbeing to local authorities, rather than providers of healthcare. Wellbeing is directed to supporting someone to continue in their caring role and may include supporting participation in activities (work, education, training, recreation) outside of their caring role. Wider carer policy such as the Carers Action Plan 2018–2020 (Department of Health and Social Care, 2018) addresses the role of wider society; for instance, businesses are encouraged to offer flexible working. In all of England's documents, the gender of unpaid carers is not specified, and this omission obscures the structural gendered inequalities we highlighted earlier.

The Consideration of Unpaid Carers and Families in Australia's Policy

We found no explicit reference to family members in Australia's national policies (Australian Government, Department of Health, 2019a, 2019b; Productivity Commission, 2017). Australian States and Territories each have a Bilateral Agreement with the Commonwealth Government on coordinated care reforms, in which integrated care is a key focus. Family members are only mentioned in the Northern Territory and Victorian documents, although details on how to involve unpaid carers in integrated care are non-existent.

At the State-level, New South Wales (NSW) and Victoria have policy documents on the topic of integrated care. The Victorian Clinical Council's Advice for Integrated Care outlines three recommendations, with no mention of the role of family members (Safer Care Victoria, 2018). The NSW Health Integrated Care Strategy makes only brief mention of family members, regarding a Chronic Disease Management Program (NSW Health, 2016). In comparison, the NSW Health Strategic Framework for Integrating Care considers family members throughout, for example, in its definition of integrated care, and in its vision: 'Integrating care—organized by, with, and for people, families and carers' (NSW Health, 2018, p. 8). As part of this framework, the first of four key outcomes is 'improved experiences for people, families and unpaid carers' (NSW Health, 2018, p. 5). Intended outcomes for this aim include involving family members in the co-design of care services and their involvement in decision-making and care planning.

Strategic plans for each Australian State and Territory were more likely to make reference to family members and unpaid carers than national policy (ACT Health, 2018; Australian Government, Department of Health, 2019b; Government of South Australia, 2017; Government of Western Australia, Department of Health, 2015; Northern Territory Government, 2018; NSW Health, 2014; Queensland Government, The Department of Health, 2018; Victorian Government, 2016). The strategic plans outlined the need to: engage families in care services and decision-making, consider family members' views, make health information accessible to families, and improve communication. Despite the consideration of the family in care planning, engagement, and outcomes, families are consistently referenced in conjunction with other stakeholders, that is, 'the individual and their family and carers' (Government of Western Australia, Department of Health, 2015, p. 10). Reference to family members is largely superficial with little information on how to involve unpaid carers in integrated care. Moreover, the role of family and unpaid carers as integrators of care, and their unpaid work, is not acknowledged in any of the documents.

Turning to carer-specific federal policies and reports, the National Carer Recognition Act (2010) aims to 'increase recognition and awareness of carers and to acknowledge the valuable contribution they make to society' (Australian Government, 2016, p. 2). Carers are those who provide personal care, support, and assistance to other individuals, including people who are 'frail and aged', outside contracted or formal volunteer work. The Act states that 'carers should be considered as partners with other care providers' (Australian Government, 2016, p. 3). The Australian Royal Commission into Aged Care Quality and Safety's recent background paper, 'Carers of Older Australians' (Commonwealth of Australia, 2019), details the role of unpaid family caregivers; the diversity of carers; support services for carers; the rewards of caregiving (e.g., strengthening relationships and development of new skills); and the detrimental effects of caregiving (e.g., lower social wellbeing, depression/anxiety, deterioration of health, financial strain, and loss of income). Australia's national carer-specific policy largely fails to acknowledge the gender imbalance of unpaid family carers. Of the documents cited, only the Royal Commission's background paper recognises the fact that the majority of unpaid carers are women, particularly daughters.

Case Accounts

Overall, the policy documents from England and Australia reflect 'work-as-imagined' (Hollnagel, 2015). If things went well, care systems would be more integrated, care would be joined up, and service users would not fall through the cracks. However, the challenge lies with implementation, that is, making the system work ('work-as-done'). To understand this, we turn to the lived experiences of daughters-as-carers, who we describe as 'dutiful daughters'. The following case accounts are of daughters who provide care for older parents and other family members. The first two are English cases, the second two, Australian. These cases serve as illustrations, drawn from experience, of the implementation challenges.

Case Account 1: The Mobilisation of My Mother (UK)

Mum (80 years) needed to see a dentist (May 2019). She had moved to Brighton a few years ago but had kept her dentist in Guildford, and travelled up there by train for appointments. After a stroke (2017), she moved into a care home and could not travel independently so had not seen the dentist. I sent an email to her friends in Guildford to see who might be able to help with transport. A couple of friends rang Mum and offered help. They hatched a plan. Anna (50 years) was going to drive to Brighton, pick up Mum, drive her to Guildford, take Mum to the dentist, and then take her to Maureen's house. Maureen (71 years) cared for her husband before he died so had a bed downstairs that Mum could sleep in. Mum planned to stay there a few days then get a lift back to Brighton.

I saw a number of problems with the plan. Mum had underestimated her physical support needs and it was very unlikely that Maureen was going to be able to care for her without injury to one or both of them, for example, getting her in and out of a domestic bed. I knew Mum could get in and out of a car but is in a lot of pain and tires very easy, so I wasn't sure if she could tolerate the journey. Also, no one had thought to check if the dental surgery had steps leading up to it and so Mum might get there and not be able to get in the building. There had been no thought given to her complicated medication regimen and Mum had not discussed her plans with the care home.

I had to undo the plan—and felt horrible about it. It was hard to discuss this in advance with Mum because of the mismatch between what is possible and what she believes is possible. I raised concerns about feasibility and she scoffed at them. I talked to the care home's lead nurse, Lucy, who agreed with my concerns and that her telling Mum 'no' would hold more weight than my doing so. I contacted the friends who had agreed to help and I explained that the plan would not go ahead. I cancelled the dentist's appointment.

That closed the door to one problem and opened another. I still needed to work out how Mum could get to see a dentist and also, was there a way to still get her to Guildford? Clearly she had been looking forward to being back there again and seeing her old friends. I didn't know why the care home didn't have dental health as part of its remit, but it seemed to be something that wouldn't otherwise get sorted out. Once I had found a dentist, made an appointment and got the registration forms, the home arranged her appointment.

Case Account 2: On Creams and Responsibility (UK)

Dad (80+ years) has an itchy back and has been scratching. There is dried blood under his fingernails as evidence of his successful scraping of the areas he can reach. After a phone call to the GP, and a complicated excursion to see a dermatologist, he is prescribed some cream to treat the rash. The rash is un-named and ill-diagnosed, but we have established a medical solution. The instructions are that the cream should be liberally applied four times a day and ideally 'allowed to soak in' before covering.

Dad sits in an upholstered armchair for 14–16 hours a day, mobilising very occasionally to toilet. He eats, sleeps, and watches TV from the chair, wrapped in a dressing gown and a blanket because, having lost considerable weight over recent years, he constantly feels cold. The central heating thermostat is turned up to the maximum even in summer, so the environment is not conducive to skin cooling at the best of times. However, there is a more pressing and insurmountable problem. Who will apply the cream? The carers from the social care agency say they are not allowed to touch the cream because it is prescribed medicine. This makes it a healthcare intervention. They are responsible for meals and personal care (washing and dressing), but this expansion of their duties is a step too far. Taking them at their word, I relay this to the GP, and suggest that the District Nurse team may need to step in.

After three phone calls to different parts of the care system, the answer comes: The District Nurses 'do not apply creams'. We are at an impasse. I send another ever-despairing email to the GP stating the facts: Cream has been prescribed. The itch persists. No one can apply the remedy. She sends one of her usual empathetic and shocked responses, copying in the relevant members of the health and social care team and this produces a care miracle. The agency carers will, prompted by the GP, apply the cream. Whether they will do this on their often-perfunctory visits remains to be seen, but this feels like a victory. After all, Dad has been scratching his back for about eight weeks.

Case Account 3: Will the Guilt Ever Ease? (Australia)

Over the years, Jen (60 years) has held many caregiving roles: mother, aunt, wife, and grandmother. The most difficult caregiving role that she has faced has been that of daughter. When Jen's mum Elizabeth was 68 years old she lost her husband. Widowed and lonely, she moved into the granny flat on Jen's property. For the first ten years of living with her daughter, Elizabeth was very independent. That eleventh year, over the space of a couple of months, things started to change. Cooking became too much of an effort for Elizabeth, so Jen prepared her meals for her. The vacuuming hurt Elizabeth's back, so Jen took on this job. Shopping was tiring for Elizabeth, so Jen added this to her list of errands. Within six months, Elizabeth was dependent on Jen for most of her domestic care. Looking back, Jen sees that these changes were the early signs of her mother's dementia; however, at the time, Elizabeth's diminishing ability to care for herself was put down to tiredness as a result of ageing.

Fast forward three more years and Elizabeth and Jen were living with Elizabeth's diagnosis of dementia. Elizabeth could no longer complete simple everyday tasks, she was often confused, and she relied heavily on Jen. Elizabeth needed Jen to drive her to all of her doctors' appointments, requiring Jen to leave work early or take an extended lunch break. During these appointments, Elizabeth often had no idea why she was visiting the doctor and when she was reminded, she played down her symptoms. Jen became her mother's advocate; explaining the reality of Elizabeth's health conditions, which was often not in line with how Elizabeth perceived her ailments. Jen would ask the doctors questions on behalf of her mum and would need to re-explain to Elizabeth what the doctor was saying. Without Jen's input, Elizabeth would not have received the medical care she needed. Jen was struggling to manage full-time work, care for her mother, and look after her grandson.

For two more years, Jen agonised about putting her mother into a care home. On the days where it all got too much and she revisited the idea of nursing home care, she kept telling herself, 'it's not time yet' or 'I can handle it'. Eventually the day came when Elizabeth started living in a formal care home, a day that broke Jen's heart. The guilt was overwhelming; she felt as though she had failed her mother. Although Elizabeth never said anything to Jen about it, Jen could sense the resentment burning inside her mother when visiting her. No matter how many times her co-workers, friends, and family reassured her that she had made the right decision, she asked herself—had she put her mum into care too early? Couldn't she have held out a little longer? She wondered: will the guilt ever ease?

Case Account 4: Multi-generational Caregiving (Australia)

Helen (56 years) lives with her husband, Cam, one of her three adult children, Jessie, her 4-year-old grandson, Brydon, and her mother-in-law Adelita. Brydon was born when Jessie was 19 years old. Helen took leave from her job as an accountant in order to help care for Brydon. This was supposed to be a temporarily leave of absence; however, Helen decided she couldn't go back to work until Brydon started school. She is helping raise Brydon, looking after him on weekdays so that Jessie can finish her university degree.

Helen's mother-in-law, Adelita, has arthritis which limits her ability to venture out on her own. Throughout the week, Helen runs errands for her mother-in-law, including picking up her prescription medication and buying groceries. She drives Adelita to all of her physiotherapy and doctors' appointments—on average, twice a week with her various health problems. Adelita was born in Spain, and although her English is good, it is her second language. Helen needs to sit in on Adelita's appointments to help facilitate conversations between Adelita and the doctor.

Last year, Helen's father, Richard, was diagnosed with dementia which has progressed quicker than anyone was expecting. Her mother, Anne, has taken on the role of primary caregiver for Richard, who now needs daily care. Helen has taken on yet another caring role—looking after her mother. As Anne's time is consumed by looking after Richard, she neglects herself. Helen has to remind her mother to look after her own health. She also provides emotional support to Anne, speaking with her on the phone twice a day and visiting her most afternoons. Anne doesn't drive, and since Richard's driver's licence was cancelled, the responsibility fell on Helen to fill this role.

Helen has always prided herself in being the glue that holds her household, and her family, together. Lately though, she feels as if she is unravelling. With the extra duties of caring for her own parents, she has been feeling extremely overwhelmed with life. She stays awake most nights thinking about the tasks that lay ahead in the upcoming days, worrying about each of her loved ones. Recently she visited her doctor who prescribed medication to help with her sleep troubles. Helen is finding that every day feels like a struggle—there is no down-time, no chance of a holiday, no relief, and absolutely no time to get sick. If Helen isn't there to look after everyone, to coordinate everyone's lives, to support her family, then who will?

The Experiences and Contributions of Daughters Across Case Accounts

Viewed together, the case accounts of daughters' experiences highlight the vital role that daughters play in coordinating care for older family members. Daughters are at the frontline, keeping older people healthy and living well. They are averting the disasters that would likely occur if the only support on offer was provided by fragmented formal care systems. In these narratives, the peripheral role that formal agencies play in maintaining health and wellbeing of each older person is striking. Without integration work by daughters, the care on offer would not fully meet the needs of the individual older person. Daughters do this work in addition to carrying out the paid and unpaid work of their other roles and responsibilities in life. Echoing the findings from the research studies we presented earlier in this chapter, daughters were found to organise care across siloed services, advocate for older adults' needs, provide domestic services, and emotionally support their parents. The role of caregiving was found to have negative effects on emotional, mental, and physical wellbeing of daughters, resulting in stress, frustration, sleeping problems, and feelings of immense guilt. This finding aligns with the Australian Royal Commission into Aged Care Quality and Safety's background paper on 'Carers of Older Australians' (Commonwealth of Australia, 2019).

Concluding Comments

Rosalynn Carter, former first lady of the United States of America, said, 'I like to say that there are only four kinds of people in the world: those who have been caregivers, those who are currently caregivers, those who will be caregivers and those who will need caregivers'. We think she mostly meant women.

This chapter set out to examine and contrast how care integration is imagined in policy and experienced in practice. We found a wealth of policy that asserts the need for care to be integrated and that sets out high-level visions for care systems and associated organisational forms to enable this to happen. For the most part however, we found that written policy neglects the role of family caregivers as integrators of care, and in particular the gender imbalance in caregiving. In a select number of documents, recommendations were put forward that unpaid carers should be identified, supported, and their caring role preserved; however, minimal detail was provided on how to achieve this. Our findings highlight the need for policymakers, managers, leaders, and dutiful daughters to work cohesively to create integrated care for older adults on an ongoing basis.

The unpaid work that women do to integrate care is largely invisible, highlighting inadequacies of formal models of integrated care set out in current health, social, and aged care policy. To formally acknowledge this silent workforce potentially shatters assumptions that women are, and will continue, to be 'naturally' caring and responsible for the welfare of others at any cost. In our case accounts, daughters were often unsupported in their attempts to integrate care (although other family members sometimes helped with care tasks). Reflecting on the stress of the family carer role, Bartlett and Brannelly note:

> Caring for and about a person with dementia who lives at home is a shared responsibility. The changing and progressive nature of the condition and the multifaceted complexities of care it entails makes a single source of support inadequate. It is like expecting a lone parent to care single-handedly for a child with multiple disabilities. (Bartlett & Brannelly, 2019, p. 116)

We echo these conclusions. If the responsibility for care and its integration is held by a single family member, these gendered patterns of work will persist. Our policy analysis suggests that the perceived responsibility of health and other care services is to support family members to continue in their caring role, and to respond and adapt to the individual circumstances in which they find themselves. In contrast, previous research and our case accounts of dutiful daughters suggest that persistent structural inequalities should be the focus of policy (and formal services') attention. Future developments in policy and practice need to focus on who is doing the integrating and ensure that unpaid carers are offered real choice in whether or not they continue in the caring role.

Responding to a growing recognition of the social, political, and economic circumstances of people's lives in determining their health, Bridges and Lynam (1993) highlighted the contribution that frontline nurses could make to tackling the structural gender inequalities of family care for older people. We support Bridges and Lynam's (1993) conclusions that care providers have a legitimate role in highlighting and helping to tackle some of the structural forces that underpin gender inequalities.

However, a quarter of a century on, we see no evidence in policy that health and social care services are seen to have such a role.

We have shown the gap between the way care integration is imagined in policy and experienced by those providing everyday care for older people. Across both England's and Australia's policy documents, there was a lack of recognition or consideration for the unpaid work family caregivers, particularly daughters, do to coordinate and integrate care for family members. Policy provides minimal detail on how to support these caregivers in their roles, nor does it advocate for alternative care arrangements to reduce the burden experienced by family caregivers. Previous research, and the four illustrative case accounts of dutiful daughters we examined, highlight the magnitude of unpaid, invisible work women do to care for their parents, parents-in-law, children, and grandchildren, often simultaneously, while also undertaking paid work. Comparing this to our analysis of policy documents, we reveal the disconnect between how policymakers recommend integrated care *should* be achieved and how dutiful daughters (and other family carers) struggle to *actually* achieve integration on the frontlines of care.

References

ACT Health. (2018). *ACT health quality strategy 2018–2028*. ACT Health. Retrieved from Canberra, Australia: https://www.health.act.gov.au/sites/default/files/2018-10/Quality%20Strategy%20Booklet.pdf

Adjei, N. K., & Brand, T. (2018). Investigating the associations between productive housework activities, sleep hours and self-reported health among elderly men and women in western industrialised countries. *BMC Public Health, 18*(1), 110–120. https://doi.org/10.1186/s12889-017-4979-z

Allan, G., & Crow, G. (Eds.). (2001). *Families, households and society*. Palgrave.

Australian Bureau of Statistics. (2019). *Disability, ageing and carers, Australia: Summary of findings*. Retrieved from Canberra, Australia: https://www.abs.gov.au/statistics/health/disability/disability-ageing-and-carers-australia-summary-findings/latest-release#carers

Australian Government. (2016). *Carer Recognition Act 2010 guidelines*. Australian Government. Retrieved from Canberra, Australia: https://www.

dss.gov.au/our-responsibilities/disability-and-carers/publications-articles/carer-recognition-act-2010-guidelines

Australian Government, Department of Health. (2019a). *Australia's long term national health plan*. Retrieved from Canberra, Australia: https://www.health.gov.au/sites/default/files/australia-s-long-term-national-health-plan_0.pdf

Australian Government, Department of Health. (2019b). *Integrated team care. Program implementation guidelines*. Australian Government. Retrieved from Canberra, Australia: https://www.murrayphn.org.au/wp-content/uploads/2015/07/Integrated-Team-Care-Activity-Implementation-Guidelines-201617-to-201718.pdf

Australian Government, Department of Health. (2019c). *Tasmanian health plan. Improved health care for all Tasmanians*. Australian Government. Retrieved from Canberra, Australia: https://www1.health.gov.au/internet/main/publishing.nsf/Content/tas-health-plan.htm

Bartlett, R., & Brannelly, T. (2019). *Life at home for people with a dementia*. Routledge.

Boniol, M., McIsaac, M., Xu, L., Wuliji, T., Diallo, K., & Campbell, J. (2019). *Gender equity in the Health workforce: Analysis of 104 countries*. Health workforce working paper 1. World Health Organisation. Retrieved from Geneva, Switzerland: https://apps.who.int/iris/bitstream/handle/10665/311314/WHO-HIS-HWF-Gender-WP1-2019.1-eng.pdf

Bookman, A., & Harrington, M. (2007). Family caregivers: A shadow workforce in the geriatric health care system? *Journal of Health Politics, Policy and Law, 32*(6), 1005–1041. https://doi.org/10.1215/03616878-2007-040

Boyd, S. L., & Treas, J. (1989). Family care of the frail elderly: A new look at 'women in the middle'. *Women's Studies Quarterly, 17*(1/2), 66–74.

Braithwaite, J., Wears, R. L., & Hollnagel, E. (Eds.). (2017). *Resilient health care, volume 3: Reconciling work-as-imagined and work-as-done*. CRC Press/Taylor & Francis.

Bridges, J., & Lynam, M. J. (1993). Informal carers: A Marxist analysis of social, political, and economic forces underpinning the role. *Advances in Nursing Science, 15*(3), 33–48. https://doi.org/10.1097/00012272-199303000-00006

Chisholm, J. F. (1999). The sandwich generation. *Journal of Social Distress and the Homeless, 8*(3), 177–191. https://doi.org/10.1023/A:1021368826791

Coleman, E. A. (2003). Falling through the cracks: Challenges and opportunities for improving transitional care for persons with continuous complex care needs. *Journal of the American Geriatrics Society, 51*(4), 549–555. https://doi.org/10.1046/j.1532-5415.2003.51185.x

Commonwealth of Australia. (2019). Carers of older Australians. Commonwealth of Australia. Retrieved from Adelaide, SA: https://agedcare.royalcommission.gov.au/publications/Pages/default.aspx

Department of Health and Social Care. (2018). *Carers action plan 2018–2020: Supporting carers today*. Department of Health and Social Care. Retrieved from London, UK: https://assets.publishing.service.gov.uk/government/uploads/system/uploads/attachment_data/file/713781/carers-action-plan-2018-2020.pdf

DeRigne, L., & Ferrante, S. (2012). The sandwich generation: A review of the literature. *Florida Public Health Review, 9*, 95–104.

Do, E. K., Cohen, S. A., & Brown, M. J. (2014). Socioeconomic and demographic factors modify the association between informal caregiving and health in the sandwich generation. *BMC Public Health, 14*(1), 362–369. https://doi.org/10.1186/1471-2458-14-362

Doress-Worters, P. B. (1994). Adding elder care to women's multiple roles: A critical review of the caregiver stress and multiple roles literatures. *Sex Roles: A Journal of Research, 31*(9–10), 597–616. https://doi.org/10.1007/BF01544282

Ellis, C., Adams, T. E., & Bochner, A. P. (2011). Autoethnography: An overview. *Historical Social Research, 36*(4), 273–290. https://doi.org/10.2307/23032294

Evans, K. L., Millsteed, J., Richmond, J. E., Falkmer, M., Falkmer, T., & Girdler, S. J. (2016). Working sandwich generation women utilize strategies within and between roles to achieve role balance. *PLoS One, 11*(6), e0157469. https://doi.org/10.1371/journal.pone.0157469

Evans, K. L., Millsteed, J., Richmond, J. E., Falkmer, M., Falkmer, T., & Girdler, S. J. (2019). The impact of within and between role experiences on role balance outcomes for working sandwich generation women. *Scandinavian Journal of Occupational Therapy, 26*(3), 184–193. https://doi.org/10.1080/11038128.2018.1449888

Ferrant, G., & Thim, A. (2019). *Measuring women's economic empowerment: Time use data and gender inequality*. OECD. Retrieved from Paris, France: http://www.oecd.org/dev/development-gender/MEASURING-WOMENS-ECONOMIC-EMPOWERMENT-Gender-Policy-Paper-No-16.pdf

Gillett, J. E., & Crisp, D. A. (2017). Examining coping style and the relationship between stress and subjective well-being in Australia's 'sandwich generation'. *Australasian Journal on Ageing, 36*(3), 222–227. https://doi.org/10.1111/ajag.12439

Government of South Australia. (2017). SA health strategic plan 2017 to 2020. Government of South Australia. Retrieved from Adelaide, Australia: https://www.sahealth.sa.gov.au/wps/wcm/connect/public+content/sa+health+internet/about+us/about+sa+health/sa+health+strategic+plan

Government of Western Australia, Department of Health. (2015). *WA health networks strategic direction 2015–2020. Collective input for collective action.* Government of Western Australia. Retrieved from East Perth, Australia: https://ww2.health.wa.gov.au/~/media/Files/Corporate/general%20documents/Health%20Networks/PDF/Health-Networks-Strategic-Direction-2015-2020.pdf

Grigoryeva, A. (2017). Own gender, sibling's gender, parent's gender: The division of elderly parent care among adult children. *American Sociological Review, 82*(1), 116–146. https://doi.org/10.1177/0003122416686521

Hajek, A. M. (2013). Breaking down clinical silos in healthcare. *Frontiers of Health Services Management, 29*(4), 45–50.

Health and Social Care Committee, House of Commons. (2018). *Integrated care: Organisations, partnerships and systems.* Seventh Report of Session 2017–19. Health and Social Care Committee. Retrieved from London, UK: https://publications.parliament.uk/pa/cm201719/cmselect/cmhealth/650/650.pdf

Hollnagel, E. (2004). *Barriers and accident prevention.* Ashgate.

Hollnagel, E. (2015). Why is work-as-imagined different from work-as-done? In R. L. Wears, E. Hollnagel, & J. Braithwaite (Eds.), *Resilient health care, volume 2: The resilience of everyday clinical work* (pp. 249–264). Ashgate.

Hooyman, N. R., & Gonyea, J. (1995). *Perspectives on family care. Policies for gender justice.* Sage Publications.

Hooyman, N. R., & Gonyea, J. G. (1999). A feminist model of family care: Practice and policy directions. *Journal of Women & Aging, 11*(2–3), 149–169. https://doi.org/10.1300/J074v11n02_11

Huvent-Grelle, D., Boulanger, E., Beuscart, J. B., Martin, T., Podvin, J., & Puisieux, F. (2015). 'Women in the middle': An observational study of a generation story in Alzheimer disease in France. *European Geriatric Medicine, 6*(2), 124–127. https://doi.org/10.1016/j.eurger.2014.10.001

International Labour Organization. (2019). *Care work and care jobs for the future of decent work.* ILO. Retrieved from Geneva, Switzerland: https://www.ilo.org/wcmsp5/groups/public/%2D%2D-dgreports/%2D%2D-dcomm/%2D%2D-publ/documents/publication/wcms_633135.pdf

Ludlow, K., Churruca, K., Mumford, V., Ellis, L. A., & Braithwaite, J. (2020a). Staff members' prioritisation of care in residential aged care facilities: A Q methodology study. *BMC Health Services Research, 20*, 423. https://doi.org/10.1186/s12913-020-05127-3

Ludlow, K., Churruca, K., Ellis, L. A., Mumford, V., & Braithwaite, J. (2020b). Family members' prioritisation of care in residential aged care facilities: A case for individualised care. *Journal of Clinical Nursing, 29*, 3272–3285. https://doi.org/10.1111/jocn.15352

Miller, D. A. (1981). The 'sandwich' generation: Adult children of the aging. *Social Work, 26*(5), 419–423. https://doi.org/10.1093/sw/26.5.419

Montgomery, R. J. V., Gonyea, J. G., & Hooyman, N. R. (1985). Caregiving and the experience of subjective and objective burden. *Family Relations, 34*(1), 19–26. https://doi.org/10.2307/583753

NHS. (2014). *Five year forward view*. NHS. Retrieved from Leeds, UK: https://www.england.nhs.uk/wp-content/uploads/2014/10/5yfv-web.pdf

NHS. (2017). *Next steps on the NHS five year forward view*. NHS. Retrieved from Leeds, UK: https://www.england.nhs.uk/wp-content/uploads/2017/03/NEXT-STEPS-ON-THE-NHS-FIVE-YEAR-FORWARD-VIEW.pdf

NHS. (2019a). *The NHS long term plan*. NHS. Retrieved from Leeds, UK: https://www.longtermplan.nhs.uk/wp-content/uploads/2019/01/nhs-long-term-plan-june-2019.pdf

NHS. (2019b). *Breaking down barriers to better health and care*. NHS. Retrieved from Leeds, UK: https://www.england.nhs.uk/wp-content/uploads/2019/04/breaking-down-barriers-to-better-health-and-care-march19.pdf

NHS. (2019c). *Designing integrated care systems (ICSS) in England*. NHS. Retrieved from Leeds, UK: https://www.england.nhs.uk/wp-content/uploads/2019/06/designing-integrated-care-systems-in-england.pdf

Northern Territory Government. (2018). *Northern Territory Health strategic plan 2018–2022*. Northern Territory Government. Retrieved from Darwin City, Australia: https://digitallibrary.health.nt.gov.au/prodjspui/handle/10137/2729

NSW Health. (2014). *NSW state health plan: Towards 2021*. NSW Health. Retrieved from North Sydney, Australia: https://www.health.nsw.gov.au/statehealthplan/Pages/NSW-State-Health-Plan-Towards-2021.aspx

NSW Health. (2016). *Integrated care strategy. Updated monitoring & evaluation framework*. NSW Health. Retrieved from North Sydney, Australia: https://www.health.nsw.gov.au/integratedcare/Documents/ic-mef-2016.pdf

NSW Health. (2018). *Strategic framework for integrating care*. NSW Health. Retrieved from North Sydney, Australia: https://www.health.nsw.gov.au/integratedcare/Pages/strategic-framework.aspx

Oakley, A. (Ed.). (1974). *The sociology of housework*. Pantheon Books.

Patterson, S. E., & Margolis. (2019). The demography of multigenerational caregiving: A critical aspect of the gendered life course. *Socius: Sociological Research for a Dynamic World, 5*, 1–19. https://doi.org/10.1177/2378023119862737

Petrie, K., & Kirkup, J. (2018). *Caring for carers: The lives of family carers in the UK*. Social Market Foundations. Retrieved from London, UK: https://www.smf.co.uk/wp-content/uploads/2018/07/Caring-for-Carers.pdf

Productivity Commission. (2017). *Integrated care, shifting the dial: 5 year productivity review, supporting paper no. 5*. Productivity commission. Retrieved from Canberra, Australia: https://www.pc.gov.au/inquiries/completed/productivity-review/report/productivity-review-supporting5.pdf

Puurveen, G., Baumbusch, J., & Gandhi, P. (2018). From family involvement to family inclusion in nursing home settings: A critical interpretive synthesis. *Journal of Clinical Nursing, 24*(1), 60–85. https://doi.org/10.1177/1074840718754314

PwC. (2019). *Women in the work index 2019*. PwC. Retrieved from London, UK: https://www.pwc.co.uk/services/economics-policy/insights/women-in-work-index.html

Queensland Government, The Department of Health. (2019). *The Department of Health strategic plan 2019–2023*. Queensland Government. Retrieved from Brisbane, Australia: https://www.health.qld.gov.au/system-governance/strategic-direction/plans/doh-plan

Rajan, S., & McKee, M. (2019). NHS is picking up the pieces as social safety nets fail. *BMJ, 365*, l2360. https://doi.org/10.1136/bmj.l2360

Raphael, D., & Schlesinger, B. (1994). Women in the sandwich generation. *Journal of Women & Aging, 6*(1–2), 21–45. https://doi.org/10.1300/J074v06n01_03

Riley, L. D., & Bowen, C. P. (2005). The sandwich generation: Challenges and coping strategies of multigenerational families. *The Family Journal, 13*(1), 52–58. https://doi.org/10.1177/1066480704270099

Safer Care Victoria. (2018). *Victorian Clinical Council advice: Integration of care: From fragmented to seamless*. Safer Care Victoria. Retrieved from Melbourne, Australia: https://www.bettersafercare.vic.gov.au/reports-and-publications/advice-integration-of-care

Sikes, P. (2015). Ethical considerations in autoethnographic research. https://www.sheffield.ac.uk/polopoly_fs/1.586562!/file/SREGP-Autoethnography-2015.pdf

Smith, A. E., & Humphreys, M. S. (2006). Evaluation of unsupervised semantic mapping of natural language with Leximancer concept mapping. *Behavior Research Methods, 38*(2), 262–279. https://doi.org/10.3758/BF03192778

Solberg, L. M., Solberg, L. B., & Peterson, E. N. (2014). Measuring impact of stress in sandwich generation caring for demented parents. *GeroPsych: The Journal of Gerontopsychology and Geriatric Psychiatry, 27*(4), 171–179. https://doi.org/10.1024/1662-9647/a000114

Steiner, A. M., & Fletcher, P. C. (2017). Sandwich generation caregiving: A complex and dynamic role. *Journal of Adult Development, 24*(2), 133–143. https://doi.org/10.1007/s10804-016-9252-7

Stephens, M. A., Franks, M. M., & Townsend, A. L. (1994). Stress and rewards in women's multiple roles: The case of women in the middle. *Psychology and Aging, 9*(1), 45–52.

Szinovacz, M. E., & Davey, A. (2013). Prevalence and predictors of change in adult-child primary caregivers. *International Journal of Aging and Human Development, 76*(3), 227–249. https://doi.org/10.2190/AG.76.3.d

United Nations General Assembly. (2019). *Women in development: Report of the Secretary General.* UN General Assembly. Retrieved from New York, NY: https://www.unwomen.org/en/digital-library/publications/2019/08/a-74-279-sg-report-women-in-development#view

Victorian Government. (2016). *Health 2040: Advancing health, access and care.* Victorian Government. Retrieved from Melbourne, Australia: https://www2.health.vic.gov.au/about/publications/policiesandguidelines/Health-2040-advancing-health-access-and-care

Willis, R. (2019). The use of composite narratives to present interview findings. *Qualitative Research, 19*(4), 471–480. https://doi.org/10.1177/1468794118787711

Wong-Cornall, C., Parsons, J., Sheridan, N., Kenealy, T., & Peckham, A. (2017). Extending 'continuity of care' to include the contribution of family carers. *International Journal of Integrated Care, 17*(2), 11. https://doi.org/10.5334/ijic.2545

5

What Is Context? Methodological Reflections on the Relationship Between Context, Actors, and Change

Ninna Meier and Sue Dopson

Introduction

In this chapter, we present reflections on what context is, how context can be studied, and why the approach we take to studying context matters for what we can investigate and understand. We start by a presenting a broad definition of context as a theoretical construct and show how this leads us to methodological considerations regarding how researchers can show what they understand by context in a given study, how they operationalize and study this, and what the consequences of these choices are for their results. We use examples from the Covid-19 pandemic to

N. Meier (✉)
Department of Sociology and Social Work, Aalborg University, Aalborg, Denmark
e-mail: meier@socsci.aau.dk

S. Dopson
Saïd Business School, University of Oxford, Oxford, UK
e-mail: sue.dopson@sbs.ox.ac.uk

R. Kislov et al. (eds.), *Managing Healthcare Organisations in Challenging Policy Contexts*, Organizational Behaviour in Healthcare,
https://doi.org/10.1007/978-3-030-81093-1_5

illustrate the relevance of a nuanced and reflective approach to context for studying health policy and management. We end the chapter with reflections on how researchers can operationalize context in collaborative research projects and when studying multi-level phenomena and reflect on implications of our approach to context for healthcare managers and leaders.

What Is Context and How Can We Study It?

The concept of context is often used to give meaning to a specific phenomenon or event. Etymologically, the term *context* means weaving or knitting together, to make a connection between a phenomenon and what is relevant for understanding the said phenomenon (Rousseau & Fried, 2001, p. 1). We propose a distinction between context as a theoretical construct, on the one hand, and context as methodological approach—how we operationalize and use the concept in the research process—on the other, and suggest the following definition of context:

> Context is a relational construct that specifies what is at any given point considered the background for understanding a phenomenon or event. This background/foreground relationship is continually constructed by people, as they make sense of their experiences and the social worlds in which they engage. (Meier & Dopson, 2019, p. 3)

Understood in this way, *context* and *phenomenon/event* mutually constitute each other. In other words, what we construct as context in our research will depend on the phenomenon or event we are trying to understand and give meaning to and vice versa. In research, the term 'context' specifies against which background a given phenomenon must be understood or has been researched and is an important aspect of the boundary conditions of research (Suddaby, 2010). In much of healthcare management research, the phenomena or events studied will consist of actors' actions, for example the development and implementation of a policy. Thus, if we aim to understand healthcare managers' attempts to implement a healthcare policy, we need to understand *what* context refers to and *how* we capture this empirically and analytically, given that research have demonstrated that implementation vary across contexts (Nilsen et al., 2013; Meier, 2012; Dopson & Fitzgerald, 2005).

Below we present a modified version of the Framework for Studying Context in Action (Meier & Dopson, 2019), which we developed to illustrate how the phenomenon/context relationship arise from the many choices a researcher makes with regard to research question, unit of analysis, philosophy of science approach, theoretical concepts, design, method, and analytical approach (Fig. 5.1). The framework starts with the researcher; their vantage point for conducting a study; the approach; and the representation of social reality that these choices afford. From here, the framework proposes three main pathways, each leading to a question addressing the context-action-change relationship.

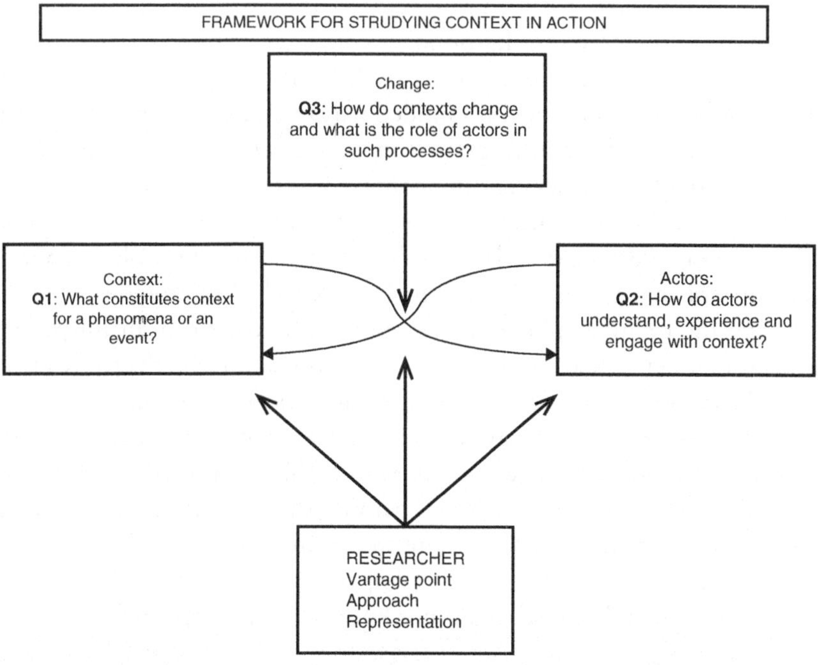

Fig. 5.1 Framework for studying context in action. (Source: Adapted from Meier & Dopson, 2019)

Most approaches to context attempt to ascertain what constitutes the context for a phenomenon or an event (the Q1 pathway). This approach to context usually assumes both phenomena and context as relatively stable entities that can be identified and studied with relative ease. However, the challenging policy contexts, which healthcare organizations are part of, change over time, and are dynamic and 'crowded' by several organizations and organizational change initiatives that are directed at multiple levels and impact organizations across the healthcare system. Thus, this approach—while useful for exploring contextual factors and explaining how they might impact the phenomena under study—is less useful for exploring processual, enacted, and dynamic features of the context-action-change relationship that are assumed in Q2 and Q3. Methodologically, we need other approaches to the phenomena-context relationship if we are interested in understanding how people enact, relate to, and understand the contexts they are part of. Regardless of our methodological approach, we need to specify what we focus on as phenomena and what we therefore 'background' as context.

Thus, as evidenced above, we argue that analyses of context are made particularly difficult by the unbounded nature of the concept: 'To understand anything well we must grasp it in its context. However, the attempt to be thorough in understanding context leads to a total contextualization, in which everything becomes the context of everything else' (Scharfstein, 1989, p. xxi). This produces a paradoxical problem: context is a concept that is central to producing research that provides meaning to a specific event or phenomenon, but is often used in an unspecific, general manner (Meier & Dopson, 2019; Johns, 2017) effectively creating a 'black box' effect. As a result, if researchers do not specify what they mean by 'context', readers are left to unpack what terms such as 'policy context' or 'clinical context' might mean. This is problematic for both research and practice in healthcare, because such usages of context make comparison of findings difficult (are we comparing apples and oranges?) and this use of 'context' risks leaving significant explanatory factors under-researched, because we do not know what the term refers to.

Context and Implementation of Healthcare Policy

Within healthcare management research in general, context is often used to explain why the implementation of policy is challenging or varies across healthcare organizations. For instance, difference in approach to context could be used to explain why a policy designed to prevent transmission of Covid-19 in healthcare settings cannot un-problematically be expected to regulate interactions in social care volunteer organizations providing social support, food, and shelter for homeless people. If we wish to study implementation of a health policy in these different settings, we would need to operationalize 'primary care' and 'volunteer social work' as two different contexts for the same policy and account for how these are different and why and how that matters.

Accounting for context is not only relevant for research and researchers. Within a complex organizational setting such as healthcare, there are multiple groups, who can be said to attempt to define 'the context' for health policies. Some groups will have more access to information than others, which will aid their decision making; others have less. Some groups will act to promote or support health policies, while other groups will act to challenge them. Recent public debates and disagreements over health policies regarding vaccines or masks are examples that illustrate how different groups in the healthcare system can be in opposition to both a given policy and each other and how these differences are also evident in the way groups construct and act within these very different understandings of what the context is. In healthcare, there are also groups with different career interests (politicians, managers, clinicians) and these interests are emotive as well as cognitive. In such settings, and perhaps due to the often-unarticulated approach to context, it can be difficult to maintain a distinction between what is foreground (phenomena) and what is background (context), because these analytical distinctions shift depending on one's perspective and approach. The difference in approach might also be a source of potential misunderstanding and conflict regarding what the appropriate next action should be or how to react to a public health policy. In his discussion of context, health policy, and implementation, Chambers (2019) highlights certain features which impact how we can understand the challenges of implementing health policies: dynamism, uncertainty, short-term verses long-term focus, external impacts, and policy framing. Each of these factors could be a worthwhile starting point for exploring why health policy implementation remains to be challenging and how a more systematic and nuanced approach to context can help.

Healthcare—especially public sector healthcare—is seen as a particularly challenging 'context' for managers and leaders due to the crowded nature of this field, the complex and often conflicting policy agendas, and the tension between standardization and customization of patient care (Dopson, 2001; Bohmer, 2009; McGivern & Dopson, 2010). Healthcare management and leadership are understood to be context-dependent work practices that are shaped by the organizational context and the character of work, for example elective surgery or stroke rehabilitation and care (Meier, 2015). Examining how managerial work is practised, Korica and Nicolini (2019) show how context can be understood as 'members' concerns made continually present through particular kinds of attention and action' (p. 125) and that this task, which we all engage in throughout our day, *contextualizing action*, was an ongoing concern for the CEOs they studied. Korica and Nicolini show how context is made to matter in specific ways through individual and collective joining together of elements in action and that it is through these processes that actors make sense of and enact contexts.

Studies of innovation adoption processes in healthcare further elaborate the importance of an interactionist's view of context. Fitzgerald et al.'s (2002) study recognizes the importance of sense-making and sense-giving processes of individuals and groups in the processes of attempting organizational change in complex contexts. Dopson and Fitzgerald (2005) sought to extend and elaborate the interactions between context and action and summarized a more active and nuanced view of context as dynamic and enacted. Context, they argue, is not discrete: local contexts are multidimensional, multifaceted configurations of forces, and individuals are influenced by social relationships and history as they are part of these contexts. Thus actors interpret and enact context in many different ways, which in turn adds to the complexity.

Context, Actors, and Change: The Covid-19 Pandemic as Example

As a pressing global problem, Covid-19 constitutes one of the greatest societal challenges of our time and a radical shift in how we understand the role of health policy, public health, and healthcare systems in general. Such crises require critically organized responses and prioritizations both in the first wave of the outbreak and beyond, when society must slowly and as safely as possible be opened up again, economic factors must be attended to, while maintaining capacity for any additional lockdowns or public health crises. These efforts require coordinated actions from actors across several organizations, for example National Government, public health agencies, research facilities and laboratories, and healthcare organizations such as hospitals, GPs, and municipal social- or eldercare facilities. Moreover, healthcare leaders and managers must navigate a rapidly changing policy landscape as they handle the unfolding pandemic and its associated uncertainty. Thus, the outbreak of the Covid-19 pandemic can be understood as a radically changed context for health policies across the globe (Q1). However, depending on our approach to Covid-19, we can also examine the pandemic as a force of change in healthcare systems (Q3), or indeed investigate how actors experience and engage with—and thus enact—the pandemic as a new context for their actions (Q2).

Covid-19 as a Changed Context

If we understand Covid-19 as a changed or a changing context for healthcare systems in general and healthcare policy in particular, we view the pandemic as 'context' for the phenomenon we wish to understand. Reflecting on Covid-19 as 'changed context' for healthcare policy and practice, we can identify and explore a number of changes. For instance, Covid-19 changes the evaluation of capacity in hospitals, because the illness resulted in overwhelmed emergency departments, hospital wards, and intensive care units (ICUs) during the spring of 2020. Particularly, Covid-19 represents a changed context for evaluation of capacity not only due to the *numbers* of patients, who need treatment and care, but also due to *procedures*, for example the need for personal protective equipment (PPE) and isolation of infected patients. This changed context is essential not only for understanding evaluation of capacity in hospitals, but also for re-evaluation of procedures for managing local, regional, and national stockpiles of essential equipment, for instance, collaborations around procuring and/or producing PPE and ventilators or re-evaluation of previous outsourcing of capacity to produce, for example, N95 masks or swab tests. One important lesson from Covid-19 as context in healthcare is that previous models for supply change management may not be constructive going forward (Sharma et al., 2020).

We can also understand and examine Covid-19 as a changed context for collaboration across healthcare systems. For countries with both public and private healthcare sectors, the Covid-19 pandemic represents a changed context for the relationship and potential collaboration between the two sectors. The reason for this is that Covid-19 requires collective, coordinated actions among the organizations involved due to the scale and pace of spread of the virus and the inter-dependency of healthcare work (Nembhard et al., 2020). Collaboration and coordinated action are important during a pandemic, because the society as a whole is impacted as people's movements and activities intersect. For instance, policy and interventions aimed at minimizing spread of Covid-19 in public transportation must be understood in relation to policies and interventions in other areas, for example places of work and education.

Lastly, Covid-19 can be understood as a changed context for healthcare professionals, who work in healthcare systems, especially at the front line. Robert et al. (2020) discuss recent studies of healthcare professionals' experiences of working during Covid-19 and the impact this changed context has had on mental health. These authors show that healthcare professionals report a range of serious concerns: 'extended workloads, feelings of powerlessness when trying to contain the large number of patients, concerns about the suffering and potential poor outcomes of their patients, preoccupations about potential shortages of intensive care resources (including personal protective equipment), the fear of transmitting the disease to their loved ones, and apprehension about possible involvement in ethically difficult resource allocation decision-making' (Robert et al., 2020, p. 6). This is not surprising, but alarming. During the first wave of the pandemic healthcare professionals were called in to work from other specialties, from retirement, and students were asked to join reserves or stand by. First, the *amount* of work (hours/day or week) were radically increased in many countries to keep up with patients, who needed treatment and care. Second, the *nature* of work during Covid-19 required healthcare professionals to make decisions under radically changed conditions and concerning radically changed matters. Third, healthcare staff around the world have contracted Covid-19 in worrying numbers, in some cases due to insufficient protective equipment or to excessive exposure to virus.

Covid-19 as Enacted: A Force of Change

Covid-19 does represent not only a changed context for healthcare systems, but also an enacted force of change. Covid-19 has presented us with a changing context for understanding and talking about public health as a global phenomenon, as a 'Global Public Good' (Brown & Susskind, 2020). Public health and its relevance for the whole of society have become more evident during Covid-19, as illustrated by the intrinsic link between public health and the economy. The economic consequences of the Covid-19 pandemic, for example large-scale job loss, evictions, financial distress, business closures, are expected and indeed evidenced. Covid-19 is not only a public health crisis, but also an economic crisis in which different sectors of the economy are hit unequally (Susskind & Vines, 2020). Accompanying this, several other examples of how Covid-19 is not only a matter of public health are emerging: for example, the virus is having a profound negative impact on mental health (Hodson, 2020); the gender gap is widening during Covid-19; and young people's lives, especially concerning education, jobs, and job prospects, are impacted disproportionately relative to other age groups (Susskind & Vines, 2020). In several countries, Covid-19 hit disenfranchised populations harder and the state of a country's general level of public health came to be seen as an important indicator for how Covid-19 impacts a population, an area, or a country. This sparked renewed discussions among healthcare professionals, researchers, and in the general public debate about social inequity and socio-economic gradients in access to healthcare and the purpose and role of public health in society (Chung et al., 2020). Thus for policy makers, politicians, and public health and social care professionals working with especially vulnerable groups of people, the Covid-19 pandemic posed new and challenging ethical and political questions that urgently need to be addressed. Any such solution must be implemented *as the pandemic is unfolding* with the aim of impacting *how* the pandemic unfolds: the connections between context, action, and change across parts of society quickly became evident. Understood this way, Covid-19 is not something that only 'happens' to society; the actions of ordinary citizens, for example the way in which we enact public health policies in everyday life, shape the development of the pandemic and thus the impact on society and us all.

Regardless of scale and spread, *crises*, such as the Covid-19 pandemic, can change dramatically and rapidly and require people to act in new ways under conditions of time pressure, and radical uncertainty. Actions and decisions during crises have been subject to research drawing on organizational decision-making theory (Hodgkinson & Starbuck, 2008; Tamuz & Lewis, 2008) and sensemaking theory (Hernes & Maitlis, 2010; Maitlis & Sonenshein, 2010). Organizational decisions are susceptible to a range of biases and sources of errors and in a crisis such as Covid-19, information overload (Sutcliffe & Weick, 2008) is likely to occur. Data has played a significant role in health policy formation and implementation during Covid-19 and we suspect the amount and pace with which data is produced and used during Covid-19 have amplified this challenge. Sensemaking is one important way actors manage information overload through constructing and enacting meaning out of the vast amounts of data available. However, 'the meaning of a particular piece of data depends on what else is going on, what else could be going on, what has gone on, and [what] the observer expects or intends to happen' (Woods et al., 2002: 27, quoted in Sutcliffe & Weick, 2008, p. 65). Here the significance of context is evident, because in order to decide what to do and how to act on this decision actors construct contexts for their actions even if these are not articulated and shared. This is relevant for health policy research and implementation because the way people make sense of their situation, individually and collectively, is essential to the collaborations they are part of and the decisions they make, also when they design and implement policies. This, in turn, potentially affects outcomes for everyone needing and providing care during a crisis like Covid-19.

The different national approaches to Covid-19 provide examples of how national governments and public health agencies have presented different understandings of the pandemic accompanied by a range of responses to handling the situation. Different approaches across Denmark, Norway, Finland, and Sweden can serve as examples. All four countries are Scandinavian countries with public healthcare sectors and strong public health agencies. Yet, their responses to the Covid-19 outbreak have been very different[1] notably concerning national lockdown as strategy and these strategies have been adjusted continually as the pandemic unfolds and 'the context' for national political action changes. Moreover, regardless of the strategy, for health policies to have any effect they must be implemented and adhered to in practice. Here it is important to remember that it is by no means certain that the people involved in making or implementing health policy agree on what 'the context' is or where the boundaries of context to solve such a complex problem lie. 'Meaning is not self-evident but must be constructed and shared. Many different interpretations are both supportable and refutable' (March et al., 1991, p. 6). Press coverage and social media posts during the pandemic illustrate the variety of interpretations of what the problem is, what should be done about it, and how.

In sum, policy makers are continually constructing contexts for actions during Covid-19 that provide citizens with guidelines for 'enacting' health policies such as social distancing or mask wearing. However, compliance with such guidelines is not guaranteed. This is evident in the different ways people form opinions on what Covid-19 *is*, what the *context* for understanding Covid-19 is, and therefore how one should or should not act. But actions are not only carried out by humans. Viewed as a non-human actor in healthcare systems, Covid-19 can be understood as an actant that interacts with humans and other non-human actors in ways that impact healthcare in practice. Understood this way, we can explore

[1] https://nordics.info/show/artikel/the-nordic-countries-react-differently-to-the-covid-19-crisis/

how 'coronavirus' and 'Covid-19' act in combination with policies, humans, material artefacts, and technologies. Moreover, we can examine how such socio-material assemblages (Orlikowski, 2007) develop as the pandemic unfolds. This would require us to foreground, or focus on, Covid-19 and specify against which background/context we wanted to examine this phenomenon. One way to pursue this line of research could be to explore how 'Covid-19' is constructed and assigned agency in documents, for example policies, research, or in people's experiences of living through a lockdown.

How Can We Study Context in Action?

Having provided examples of how and why the way we approach and operationalize context matters, we now turn to discuss how we can study complex phenomena such as Covid-19 in action through qualitative methods. In this, we focus on collaborative fieldwork because widespread, complex phenomena lend themselves well to collaborative fieldwork. We also briefly discuss the multi-level nature of phenomena such as Covid-19 and how context can be operationalized in this regard.

Constructing Context in Collaborative Fieldwork

Collaborative fieldwork is one way to study complex and multi-sited phenomena that change over time, because such studies require efforts that may go beyond what an individual researcher can carry out. Barley et al. (2016) conducted a coordinated set of ethnographies in which the researchers collaborated to study technicians' work in different settings. Each researcher was responsible for an occupation and for presenting this to the team. Then team members collaborated during iterations of data analysis to surface shared themes across the data. These authors do not specify how they constructed 'the context' for their study. However, in their study, 'context' is primarily used as a term to refer to 'the context of everyday work', 'the situational context', and 'contextual knowledge', which again refers to knowledge of work practices within a given occupation.

This term, 'context of everyday work', seems to have been constructed through a series of methodological and analytical choices. First, each individual researcher produced 'a detailed portrait of the occupation's work *as they currently understood it*' (ibid., p. 133, italics added). This move involved repeated engagement with people in the field and initial data analysis to decide what to include and what to exclude from the detailed portrait. Then each researcher presented the account of the occupation's work to team members, who asked questions to fill out gaps in the account. The purpose of this move was to 'develop familiarity with the details of practice in various settings' (p. 133). Although this is not specifically addressed as a strategy for operationalizing what they meant by context and how they wanted to study it, we suggest that this is one of the central outcomes of the exercise. Moreover, by operationalizing context this way, these authors could produce *comparable* 'backgrounds' for analysing their phenomenon (technical work) and certain elements of it (professional talk). This, in turn, allows the reader to understand the premise and conditions of their research. These insights into how a collaborative fieldwork can be organized and carried out with a shared approach to context may serve as inspiration for groups of researchers that face the challenge of examining aspects of healthcare, for example implications of policies, organizational change processes, or the role of specific actions or groups of actors in change initiatives.

Context and the (Changing) Micro-foundations of Institutions

In this section, we focus on how operationalizing context can help researchers, who wish to examine the multi-level nature of the phenomenon and its link to several institutions, for example medicine, the market, government, or education. We discussed in the sections above how Covid-19 can be understood as a changed and changing context for healthcare systems, as 'enacted phenomenon' and as source of 'change' in healthcare systems, society, or our everyday life. In all these regards,

Covid-19 is linked to institutions. National governments and public health agencies draw on and develop regulatory frameworks for handling the pandemic, often heavily inspired by initiatives from institutional actors such as the WHO, drawing on scientific knowledge produced before and during the pandemic. Scientific evidence may be seen as a source of legitimacy, but the legitimacy accompanying evidence has been, and is still, subject to debate and political interests. Institutional norms are significantly impacted across institutions, as guidelines travel with public health policies from the field of medicine to, for example, education or volunteering. Lastly, while this development is still ongoing, our taken-for-granted assumptions about the world, how it works, and what it means to be, for example a school teacher, a local politician, or a public health scientist, are also changing with Covid-19. Such matters are never just a question of what happens during 'micro-interactions'. Rather, if we want to understand people and their interactions, we need to situate them within their broader context and explore the dynamic relationships that constitute what we understand as 'context' across analytical levels.

Zilber (2020) suggests ethnography as one of several constructive approaches to analysing people and their interactions within a broader institutional context. She argues that '[t]he ultimate test of any microfoundations approach is in its ability to allow the capturing of both micro and macro. Such a challenge necessitates creativity, flexibility and rigour. We need to dedicate more efforts to explicate the methodological choices—regarding research strategy, case study, data collection and data analysis—that are made before the study begins, and during its early phases, and their theoretical implications' (Zilber, 2020, p. 18). Despite rich methodological reflections, Zilber uses the term 'context' in a generalized way: the social context, broader context, macro-level context, institutional context, and to refer to 'the context of' something. We hope that our explication of the different approaches to Covid-19, context, action, and change has demonstrated why systematic operationalization and explication of context are essential for research that hopes to examine complex, dynamic, and multi-level phenomena such as Covid-19. We argue that a systematic approach to what is constructed as a relevant context for a phenomenon, and why, will aid comparative studies across organizations or institutions provided the researcher tackles the challenges inherent in multi-level approaches. Zilber (2020) provides a rich discussion of methodological choices and consequences and suggestions for avenues going forward.

Implications for Healthcare Managers and Leaders

What are the implications of adopting a nuanced approach to context for healthcare managers and leaders? For one thing, the approach to context, which we have argued for in this chapter, comes with an understanding that acknowledges that context is something you construct and enact. This allows healthcare managers and leaders to surface their own assumptions and take for granted perspectives on a given situation and to use this as occasion to improve collaborative processes such as organizational change or implementation of policy.

Our approach to context and its relationship to action and change also show how disagreements about what counts as 'the change' and 'the context' of implementing a health policy can lead to conflict and misunderstandings and hamper the process. Our illustrations from using Covid-19 as an example and the insights from collaborative fieldwork can serve as inspiration from healthcare managers and leaders, hopefully sparking curiosity and discussion about the consequences of different approaches to context. It is our hope that such reflections can be used to start a dialogue and explore how the context-action-change relationship might look from others' point of view.

To summarize, research into the tasks and challenges associated with managing healthcare organizations in what we can define as 'a challenging policy context' can benefit greatly from defining and operationalizing what is meant by 'context' and how we aim to study contexts from different approaches. Throughout this chapter, Covid-19 has been used as an example to illustrate the significance of *how* we construct context and how different approaches to context will allow us to understand and study very different things. Our aim has been to raise some important issues about context and its relationship to action and change in a complex healthcare policy context. We have done this to underscore researchers' responsibility to specify what we analytically 'bound' as context in our research and the consequences that such specific constructions of context may have for the research we carry out and for how this research can be used in practice.

References

Barley, S. R., Bechky, B. A., & Nelsen, B. J. (2016). What do technicians mean when they talk about professionalism? An ethnography of speaking. *The Structuring of Work in Organizations, 47*, 125–160.

Bohmer, R. M. J. (2009). *Designing care: Aligning the nature and management of health care*. Harvard Business Press.

Brown, G. & Susskind, D. (2020). International cooperation during the COVID-19 pandemic. *Oxford Review of Economic Policy, 36*(Suppl_1), S64–S76.

Chambers, D. (2019). Context of health policies and the impact on implementation of health care and health interventions. In N. Meier & S. Dopson (Eds.), *Context in action and how to study it: Illustrations from healthcare*. Oxford University Press.

Chung, R. Y., Dong, D., & Li, M. M. (2020). Socioeconomic gradient in health and the Covid-19 outbreak. *BMJ, 369*, m1329.

Dopson, S. (2001). Applying an Eliasian approach to Organisational analysis. *Organization, 83*, 515–535.

Dopson, S., & Fitzgerald, L. (Eds.). (2005). *Knowledge to action? Evidence based health care in context*. Oxford University Press.

Fitzgerald, L., Ferlie, E., Wood, M., & Hawkins, C. (2002). Interlocking interactions, the diffusion of innovations in health care. *Human Relations, 55*(12), 1429–1449.

Hernes, T., & Maitlis, S. (2010). Process, sensemaking and organizing: An introduction. In T. Hernes & S. Maitlis (Eds.), *Process, sensemaking and organizing* (pp. 27–37). Oxford University Press.

Hodgkinson, G. P., & Starbuck, W. H. (Eds.). (2008). *The Oxford handbook of organizational decision making*. Oxford University Press.

Hodson, N. (2020, September 25). We should prepare for the mental health impact of mass unemployment. *The BMJOPINION*. https://blogs.bmj.com/

bmj/2020/09/25/nathan-hodson-we-should-prepare-for-the-mental-health-impact-of-mass-unemployment/

Johns, G. (2017). Incorporating context in organizational research: Reflections on the 2016 AMR decade award. *Academy of Management Review, 42*(4), 577–595.

Korica, M., & Nicolini, D. (2019). Tracing context as relational, discursive accomplishment: Analytical lessons from a shadowing-based study of health care chief executives. In N. Meier & S. Dopson (Eds.), *Context in action and how to study it: Illustrations from healthcare*. Oxford University Press.

Maitlis, S., & Sonenshein, S. (2010). Sensemaking in crisis and change: Inspiration and insights from Weick (1988). *Journal of Management Studies, 47*(3), 551–580.

March, J. G., Sproull, L. S., & Tamuz, M. (1991). Learning from samples of one or fewer. *Organization Science, 2*(1), 1–13.

McGivern, G., & Dopson, S. (2010). Inter-epistemic power and transforming knowledge objects in a bio medical network. *Organization Studies, 31*(2), 1667–1686.

Meier, N. (2012). Coordination in clinical managerial practice: Moving things around and making things happen. *Scandinavian Journal of Public Administration, 15*(4), 67–88.

Meier, N. (2015). Configurations of leadership practices in hospital units. *Journal of Health Organization and Management, 29*(7), 1115–1130.

Meier, N., & Dopson, S. (Eds.). (2019). *Context in action and how to study it: Illustrations from healthcare*. Oxford University Press.

Nembhard, I. M., Burns, L. R., & Shortell, S. M. (2020). Responding to Covid-19: Lessons from management research. *New England Journal of Medicine Catalyst, 1*(2). https://doi.org/10.1056/CAT.20.0111

Nilsen, P., Stahl, C., Roback, K., & Cairney, P. (2013). Never the twain shall meet?—A comparison of implementation science and policy implementation research. *Implementation Science: IS, 8*, 63. https://doi.org/10.1186/1748-5908-8-63

Orlikowski, W. J. (2007). Sociomaterial practices: Exploring technology at work. *Organization Studies, 28*(9), 1435–1448.

Robert, R., Kentish-Barnes, N., Boyer, A., Laurent, A., Azoulay, E., & Reignier, J. (2020). Ethical dilemmas due to the Covid-19 pandemic. *Annals of Intensive Care, 10*, 84.

Rousseau, M. D., & Fried, Y. (2001). Location, location, location: Contextualizing organizational research. *Journal of Organizational Behavior, 22*(1), 1–13.

Scharfstein, B. A. (1989). *The dilemma of context.* New York University Press.

Sharma, A., Gupta, P., & Jha, R. (2020). COVID-19: Impact on health supply chain and lessons to be learnt. *Journal of Health Management, 22*(2), 248–261.

Suddaby, R. (2010). Editor's comments: Construct clarity in theories of management and organization. *Academy of Management Review, 35*(3), 346–357.

Susskind, D., & Vines, D. (2020). The economics of the COVID-19 pandemic: An assessment. *Oxford Review of Economic Policy, 36*(Suppl_1), S1–S13.

Sutcliffe, K. M., & Weick, K. E. (2008). Information overload revisited. In G. P. Hodgkinson & W. H. Starbuck (Eds.), *The Oxford handbook of organizational decision making* (pp. 56–76). Oxford University Press.

Tamuz, M., & Lewis, T. E. (2008). Facing the threat of disaster: Decision making when the stakes are high. In G. P. Hodgkinson & W. H. Starbuck (Eds.), *Organizational decision making* (pp. 155–174). Oxford University Press.

Zilber, T. B. (2020). The methodology/theory interface: Ethnography and the microfoundations of institutions. *Organization Theory, 1*(2), 1–27.

Part II

Translating Healthcare Policy into Practice

6

Understanding Mission Drift in UK Health Charities with a Focus on Africa: A Realist-Informed Synthesis

Crispen Sachikonye, Naomi Chambers, and Ronnie Ramlogan

Introduction: Charities, Boards and Mission Drift

Charities that are based in the UK and support health improvement in Africa face unique opportunities, risks and complexity. They work in the region that receives the largest proportion of UK aid, which suggests that they have significant access to funding for their missions (DFID, 2018b). However, the funding is tied to policies that require these charities to promote UK values, laws and priorities even though they are operating as guests of African governments (DFID, 2015; Charities Act, 2011). In doing their work, health charities encounter deeply entrenched ethnic and

C. Sachikonye (✉) • N. Chambers • R. Ramlogan
Alliance Manchester Business School, The University of Manchester, Manchester, UK
e-mail: crispen.sachikonye@manchester.ac.uk; naomi.chambers@manchester.ac.uk; ronnie.ramlogan@manchester.ac.uk

R. Kislov et al. (eds.), *Managing Healthcare Organisations in Challenging Policy Contexts*, Organizational Behaviour in Healthcare,
https://doi.org/10.1007/978-3-030-81093-1_6

tribal cultures, influential religions, weak governance institutions and norms that may contradict their ethical standards (Parboteeah et al., 2014). At times, they struggle to manage these various influences and can become inconsistent in their actions (Charity Commission, 2019; UNHCR and Save the Children UK, 2002). There emerges a gap between the actions and the intentions of the health charity. This gap is mission drift.

Previous reviews explain mission drift as an outcome of a choice between competing charitable and business pressures (Battilana & Lee, 2014). The literature suggests that mission drift can be managed by resisting, partially accommodating or finding ways of accepting donor pressures. However, this literature is scant and drawn mainly from research on social enterprises. It is predominantly concerned with the influence of donors and pays little attention to the role of charity boards in mission drift. Boards are groups of individuals, mainly part-time outsiders, that are sanctioned to secure the mission of the charity (Judge & Talaulicar, 2017), which makes exploration of their role in mission drift particularly important.

Insights about how organisations can tackle mission drift can be found in studies investigating strategic responses to institutional processes. Studies explain, for instance, the nature of decision-making in the face of critical tensions in organisations with multiple institutional logics (Pache & Santos, 2010; Jay, 2013). Much like the mission drift literature, these studies focus on donor pressures and lack explicit attention to the role of boards. Yet, besides donors, there are other identifiable sources of mission drift at the institutional, social and organisational levels, and boards have an important role in managing mission drift (Cornforth, 2014). Greater knowledge of the various sources of mission drift, the circumstances in which these sources are relevant and board responses to them could improve our understanding of mission drift and help charity boards to tackle it.

This review synthesises evidence from health charities' annual reports with the insights from mission drift and governance literature to understand how boards operating in complex and ambiguous environments reconcile the tensions that lead to mission drift. It seeks to (1) identify the external sources of mission drift and (2) explain how, why and in what circumstances health charity boards respond. In the next section, we explain the methodological approach and introduce the theory applied to inform the review. We then turn to the literature to identify board responses to four key charity stakeholder groups. The findings are brought into a framework for board decision-making applicable to managing mission drift. The chapter concludes with a summary as well as recommendations for future research.

Methodological Approach

The review applies insights from Pfeffer and Salancik's (1978) resource dependence perspective to explain how boards can respond to external pressures that would otherwise lead to mission drift. This perspective is useful for understanding the role of boards in linking to and managing the relationship between external stakeholders and the organisation (Hillman et al., 2009). It emphasises that organisations can make active choices to control external stakeholders or negotiate an arrangement to coordinate their behaviour. When it is not possible to control or coordinate external stakeholders, organisations become political by appealing to the wider social system to help them eliminate difficulties and promote their interests. They create alliances, ingratiate themselves with others and acquiesce to more powerful players to alter their environment.

With this political aspect of resource dependence perspective as a theoretical lens, we use the scientific realist approach to identify political mechanisms in the governance and mission drift literature. Scientific realists argue that research should identify and study mechanisms, that is causal structures that generate expected and unexpected outcomes (Pawson & Tilley, 1997). Mechanisms help explain the relationship between contextual factors, such as donor pressures, and outcomes, such as mission drift. The scientific realist approach enables researchers to theorise the existence of mechanisms, going beyond empirically observable concepts, and then to test and refine the theories using empirical literature (Pawson et al., 2005).

The review was undertaken in three stages which are shown in Fig. 6.1. First, guided by the research objectives of the study, we searched and extracted the data to aid the development of a set of working hypotheses, called candidate theories, about how boards manage mission drift. Booth et al. (2018) suggest that candidate theories 'appear wherever

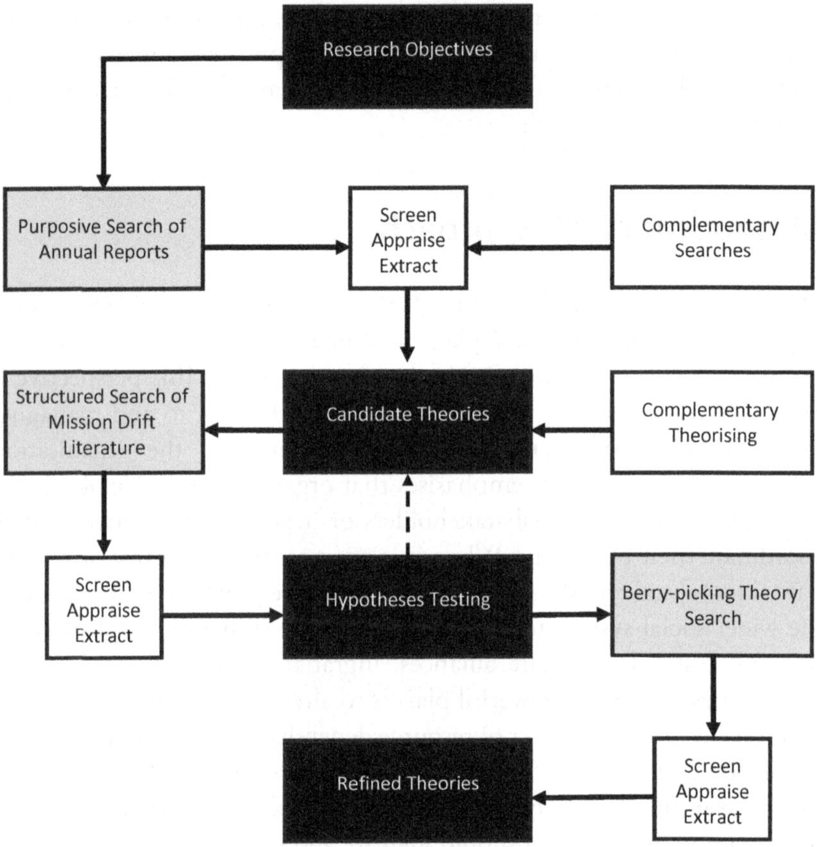

Fig. 6.1 Realist search, review and synthesis process. (Source: Authors' adaption of the realist search process described by Booth et al., 2018; Note: Complementary processes include complementary theorising with experts in interviews and at a conference)

stakeholders discuss assumptions' about their activities including in business plans and policy reports (p. 159). This suggestion led to the purposive identification of annual reports of health charities as sources of candidate theories. Data on external charity stakeholders, contexts, board responses, and intended and unintended outcomes were extracted and coded using computer-assisted qualitative data analysis software. The search stopped after extraction from twenty-seven reports of the largest health charities, at which point there was sufficient support for a set of hypotheses.

Second, a structured search of mission drift literature was conducted in the Web of Science databases to identify literature to test the candidate theories and expound the mechanisms. The search used broad search terms "mission drift" AND charity OR "social enterprise" or variations of these terms with no date limits. The results of the search were manually sifted, initially using the abstracts, and then using a full-text screen to identify literature that (1) represented primary research, (2) reported on the influence of external stakeholders and (3) involved a description of organisational responses to these external pressures.

Third, governance literature was identified through an iterative search process based on the mission drift literature. In contrast to a fixed and linear model of search where the strategy is fully formed before searching, with this 'berrypicking' approach, researchers begin with one relevant reference and use that to identify useful information and additional references (Bates, 1989). Thus, the search is not satisfied by one set of literature from a single query, but by a collection of information picked one at a time from various searches. This literature was used to refine the tested theories. The refined theories, with their respective mechanisms, are presented in the next section. While mechanisms exist at various system levels, for instance at the socio-institutional level where cultural assumptions are critical (Westhorp, 2018), this review only identifies mechanisms at the social system level which emphasises the pressure or desire for group consensus. Mechanisms at the social level are able to explain how the board, acting as a group, makes choices to manage mission drift.

Findings: Mechanisms and Variability of Board Responses to External Pressures

Mechanism 1: Boards Are Maternal Towards Beneficiaries

Maternalism is concerned with how decision-makers act on behalf of beneficiaries without their explicit permission but with regard for their autonomy and preferences (Sullivan & Niker, 2018). It is evident in 'nudge' interventions where an organisation persuades beneficiaries to do what is best for themselves without restricting their choices or forcing their decisions (Thaler & Sunstein, 2008). For example, when the health charity Absolute Return for Kids sought to reduce diarrhoeal deaths in young children in Zambia, they developed an intervention for caregivers to improve their health behaviours (Greenland et al., 2016). The health charity proceeded by first understanding the preferences and needs of beneficiaries through formative research. Then, working with the permissions of the Zambian government and the broader community, but without an explicit consent of the children or caregivers, the charity developed communications to persuade caregivers to increase breastfeeding, wash their hands and use oral rehydration salt solution.

Maternalism has not always been adopted. One example is the failure by Oxfam to protect beneficiaries from sexual abuse in Haiti (Charity Commission, 2019). Oxfam prioritised its reputation ahead of the people it pledged to protect whilst working in Haiti after the earthquakes of 2010. Another example relates to how, in pursuit of performance, microfinance institutions in Asia clandestinely charged beneficiaries higher interest rates, additional participation fees and subjected them to extensive pressure at collection (Fouillet & Augsburg, 2010). Many beneficiaries committed suicide. Both examples led to perceptions of mission drift. They highlight that even as the organisations served beneficiaries and made decisions about them, in the presence of certain organisational and environmental constraints, those decisions were not in the interest of beneficiaries. By contrast, genuine maternalism encourages boards to make decisions with beneficiaries by listening to their voices, understanding their needs and then acting on their behalf. It explains calls by policymakers for safeguarding to be prioritised in all charities operating internationally to avert mission drift (DFID, 2018a).

Mechanism 2: Boards Promote Diplomacy Towards Civil Society

UK health charities working in Africa are subject to various suspicions. They carry significant historical baggage linked to British imperialism that reflects tensions between African political groups and the charities (Manji & O'Coill, 2002). In the face of such tensions, charities adopt a diplomatic approach, appealing to the broader civil society to legitimise their existence. Diplomacy includes advocating for the rights of key constituents, shaping public opinion and developing linkages that support their missions (Jenkins, 2006).

Diplomacy may, however, require the charity to make compensatory actions such as suspending its values or shifting its goals, modes of operation and image to align with civil society (Lu, 2018). Charities may have to downplay or emphasise certain aspects of their work resulting in a coordinated form of mission drift where the charity is aware of the changes occurring as it moves away from its initial intentions. For instance, under President Rawlings in Ghana, non-governmental organisations (NGOs) were gradually excluded from operating in the political space. They were able to operate only if they agreed to be co-opted by the government and were directed to focus on specific civil society policies or programmes (Gary, 1996). This arrangement enabled them to pursue and achieve part of their mission. However, it affected their autonomy, increased their administrative burden and threatened their charitable role. Thus, while diplomacy works to support the achievement of the mission when the charity has the freedom to exercise significant influence over civil society, this approach may lead to 'coordinated' mission drift when the power and authority of the charity are constrained.

Mechanism 3: Boards Adopt a Coaching Approach Towards Donors

Donors offer financial resources to the charity in return for social value. They also provide systems that influence what the charity does and how accountable and effective it is (Tacon et al., 2017). The nature of the donor can affect organisational behaviours (Hodge & Piccolo, 2005; Khieng & Dahles, 2015), the reputation of the charity (Wright et al., 2019; Dunn, 2010), the extent to which the charity is resource- or mission-focused (Ma et al., 2018; Adams & Perlmutter, 1995), and other funding that the charity attracts (Schatteman & Bingle, 2017). Donors and the systems they promote are therefore a potential source of mission drift.

To manage mission drift, health charities adopt a coaching approach towards their donors. They assume responsibility for articulating and promoting their preferences to donors and encourage donors to act in certain ways (AbouAssi, 2013). Coaching involves shaping donor values, through some form of education, to condition the donor preferences (Henderson & Lambert, 2018; Mitchell, 2014; Batley, 2011). It works when the charity acts proactively, providing workshops for education and taking primary control of projects through strategic account management (Bennett & Savani, 2011). Coaching also involves co-optation. Through co-optation, the charity involves donors as part of decision-making and encourages them into a relationship that reduces organisational uncertainty and encourages generosity (Betzler, 2015). However, these relationships can lead to a lack of independence for the charity and demands for accountability that threaten the charity's legitimacy and responsiveness (Baur & Schmitz, 2012). They can generate battles for control, divert the attention of the leadership and lead to mission drift.

Mechanism 4: Boards Encourage Coalitions with Partners

Charities collaborate with programme partners to secure resources, improve their competences and gain new knowledge to solve complex social issues (Betzler & Gmur, 2016; Shumate et al., 2018). Programme partners meet their objectives through the charity, meaning that there is a symbiotic relationship through which partners and the charity can both achieve their goals. However, when there is more emphasis on the goals of the partners than those of the charity, the relationship is not mutually beneficial and can lead to mission drift (Jang et al., 2016; Herlin, 2015).

The mechanism identified to explain how the board can respond to pressures and opportunities from partners is coalitionism. It involves embedding certain shared practices and performance standards within a group of organisations working together. The idea is for the charity to influence its partners to adhere to specific ways of working, and to specific goals and standards, aiming to promote the charity's power and authority. Save the Children International, for instance, promotes a formal charter to promote its coalition with organisations and individuals. The charter is based on the Declaration of the Rights of the Child that the charity published in 1923 to promote cooperation and coordination around the charity's mission (Mulley, 2009). The charter has had positive effects on the charity. In its early years, it inspired growth and new relief work for the charity outside Europe. More recently, it has enabled the charity to focus on its mission to protect children while working with a large number of partners. Similarly, Comic Relief (2017) sets out a range of working principles to focus its partnerships towards its mission. Givewell, a charity that rates the performance of other charities, uses its evaluation process to encourage charities to focus on its causes (Brown, 2016).

The critical point about these coalitions is that their membership pledges to abide by specific rules that the charity sets. Control of the rules, which are open to interpretation and manipulation, means that members are open to influence and control by the charity. In this way, charities leading coalitions exercise control over important goals and can invite the participation of other organisations to help them achieve their goals. However, for charities with no control over the rules, coalitionism can reinforce, rather than reduce, mission drift. Also, when the charity and its partners have similar capacity and capability, there can be an unhealthy competition which may lead to tensions over the control of resources and impact a charity's ability to achieve its mission. As a result, charities may engage in unethical behaviours, leverage their charitable status to deal with their competitors and move away from practices related to their mission (Bousalham & Vidaillet, 2018).

Synergies and Tensions Between Stakeholder Pressures

Mechanisms overlap, interact and evolve (Williams, 2018). At any one time, each stakeholder group is presenting different interconnected opportunities and demands, some of which are more salient than others (Bradford et al., 2018). Further, supportive, complementary relationships between stakeholder groups may make it difficult to differentiate between them. For example, donor policies and pressures can manifest in civil society programmes such that it is difficult to discern whether civil society's issues are truly their own or are disguised donor pressures (Fowler, 2014). This is particularly evident in underdeveloped societies that rely on patronage. In these situations, donors can fundamentally alter local politics and the quality of democracy (Brown et al., 2002). This modifies the role of donors and has implications for the nature of mechanisms related to them.

The interconnections between stakeholders can also lead to tensions which make it difficult for charities to display accountability (Ramus & Vaccaro, 2017). For instance, charities grapple with whether they should prioritise the demands of beneficiaries and programme partners over those of civil society and donors (Calhoun, 2008). If they prioritise one over the other, what does that mean for meeting human needs versus ensuring human rights? Such questions require boards to make paradoxical choices about stakeholders, to broaden stakeholder involvement and to promote multi-perspective responses (Chambers et al., 2017). The choices that emerge, triggered by different and multiple stakeholder pressures, lead to actions that, at times, support the achievement of charity's mission, and at other times oppose it.

Radical, Incremental and Weak Responses

The mission drift literature points to variation in the nature and strength of board responses to opportunities and demands from external stakeholders. The quality of response depends, in part, on the approach to decision-making. It is influenced by the practical intelligence and the ideology to which the board is drawn (Jin, 2020; Jönsson, 2019). It also depends on the structure and processes of the board. Jones et al. (2017) explain how clinicians invited onto boards of health organisations influence board decisions on quality improvement. They find that the knowledge and skills of clinicians applied to interpreting data and linking external pressures to internal priorities contextualise information and help boards make better decisions.

Board responses can be radical, incremental or weak. A radical response involves active resistance to external stakeholder pressures. It involves instating structural or systemic barriers to provide the charity with complete control of the organisation's mission in a way that rejects stakeholder pressures. For example, when leaders are resilient, resourceful and reflexive, they can provide a radical response and outrightly reject external values and control (Darby, 2016). Also, the board may introduce drastic organisational strategies that are antithetical to their approach. It can reject funding from powerful donors and focus on commercial activities even if they lead to mission drift (Khieng & Dahles, 2015).

Incremental responses are day-to-day adjustments and routines of decision-makers to interconnect various stakeholders and the organisation to mediate any impact on the mission. They manifest as negotiated control over stakeholder pressures (Ismail & Johnson, 2019; Raisiene & Urmanaviciene, 2017; Ometto et al., 2019). In their research on organisational partnerships in sports, Peachey et al. (2018) found that actions, such as focusing on building relationships and networks as well as demonstrating benefits of the partnership, helped to align the missions of the partners.

A weak response means the board provides no resistance to stakeholder pressures and is susceptible to mission drift. The board's reasoning in response to stakeholder pressures is ineffective such that it fails to control or negotiate stakeholder pressures completely. For instance, charities can be so reliant on donor funding that they are unable to push-back on donor demands (AbouAssi, 2013).

Discussion: Managing Mission Drift

Board Responses to Mission Drift

This synthesis identifies how external stakeholders influence health charities and how boards can respond to these influences to manage mission drift. The synthesis supports the findings of previous reviews, which show that mission drift is predominantly an outcome of a choice between conflicting logics (Battilana & Lee, 2014). However, it advances the argument beyond charitable or business logics to show that mission drift can occur wherever there are stakeholders that offer different opportunities to the charity. The synthesis identifies beneficiaries, civil society, donors and programme partners as key interconnected charity stakeholders. It finds that tensions between these stakeholders become part of the context of the decision-making of the board.

Drawing on Pfeffer and Salancik's (1978) resource dependence perspective, the review uncovers four political mechanisms that can help the board make choices. These are likely rather than necessary ways for the board to act in complex, interconnected environments and suggest that the board has a significant political role. It identifies maternalism as the board's response to opportunities from beneficiaries; diplomacy as the response towards pressures from civil society; coaching for donors; and coalitionism for programme partners. The mechanisms are described individually but can act together. Consistent with Bigelow et al. (1996), these mechanisms suggest that the power and influence of charity boards lie in their political skills.

Grimes et al. (2019) propose a model that argues that mission drift can be shaped through organisational mindfulness—paying attention to noticing, encoding, interpreting and acting on environmental cues. It is concerned with the quality, rather than quantity, of attention that organisations devote to external pressures and enables nuanced responses. In reviewing this model, this synthesis suggests that adopting a mindful approach involves paying attention to the multiple, interconnected and competing stakeholder pressures, and adopting a variety of responses of different strength. This leads to mission drift that is more coordinated, where the board retains oversight of the changes occurring.

The Mission Governance Framework

The findings are drawn together into a framework about mission governance, which describes board responses to sources of mission drift (Fig. 6.2).

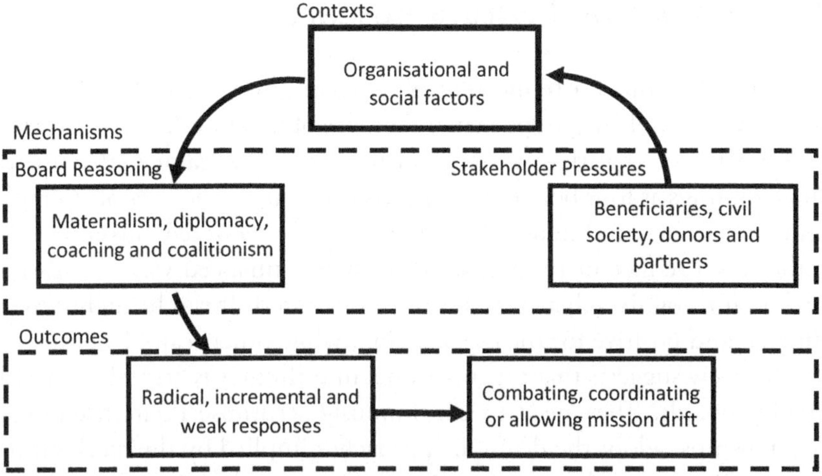

Fig. 6.2 Mission governance framework. (Source: Authors' adaption of the context, mechanism, outcomes framework by Dalkin et al., 2015)

The framework is based on realist principles about how contexts, mechanisms and outcomes interact (Dalkin et al., 2015). It argues that external stakeholders provide a range of interconnected pressures, often contradictory, that present opportunities for the board to take purposeful action. Whether and how those opportunities are taken depend on the context of decision-making and the reasoning of the board. The context includes organisational and social factors, such as board processes and the complexity of the operating environment, that contextualise stakeholder pressures and affect the choices of the board. The board may choose to be maternal, diplomatic, to coach or form coalitions. Each of these strategies can be deployed with variable degrees of strength, namely radical, incremental or weak responses, and have intended and unintended effects. A radical response blocks change, revolutionises the setting and combats mission drift. An incremental response delivers gradual change and facilitates a highly coordinated form of mission drift. It promotes collaborative and complementary relationships that can improve organisational performance such as being able to identify more efficient products through the strategy of bricolage (Kwong et al., 2017). A weak response leads to an undesirable form of mission drift as external environmental pressures are allowed to dominate.

Conclusions and Future Research

We have developed a framework of mission governance that identifies four key stakeholder groups that are sources of mission drift and explains how boards of charities can respond to them. The framework presents these findings as four board mechanisms with various degrees of strength. Under certain conditions, these mechanisms reinforce mission drift, rather than reduce or prevent it. This offers a nuanced view of mission drift that recognises that some forms of mission drift can be highly coordinated and positive for the organisation, while others can be negative.

This view suggests that organisational mindfulness is critical for health charity boards. They need to continuously scrutinise their stakeholder relationships, adopt the decision approaches implied by the mechanisms and apply measured responses. Boards may also benefit from inviting meaningful stakeholder representation into the decision-making process. Stakeholder representatives will bring to the board their knowledge and approaches to African cultures, religions, political structures and the operating environment. They can help the board improve its understanding of stakeholders, link multiple stakeholder demands to organisational objectives and modify the mission of the charity in order to avoid inconsistent organisational actions.

Given the paucity of literature on mission drift that is specific to Africa, this synthesis draws on a wide range of literature from various continents to develop the framework. The framework may, therefore, benefit from refinement using empirical data from specific African health charity contexts. While this research explains that contextual factors affect decision-making, exploring these influences empirically could be an interesting direction for future research. More specifically, further research might theorise and test how mechanisms at the socio-institutional level enhance or constrain the will of the board to act and explain how mechanisms described in this chapter are activated.

References

AbouAssi, K. (2013). Hands in the pockets of mercurial donors: NGO response to shifting funding priorities. *Nonprofit and Voluntary Sector Quarterly, 42*(3), 584–602.

Adams, C. T., & Perlmutter, F. D. (1995). Leadership in hard times—Are nonprofits well-served. *Nonprofit and Voluntary Sector Quarterly, 24*(3), 253–262.

Bates, M. J. (1989). The design of browsing and berrypicking techniques for the online search interface. *Online Review, 13*(5), 407–424.

Batley, R. (2011). Structures and strategies in relationships between non-government service providers and governments. *Public Administration and Development, 31*(4), 306–319.

Battilana, J., & Lee, M. (2014). Advancing research on hybrid organizing—Insights from the study of social enterprises. *The Academy of Management Annals, 8*(1), 397–441.

Baur, D., & Schmitz, H. P. (2012). Corporations and NGOs: When accountability leads to co-optation. *Journal of Business Ethics, 106*(1), 9–21.

Bennett, R., & Savani, S. (2011). Surviving mission drift: How charities can turn dependence on government contract funding to their own advantage. *Nonprofit Management & Leadership, 22*(2), 217–231.

Betzler, D. (2015). Factors of board governance and fundraising success: The composition of Swiss museum boards does matter. *Journal of Cultural Economy, 8*(2), 144–165.

Betzler, D., & Gmur, M. (2016). Does fundraising professionalization pay?: The impact of organizational fundraising capability on a charity's net revenue from private donations. *Nonprofit Management & Leadership, 27*(1), 27–42.

Bigelow, B., Stone, M. M., & Arndt, M. (1996). Corporate political strategy: A framework for understanding nonprofit strategy. *Nonprofit Management and Leadership, 7*(1), 29–43.

Booth, A., Wright, J., & Briscoe, S. (2018). Scoping and searching to support realist approaches. In N. Emmel, J. Greenhalgh, A. Manzano, M. Monaghan, & S. Dalkin (Eds.), *Doing realist research* (pp. 147–166). SAGE.

Bousalham, Y., & Vidaillet, B. (2018). Contradiction, circumvention and instrumentalization of noble values: How competition undermines the potential of alternatives. *Organization, 25*(3), 401–427.

Bradford, A., Luke, B., & Furneaux, C. (2018). Social enterprise accountability: Directions, dominance and developments. *Social Enterprise Journal, 14*(2), 156–179.

Brown, S. G. (2016). Supporting the best charities is harder than it seems. *Journal of Global Ethics, 12*(2), 240–244.

Brown, D. S., Brown, J. C., & Desposato, S. W. (2002). Left turn on green? The unintended consequences of international funding for sustainable development in Brazil. *Comparative Political Studies, 35*(7), 814–838.

Calhoun, C. (2008). The imperative to reduce suffering: Charity, progress, and emergencies in the field of humanitarian action. In M. Barnett & T. G. Weiss (Eds.), *Humanitarianism in question: Politics, power, ethics* (1st ed., pp. 73–97). Cornell University Press.

Chambers, N., Harvey, G., & Mannion, R. (2017). Who should serve on health care boards? What should they do and how should they behave? A fresh look at the literature and the evidence. *Cogent Business & Management, 4*(1), 1–14.

Charities Act. (2011). Retrieved February 2, 2018, from https://www.legislation.gov.uk/ukpga/2011/25

Charity Commission. (2019). *Oxfam inquiry report: Summary findings and conclusions*. Charity Commission for England and Wales. Retrieved December 8, 2020, from https://assets.publishing.service.gov.uk/government/uploads/system/uploads/attachment_data/file/807943/Inquiry_Report_summary_findings_and_conclusions_Oxfam.pdf

Comic Relief. (2017). *Comic relief international grants*. Comic Relief. Retrieved January 9, 2019, from https://www.comicrelief.com/sites/default/files/downloads/Comic_Relief_International_Grants_List.pdf

Cornforth, C. (2014). Understanding and combating mission drift in social enterprises. *Social Enterprise Journal, 10*(1), 3–20.

Dalkin, S. M., Greenhalgh, J., Jones, D., Cunningham, B., & Lhussier, M. (2015). What's in a mechanism? Development of a key concept in realist evaluation. *Implementation Science, 10*(1), 49.

Darby, S. (2016). Dynamic resistance: Third-sector processes for transforming neoliberalization. *Antipode, 48*(4), 977–999.

DFID. (2015). UK aid: Tackling global challenges in the national interest. Retrieved March 2, 2018, from https://www.gov.uk/government/uploads/system/uploads/attachment_data/file/478834/ODA_strategy_final_web_0905.pdf

DFID. (2018a). Statement from international development secretary on Oxfam and UK action to tackle sexual exploitation in the aid sector. Retrieved December 8, 2020, from https://www.gov.uk/government/news/statement-from-international-development-secretary-on-oxfam-and-uk-action-to-tackle-sexual-exploitation-in-the-aid-sector

DFID. (2018b). Statistics on international development. Provisional UK aid spend 2018. Retrieved December 8, 2020, from https://www.gov.uk/government/statistics/statistics-on-international-development-provisional-uk-aid-spend-2018

Dunn, P. (2010). Strategic responses by a nonprofit when a donor becomes tainted. *Nonprofit and Voluntary Sector Quarterly, 39*(1), 102–123.

Fouillet, C., & Augsburg, B. (2010). Profit empowerment: The microfinance institution's mission drift. *Perspectives on Global Development and Technology, 9*(3–4), 327–355.

Fowler, A. (2014). Civil society and aid in Africa: A case of mistaken identity? In *The handbook of civil society in Africa* (pp. 417–438). Springer.

Gary, I. (1996). Confrontation, co-operation or co-optation: NGOs and the Ghanaian state during structural adjustment. *Review of African Political Economy, 23*(68), 149–168.

Greenland, K., Chipungu, J., Curtis, V., Schmidt, W. P., Siwale, Z., Mudenda, M., et al. (2016). Multiple behaviour change intervention for diarrhoea control in Lusaka, Zambia: A cluster randomised trial. *Lancet Global Health, 4*(12), E966–E977.

Grimes, M. G., Williams, T. A., & Zhao, E. Y. (2019). Anchors aweigh: The sources, variety, and challenges of mission drift. *Academy of Management Review, 44*(4), 819–845.

Henderson, E., & Lambert, V. (2018). Negotiating for survival: Balancing mission and money. *The British Accounting Review, 50*(2), 185–198.

Herlin, H. (2015). Better safe than sorry: Nonprofit organizational legitimacy and cross-sector partnerships. *Business & Society, 54*(6), 822–858.

Hillman, A. J., Withers, M. C., & Collins, B. J. (2009). Resource dependence theory: A review. *Journal of Management, 35*(6), 1404–1427.

Hodge, M. M., & Piccolo, R. F. (2005). Funding source, board involvement techniques, and financial vulnerability in nonprofit organizations: A test of resource dependence. *Nonprofit Management and Leadership, 16*(2), 171–190.

Ismail, A., & Johnson, B. (2019). Managing organizational paradoxes in social enterprises: Case studies from the MENA region. *VOLUNTAS: International Journal of Voluntary and Nonprofit Organizations, 30*(3), 516–534.

Jang, H. S., Feiock, R. C., & Saitgalina, M. (2016). Institutional collective action issues in nonprofit self-organized collaboration. *Administration & Society, 48*(2), 163–189.

Jay, J. (2013). Navigating paradox as a mechanism of change and innovation in hybrid organizations. *Academy of Management Journal, 56*(1), 137–159.

Jenkins, J. C. (2006). Nonprofit organizations and political advocacy. *The Nonprofit Sector: A Research Handbook, 2*, 307–331.

Jin, B. (2020). The practical intelligence of social entrepreneurs: Managing the hybridity of social enterprises. *Entrepreneurship Research Journal, 10*(1), 1–19.

Jones, L., Pomeroy, L., Robert, G., Burnett, S., Anderson, J. E., & Fulop, N. J. (2017). How do hospital boards govern for quality improvement? A mixed methods study of 15 organisations in England. *BMJ Quality & Safety, 26*(12), 978–986.

Jönsson, J. (2019). Logic salience in ideologically-torn nonprofit hybrids. In *Nonprofit policy forum, 2019* (Vol. 10, Vol. 3). De Gruyter.

Judge, W. Q., & Talaulicar, T. (2017). Board involvement in the strategic decision making process: A comprehensive review. *Annals of Corporate Governance, 2*(2), 51–169.

Khieng, S., & Dahles, H. (2015). Resource dependence and effects of funding diversification strategies among NGOs in Cambodia. *VOLUNTAS: International Journal of Voluntary and Nonprofit Organizations, 26*(4), 1412–1437.

Kwong, C., Tasavori, M., & Cheung, C. W. M. (2017). Bricolage, collaboration and mission drift in social enterprises. *Entrepreneurship and Regional Development, 29*(7–8), 609–638.

Lu, J. H. (2018). Organizational antecedents of nonprofit engagement in policy advocacy: A meta-analytical review. *Nonprofit and Voluntary Sector Quarterly, 47*(4), 177S–203S.

Ma, J., Jing, Y., & Han, J. (2018). Predicting mission alignment and preventing mission drift: How revenue sources matter? *Chinese Public Administration Review, 9*(1), 25–33.

Manji, F., & O'Coill, C. (2002). The missionary position: NGOs and development in Africa. *International Affairs, 78*(3), 567–583.

Mitchell, G. E. (2014). Strategic responses to resource dependence among transnational NGOs registered in the United States. *Voluntas: International Journal of Voluntary and Nonprofit Organizations, 25*(1), 67–91.

Mulley, C. (2009). *The woman who saved the children: A biography of Eglantyne Jebb: Founder of save the children*. Simon and Schuster.

Ometto, M. P., Gegenhuber, T., Winter, J., & Greenwood, R. (2019). From balancing missions to mission drift: The role of the institutional context, spaces, and compartmentalization in the scaling of social enterprises. *Business & Society, 58*(5), 1003–1046.

Pache, A. C., & Santos, F. (2010). When worlds collide: The internal dynamics of organizational responses to conflicting institutional demands. *Academy of Management Review, 35*(3), 455–476.

Parboteeah, K. P., Seriki, H. T., & Hoegl, M. (2014). Ethnic diversity, corruption and ethical climates in sub-Saharan Africa: Recognizing the significance of human resource management. *The International Journal of Human Resource Management, 25*(7), 979–1001.

Pawson, R., & Tilley, N. (1997). *Realistic evaluation*. SAGE Publications.

Pawson, R., Greenhalgh, T., Harvey, G., & Walshe, K. (2005). Realist review: A new method of systematic review designed for complex policy interventions. *Journal of Health Services Research & Policy, 10*(1_suppl), 21–34.

Peachey, J. W., Cohen, A., Shin, N., & Fusaro, B. (2018). Challenges and strategies of building and sustaining inter-organizational partnerships in sport for development and peace. *Sport Management Review, 21*(2), 160–175.

Pfeffer, J., & Salancik, G. R. (1978). *The external control of organizations: A resource dependence approach*. Harper and Row Publishers.

Raisiene, A. G., & Urmanaviciene, A. (2017). Mission drift in a hybrid organization: How can social business combine its dual goals? *Ekonomski Vjesnik, 30*(2), 301–310.

Ramus, T., & Vaccaro, A. (2017). Stakeholders matter: How social enterprises address mission drift. *Journal of Business Ethics, 143*(2), 307–322.

Schatteman, A. M., & Bingle, B. (2017). Government funding of arts organizations: Impact and implications. *Journal of Arts Management Law and Society, 47*(1), 34–46.

Shumate, M., Fu, J. S., & Cooper, K. R. (2018). Does cross-sector collaboration lead to higher nonprofit capacity? *Journal of Business Ethics, 150*(2), 385–399.

Sullivan, L. S., & Niker, F. (2018). Relational autonomy, paternalism and maternalism. *Ethical Theory and Moral Practice, 21*(3), 649–667.

Tacon, R., Walters, G., & Cornforth, C. (2017). Accountability in nonprofit governance: A process-based study. *Nonprofit and Voluntary Sector Quarterly, 46*(4), 685–704.

Thaler, R. H., & Sunstein, C. R. (2008). *Nudge: Improving decisions about health, wealth, and happiness*. Yale University Press.

UNHCR and Save the Children UK. (2002). *Sexual violence and exploitation: The experience of refugee children in Guinea, Liberia and Sierra Leone*. UNHCR and Save the Children UK Geneva. Retrieved December 8, 2020, from https://www.parliament.uk/globalassets/documents/commons-committees/international-development/2002-Report-of-sexual-exploitation-and-abuse-Save-the-Children.pdf

Westhorp, G. (2018). Understanding mechanisms in realist evaluation and research. In N. Emmel, J. Greenhalgh, A. Manzano, M. Monaghan, & S. Dalkin (Eds.), *Doing realist research* (pp. 41–57). SAGE.

Williams, M. (2018). Making up mechanisms in realist research. In N. Emmel, J. Greenhalgh, A. Manzano, M. Monaghan, & S. Dalkin (Eds.), *Doing realist research* (pp. 25–40). SAGE.

Wright, K., Scott, M., & Bunce, M. (2019). Foundation-funded journalism, philanthrocapitalism and tainted donors. *Journalism Studies, 20*(5), 675–695.

7

Work-as-Imagined Versus Work-as-Done: The Disconnect Between Policy Expectations and Staff Experiences in Hospital Redevelopment

Chiara Pomare, Kate Churruca, Janet C. Long, Louise A. Ellis, and Jeffrey Braithwaite

Background

Hospital Redevelopment

Hospital redevelopment is a large-scale change to the physical infrastructure and organisational processes of a hospital. It is a recurring and inevitable organisational change in the complex and adaptive world of health care, which intends to improve hospital functioning and modernise the delivery of safe and high-quality care. Redeveloping hospitals—revitalising, improving, renovating, or building new hospital buildings—is a

C. Pomare (✉) • K. Churruca • J. C. Long • L. A. Ellis • J. Braithwaite
Centre for Healthcare Resilience and Implementation Science, Australian Institute of Health Innovation, Macquarie University, Sydney, NSW, Australia
e-mail: chiara.pomare@mq.edu.au; kate.churruca@mq.edu.au; janet.long@mq.edu.au; louise.ellis@mq.edu.au; jeffrey.braithwaite@mq.edu.au

R. Kislov et al. (eds.), *Managing Healthcare Organisations in Challenging Policy Contexts*, Organizational Behaviour in Healthcare,
https://doi.org/10.1007/978-3-030-81093-1_7

necessary component of health systems improvement to address the many challenges facing contemporary health care systems. We need to constantly change and modernise hospital infrastructure to address: the rising demands of ageing populations and overall population growth, changing trends and technological advances in medicine, and inadequate infrastructure that may compromise staff safety or infection control for patients (World Health Organization, 2014; Morris, 2016; Braithwaite et al., 2018).

In Australia, which has a largely publicly funded hospital system, there is continuous investment in world-class hospitals and health services (NSW Government, 2018). For example, in 2015–16, AUD$10 billion was spent on capital expenditure (Australian Institute of Health and Welfare, 2018), with commitments made for this level of funding to continue into the future (Australian Government, 2019). Similar trends have been witnessed in other high-income countries such as the United States (Ulrich et al., 2004) and across Europe (Rechel et al., 2009).

Funding Capital Infrastructure in Australian Hospitals

The complexity of health care is reflected in its funding arrangements, with different entities responsible for funding different levels and components of the health system. In Australia, funding of health care is shared across federal, state, and territory governments, and managed by state and territory governments (Australian Institute of Health and Welfare, 2016). Administration of public hospitals is typically decentralised to local health districts (LHDs)—geographic arrangements similar to acute NHS Trusts. LHDs are responsible for the coordination, management, planning, and delivery of capital investments up to AUD$10M. When a health sector capital investment exceeds AUD$10M, state health departments take the lead. In the case of a health facility investment such as a hospital redevelopment, a state government agency of the Ministry of Health is responsible for the planning, design, procurement, and construction of the facility. This shared funding model means that different Australian state and territory governments have different approaches to funding health expenditure, and specific to this chapter—capital infrastructure.

For illustration purposes, we turn to the state with the highest population, New South Wales (NSW). In NSW, the building of a new hospital is outlined in policy as a three-step process: (1) planning, (2) design, and (3) delivery (NSW Government, 2017). The policy description is overtly linear, with the completion of one phase instigating the next. Within each phase it is expected that there is consultation with local government, LHD, hospital, and other key stakeholders. The process begins when the hospital is allocated funding. Following this, the relevant LHD, in consultation with the state government, creates a clinical services plan outlining contemporary and future models of care to align with the needs of the community. Next, master planning occurs in consultation with local government and government planning agencies, clinicians and other staff of the hospital, and local members of the community. Different stakeholders have the opportunity to contribute to the clinical and site planning from the commencement of this first phase. The next stage is the development of the functional brief that looks beyond the physical building and begins to consider what services will be provided. During this time, the state government agency works with the LHD and the hospital to create a business case that must be submitted to the government to demonstrate value for money. Following approval of this case, the design phase commences, including schematic designs specific to rooms and services. Then, a detailed design is produced, considering the placement of equipment, furniture, and fittings. Last is the delivery phase: procurement and construction (NSW Government, 2017).

A Challenging Policy Context: "Work-as-Imagined" Versus "Work-as-Done"

A source of potential tension in planning and effectively undertaking hospital redevelopment is that there are many entities (e.g., government personnel, project managers, hospital staff, consumers) involved in the planning, design, and delivery of new hospital infrastructure. According to the literature, there may be some disconnect between what policy declares (e.g., that these entities work together) and the day-to-day functions of a health organisation. This is otherwise known as "work-as-imagined" (WAI) versus "work-as-done" (WAD) (Braithwaite et al., 2016); the tension between what the policy recommends and what is possible or feasible for people to implement in the complex reality of health care systems.

Applying this lens can aid in the identification and then rectification of disconnect between policy and practice. For example, a scoping review of nurses' workarounds in acute care found that deviations from policy and procedure are common (Debono et al., 2013). One example of this is that while policy mandates that nursing staff administer medication at the bedside by wheeling the computer into a patient's room and scanning a patient's wristband, a lack of wireless connectivity may make this infeasible. Nurses instead use other methods to verify the patients' identity, such as bed numbers or writing down information on a piece of paper (Debono et al., 2018). Another example includes clinicians bypassing workflow blocks of barcode medication administration systems to save time (Patterson et al., 2006; Koppel et al., 2008). Through identification of these differences between what staff do in their day-to-day work (WAD) and what they are expected to do based on policy and procedure (WAI), managers can work with staff to make necessary changes.

While researchers have reported multiple instances of the disjuncture between WAI and WAD in health care (Braithwaite et al., 2016; Ellis et al., 2019), there is a gap in the literature in examining the extent that this distinction applies to policy and procedures surrounding hospital redevelopment. It is important that we explore the experiences and perspectives of staff during a hospital redevelopment project to understand where their experiences are at odds with what is envisaged in policy. Thus, this chapter uses WAI/WAD as an interpretive lens to explore the concerns that may arise during an Australian hospital redevelopment and potential areas of misalignment between what is stated in policy and what hospital staff experience.

The Case Study

The hospital site where this study was conducted was a large metropolitan, public hospital in Australia, undergoing a multimillion-dollar redevelopment project. At the time of data collection, the hospital was preparing to open a new acute services building, which would include the relocation of several wards to this new building (e.g., emergency department, maternity services, theatres, intensive care unit). In addition to these physical changes, there were also expected operational and behavioural changes such as an increase in resources (e.g., more equipment and staffing for the new building) and the adoption of new ways of working.

We used an exploratory sequential mixed methods case design consisting of semi-structured interviews, key informant discussions, document analysis (e.g., hospital and government documents), and survey responses about experiences of the hospital redevelopment. Semi-structured interviews were conducted with 46 clinical and non-clinical staff working at the hospital. The hospital staff were purposively recruited by department heads and snowballing techniques were used whereby participants were asked to nominate other staff. Interviews were conducted in ward/department interview rooms or private offices at the hospital. Interviews were conducted face-to-face or over the phone and informed consent was provided by all participants prior to participation. During the interview, participants were asked about their concerns, experiences, and expectations regarding the hospital redevelopment.

All interviews were audio-recorded and transcribed verbatim by the first author. Participants were deidentified in the storing of data and throughout the analysis. Pseudonyms were created whereby participants were coded according to their profession (AD: Administrative staff; PRMG: Project management team staff; DR: Medical staff; GS: General services staff; MW: Midwifery staff; N: Nursing staff; OTH: Other profession). Ethics approval was granted by the relevant ethics committee in Australia (no: 18/233). Interviews ranged from 7 to 33 minutes in length ($M = 17$ minutes).

Over half of the participants were nursing and midwifery staff (56.5%), followed by medical (15.2%). Other interview participants worked in general services (e.g., coordinator, supervisor, cleaner, wards person), administration, and allied health. Three project management staff were also interviewed; these individuals were employed by the state government department and considered external to the hospital (i.e., they do not report to hospital executives).

Key informant discussions, document analysis, and surveys were used to support the interview data. Key informant discussions were conducted with three hospital executives whereby detailed notes were taken. Document analysis consisted of hospital and government reports, as well as media outputs, published in relation to the hospital where this case study was conducted. These documents were sourced through a grey literature search using Google. Lastly, an online survey was distributed to all hospital staff with closed-ended statements querying their sense of involvement in the redevelopment change process and open-ended questions for staff to express any concerns or issues related to the development. A total of 153 staff members participated in the survey.

Semi-structured interviews were analysed using six phases of thematic analysis: familiarise, generate initial codes, develop themes, review potential themes, define and name themes, produce the report (Braun & Clarke, 2006). Data were read multiple times by the first author, then inductively coded into themes to represent patterns in the semantic features of the data. Frequent discussions concerning the categorisation of codes and themes were conducted with the broader research team. Once themes were developed from the interview data, key informant discussions, open-ended survey responses, and documents were examined to contextualise discussions of policy. The first author scanned the notes from key informant discussions, the open-ended survey responses, and relevant documents in direct context of the interview data. This was used as a checking process to evaluate if certain experiences identified in the interview data were supported by other sources, and whether this clashed with what was written in policy or other documents. Close-ended survey responses were analysed using IBM SPSS v22 to describe the degree of perceived involvement and feeling informed throughout the hospital redevelopment.

Results

The majority of staff (n = 119, 79.4%) who participated in our survey reported that they had not been involved in decision-making about the new hospital building. Over one third (n = 54, 36.0%) indicated that they were "very" or "somewhat" uninformed about the hospital redevelopment project. Findings revealed that staff reported feeling both uninformed and not involved in the hospital redevelopment process despite being a clinician (n = 90, 70.3%) or non-clinician (n = 38, 29.7%), and that being involved in design decisions did not necessarily mean staff felt informed about the redevelopment. Thematic analysis of interview data, supported by key informant discussions, open-ended survey responses, and document analysis, led to the development of three themes that encompassed the concerns frequently expressed by staff regarding the hospital redevelopment: lack of consultation, uncertainty, and constant change.

Lack of Consultation

A notable point of tension was that staff indicated they had not been consulted throughout the design process of the hospital redevelopment, despite policy setting a clear expectation for consultation between designers and hospital staff throughout the stages of design, planning, and delivery. This perceived lack of consultation contributed to feelings and experiences associated with burnout and fatigue:

> *I think staff are very beaten and worn out and change fatigued and feel like they're not listened to and that—and not from me but from above us.* (NMG1)

> *Burnout is a real problem, and that staff feel that they're not really listened to or heard.* (DR2)

The frustration staff were experiencing was directed towards the state government department responsible for the design of the new building. For instance, in key informant discussions, hospital executives indicated that department heads or staff on wards were not consulted to gather insights on, for example, the appropriate placement of resources. While some design decisions were evidence-based, key informants highlighted that design cannot be strictly led by evidence, it needs also to consider the insights of the people on the frontlines working in the context that is undergoing change.

In contrast to this, members of the project management team (i.e., those who work for the relevant state department responsible for the capital investment) indicated that hospital staff were invited to attend meetings about the design of the new building to share their insights and opinion. According to these interview participants, it was up to the staff to be engaged, and many chose not to be. Hospital executives and frontline clinicians argued that the meetings had not been scheduled to accommodate clinicians, who often work in under-staffed wards and needed to prioritise patient care:

> *We don't even have time to look at these things! We are so much into the ward, busy, doing overtime. Who gets time? We don't even go out for lunch.* (N3)

Uncertainty

The new building required a larger number of staff to provide safe care (due to more beds and larger areas to clean and service). Hospital staff were uncertain about securing the operational funding for the new staff required to work safely in the new building. While funding for the infrastructure was confirmed and the construction of the new facility was well underway, participants expressed that little was known regarding how much additional salary expenditure would be available. This concern was shared by various clinical and non-clinical staff and was directed externally towards government funding entities:

> *I don't know if we're going to get more staff, and that's really the main issue.* (N1)

> *The issues stem from the fact that you never know how many beds we are able to open based on the funding from the government, and that is what is still up in the air.* (DR1)

Uncertainty as a key concern maintained throughout the hospital redevelopment was corroborated by hospital executives during key informant discussions who, despite their higher level of responsibility within the hospital, also detailed that they were uncertain about funding for staff up until weeks before the planned move. This uncertainty was a substantial source of stress for hospital staff, as it hindered planning for the transition process. According to key informants, there was a rush from government to build the new hospital infrastructure, with little concern for how the new building would be staffed. Consistently, the project management team also acknowledged that hospital staff were concerned about government funding and that this was due to the hierarchy and bureaucracy tied up in government funding:

> *The biggest problem is staffing, and people are nervous and it's almost because they haven't gotten an answer yet. And it has to go through all the levels of government and all that stuff in public health.* (PRMG1)

Constant Change

Interview participants also expressed concern about the iterative nature of change initiatives at the hospital. Some staff discussed that their workplace was indeed an environment of churn with a never-ending cycle of change being implemented: "It's sort of from one thing to the next that ... Again, what's changing now? What do I have to do now? What don't I have to do now? It's just very hard to keep on top of it all" (MG2). Many changes were experienced concurrently; that is, not only was the physical environment changing in the redevelopment project, but new procedures and policy were also being implemented (i.e., organisational changes) that required staff to adapt to new ways of working.

While many staff recognised change as an integral part of health care, others reported being tired of working in an environment of constant physical and organisational change that was, at times, a disruption to their work:

> *If I hear another pneumatic drill I think I will go crazy. It's the construction and the disruption of the site that you work in for such an extended period of time. I'm wishing all the scaffolding and the cranes and all the siding and all the, everything to be gone, I'm over it. I have construction fatigue.* (N4)

Key informants highlighted that implementers of change (policy makers and internal staff) need to understand the limits of those at the frontlines on whom they are attempting to push change. It was likely, everyone agreed, that this situation would continue until the redeveloped building was handed over and occupied.

Discussion

Misalignment Between Hospital Redevelopment Policy and Staff Experiences

The purpose of this study was to explore the concerns of hospital staff during a hospital redevelopment and examine the potential for misalignment between the policy for redevelopment (WAI) and staff experiences (WAD). In general, a disjuncture was identified between policy and the experiences of hospital staff. Three specific concerns were identified: lack of consultation, uncertainty, and constant change.

The majority of staff interviewed felt that despite the building infrastructure being ready, whether the move would take place at the planned date was still not clear because of the continuing uncertainty around securing funding to staff the new building. In addition to uncertainty, staff were frustrated as they felt they were not appropriately consulted regarding the design of the new building. This contradicted the experiences reported by the project management team, who claimed that staff were invited to meetings to be involved in design decisions. One reason for this incongruence may be a lack of understanding about clinical work (e.g., a nurse on the floor cannot leave patients unattended to participate in a meeting). Therefore, the experiences of staff at the hospital under investigation seem to contradict how this process should be conducted according to the policy.

This supports the notion of disjuncture between policy, designed by those at the "blunt end" (WAI), and the delivery of care, conducted by those at the "sharp end" (WAD) (Braithwaite et al., 2016) (Fig. 7.1). Our findings show that there is disconnect between the policy ("blunt end"), which states that all staff should be involved by way of consultation, and what staff actually experience in practice (i.e., at the "sharp end"). This is not an unusual experience in health care where there is often a disconnect between what is postulated in policy and what is enacted by health care

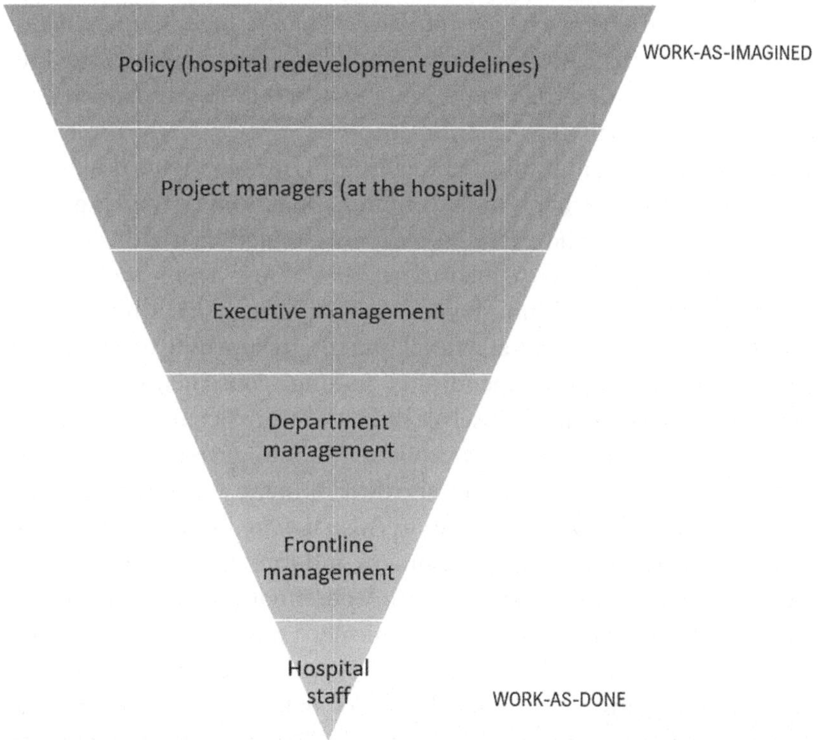

Fig. 7.1 Work-as-imagined versus work-as done: an Australian hospital redevelopment. (Source: Adapted from Hollnagel (2015))

workers in their day-to-day work (Leggat et al., 2011; Kislov et al., 2019; Chinitz & Rodwin, 2014). While it is clear that policy makers see the importance of clinician involvement—as is articulated in policy documentation—there is a potential issue of ownership and adoption by the different management entities, to action what the policy states (i.e., organise the consultation with staff).

Another concern expressed by hospital staff was regarding the constancy of change in the hospital where they work. The redevelopment or building of hospital infrastructure is described in government documents as a linear process comprised of three phases: planning, design, and delivery (NSW Government, 2017). However, hospital staff reported experiencing the hospital redevelopment process as dynamic and complex, with multiple changes occurring at once, with little time between the implementation of the next change initiative. Change here is stochastic and iterative rather than measured and predictable. For example, the initial plan of which wards would move into the new building and at what time was constantly changing, and this information was rarely perceived as being adequately communicated to all staff. This highlights the dynamic nature of health care that is more complex and less linear than is generally conceptualised in policy and procedures. Change in health care rarely progress through linear sequential stages because there are too many interdependencies and unintended consequences (Braithwaite et al., 2017). In the case of hospital redevelopment, the opening of a new building is dependent upon expenditure, staffing, construction, and many other factors that are in themselves difficult to predict and influenced by other issues (e.g., election cycles, economic factors, government decisions).

A major concern in this hospital redevelopment was the complexity of funding, that is, hospital resources in Australia are funded from different sources by separate levels of government and capital expenditure is managed separately to salary expenditure. A potential source of this problem is that funding for infrastructure is typically a one-off payment, set aside for that specific purpose, whereas funding of hospital staff is a sustained commitment going forward. Ideally, salary expenditure should increase if the hospital infrastructure expands because there is more space to be covered (e.g., cleaners will have greater square metreage of floor to cover; consequently, the number of domestic staff will need to increase). Thus, more complex than actually building the new hospital infrastructure is sustaining the salary expenditure to staff it for many years to come. Interestingly, this disconnect between capital and salary expenditure referred to by participants of this study is not referred to in policy documents, suggesting little consideration for the long-term effects of redevelopment for those at the "sharp end".

Recommendations for Managing Hospital Redevelopment Projects

During policy-led change there may be a breakdown between what policy declares for hospital redevelopment and the experiences of staff. In the case examined here, rather than a smooth linear transition of planning, design, and delivery, staff experienced uncertainty, stress, and indications of burnout and frustration regarding their lack of involvement in the change process.

In order to make improvements, we need to find ways to realign policy around hospital redevelopment with hospital staff experiences of their work during this change process (Braithwaite, 2018). In other words, to bridge the gap between WAI and WAD. A middle ground needs to be sought between what the policy states and what is feasible in the time-restricted, pressurised environment of acute care. A key finding of this study is that staff need to be more involved in the design of new hospitals and informed throughout the process of planning, design and delivery. Designated time needs to be allocated during work hours for staff consultation in the building design. This should ideally be at a time where staff can be covered so that patient care is not disrupted; such contingencies are commonly implemented when staff are required to attend mandatory training.

These recommendations draw directly from the present case, where project managers attempted to run meetings and involve staff in the stages of hospital design; however, the reality was that staff did not have the time to attend despite their desire to be involved. A strategy like this might better foster staff engagement in the redevelopment and the array of other challenges going along with this change. However, with this level of complexity it is difficult to ensure that all the different stakeholders and entities will feel involved, informed, and be satisfied. Indeed, staff may not be able to be informed about all aspects of the change because in reality many aspects of health care are uncertain and cannot be known (Pomare et al., 2019), but it is important that managers and key stakeholders acknowledge this uncertainty and inform staff even when there are no updates so that everyone feels in the loop.

Strengths and Limitations

A key strength of this study was that both clinical and non-clinical staff were invited to participate in interviews and the online survey, resulting in the inclusion of a broad range of hospital staff experiences. A weakness of the study was that it did not explicitly seek to test the WAI/WAD theory, but uses the theory as a lens in the interpretation of the findings. The findings may be limited to the one Australian hospital where the case study was conducted, as experiences of staff may be reflective of the culture and context of the specific hospital redevelopment under investigation. However, the grey literature search of government reports, policy, and media outputs suggests that the findings are transferable to the Australian context of hospital redevelopment and, most likely, beyond (e.g., Carpenter & Hoppszallern, 2006).

Conclusions

This case shows how pivotal it is to reconcile the two worlds of WAI and WAD—in this case, those of the policy maker and project manager doing the imagining and the presumption of how the redevelopment should work, and the gritty, realistic world of the staff trying to make things work on the ground. In this study we argue that there is a misalignment between what policy dictates and how hospital redevelopment is actually enacted. A major concern identified in this study was that staff felt they were not consulted throughout the redevelopment process and were thus uninvolved, uninformed, and uncertain preceding the opening of the new hospital building. Further, the policies and decision-making related to infrastructure and staffing are fragmented and not considered together despite their dependencies, which may heighten uncertainties experienced by staff during large hospital redevelopment projects. This may have negative ramifications as uncertainty, being a substantial source of stress for staff, coupled with negative experiences of change, could disrupt the delivery of safe of high-quality care. Future hospital redevelopment projects should ensure infrastructure and staffing are considered concurrently, uncertainties are acknowledged, staff are more appropriately consulted throughout the process of redevelopment, and staff are informed that the redevelopment may have unexpected turns and not be a strictly linear process.

References

Australian Government. (2019). Supporting our hospitals—Additional infrastructure and services. In Department of Health (Ed.), *Budget 2019–20*.

Australian Institute of Health and Welfare. (2016). *Australia's health 2016*. Canberra: AIHW.

Australian Institute of Health and Welfare. (2018). How much does Australia spend on health care? In A. s. h. 2018 (Ed.). Canberra: AIHW.

Braithwaite, J. (2018). Changing how we think about healthcare improvement. *British Medical Journal, 361*, k2014. https://doi.org/10.1136/bmj.k2014

Braithwaite, J., Churruca, K., Ellis, L. A., Long, J. C., Clay-Williams, R., Damen, N., et al. (2017). *Complexity science in healthcare-aspirations, approaches, applications and accomplishments: A white paper*. Macquarie University.

Braithwaite, J., Mannion, R., Matsuyama, Y., Shekelle, P. G., Whittaker, S., & Al-Adawi, S. (2018). *Healthcare systems: Future predictions for global care*. CRC Press.

Braithwaite, J., Wears, R. L., & Hollnagel, E. (2016). *Resilient health care, volume 3: Reconciling work-as-imagined and work-as-done*. CRC Press.

Braun, V., & Clarke, V. (2006). Using thematic analysis in psychology. *Qualitative Research in Psychology, 3*(2), 77–101.

Carpenter, D., & Hoppszallern, S. (2006). 2006 hospital building report. The boom goes on. *Hospitals & Health Networks, 80*(3), 48–50, 52–44, 42.

Chinitz, D. P., & Rodwin, V. G. (2014). On Health Policy and Management (HPAM): Mind the theory-policy-practice gap. *International Journal of Health Policy and Management, 3*(7), 361.

Debono, D., Clay-Williams, R., Taylor, N., Greenfield, D., Black, D., & Braithwaite, J. (2018). Using workarounds to examine characteristics of resilience in action. In *Delivering resilient health care* (pp. 44–55). Routledge.

Debono, D., Greenfield, D., Travaglia, J. F., Long, J. C., Black, D., Johnson, J., et al. (2013). Nurses' workarounds in acute healthcare settings: A scoping review. *BMC Health Services Research, 13*(1), 175.

Ellis, L. A., Churruca, K., Clay-Williams, R., Pomare, C., Austin, E. E., Long, J. C., et al. (2019). Patterns of resilience: A scoping review and bibliometric analysis of resilient health care. *Safety Science, 118*, 241–257.

Hollnagel, E. (2015). Why is work-as-imagined different from work-as-done. In *Resilience in everyday clinical work*. Ashgate.

Kislov, R., Wilson, P., Cummings, G., Ehrenberg, A., Gifford, W., Kelly, J., et al. (2019). From research evidence to "evidence by proxy"? Organizational enactment of evidence-based health care in four high-income countries. *Public Administration Review, 79*(5), 684–698. https://doi.org/10.1111/puar.13056

Koppel, R., Wetterneck, T., Telles, J. L., & Karsh, B.-T. (2008). Workarounds to barcode medication administration systems: Their occurrences, causes, and threats to patient safety. *Journal of the American Medical Informatics Association, 15*(4), 408–423. https://doi.org/10.1197/jamia.M2616

Leggat, S. G., Bartram, T., & Stanton, P. (2011). High performance work systems: The gap between policy and practice in health care reform. *Journal of Health Organization and Management, 25*(3), 281–297. https://doi.org/10.1108/14777261111143536

Morris, M. (2016). Global health care outlook: Battling costs while improving care. London: Deloitte.

NSW Government. (2017). Health infrastructure: How to build a hospital.

NSW Government. (2018). Health infrastructure. https://www.hinfra.health.nsw.gov.au/our-projects/project-search

Patterson, E. S., Rogers, M. L., Chapman, R. J., & Render, M. L. (2006). Compliance with intended use of bar code medication administration in acute and long-term care: An observational study. *Human Factors, 48*(1), 15–22.

Pomare, C., Churruca, K., Ellis, L. A., Long, J. C., & Braithwaite, J. (2019). A revised model of uncertainty in complex healthcare settings: A scoping review. *Journal of Evaluation in Clinical Practice, 25*(2), 176–182. https://doi.org/10.1093/intqhc/mzy242

Rechel, B., Wright, S., & Edwards, N. (2009). *Investing in hospitals of the future* (Vol. 16). WHO Regional Office Europe.

Ulrich, R., Zimring, C., Quan, X., Josephh, A., & Choudhary, R. (2004). The role of the physical environment in the hospital of the 21st century: A once-in-a-lifetime opportunity. Concord, CA: The Center for Health Design.

World Health Organization. (2014). Everybody's business: Strengthening health systems to improve health outcomes: WHO's framework for action. Geneva: WHO; 2007.

8

Changing Organisational Practices through the Integration of Health and Social Care: Implications for Boundary Work and Identity Tactics

Abigail Tazzyman, Claire Mitchell, and Damian Hodgson

Introduction

Healthcare faces well-documented pressures due to ageing populations, a shrinking fiscal base, new technologies, and the rising cost of treatment (Exworthy, 2015; Dixon-Woods et al., 2011). In response to these pressures, many countries have explored new 'integrated' models for the provision of health and care. In England, integration has long been the direction of travel for health and care policy, in the expectation that

A. Tazzyman (✉)
Sheffield Methods Institute, University of Sheffield, Sheffield, UK
e-mail: a.tazzyman@sheffield.ac.uk

C. Mitchell
Faculty of Biology, Medicine and Health,
The University of Manchester, Manchester, UK
e-mail: claire.mitchell@manchester.ac.uk

R. Kislov et al. (eds.), *Managing Healthcare Organisations in Challenging Policy Contexts*, Organizational Behaviour in Healthcare,
https://doi.org/10.1007/978-3-030-81093-1_8

integrated models will break down barriers between the health and social care systems, delivering joined-up and personalised services designed around population needs which can be made financially sustainable into the long term.

However, efforts to integrate health and social care present deep challenges to professional and organisational practices in both health and care. Well-documented enduring and hierarchical boundaries of professional expertise and practices between health and social care present a risk of unwillingness to integrate, while separate budgets for each sector, different statutory responsibilities, and delivery distribution by differing geographical territories limit integration possibilities. In this chapter we seek to answer the question *how can work be fully integrated when each sector is funded to do different work, with its workforces being placed on different contracts with different legal obligations, and required to deliver services for geographical areas which do not match up?*

Indeed, it might be argued that integration could succeed only by disrupting or transforming the kinds of professional institutions upon which both health and care are founded. Integrated care therefore presents an ideal opportunity to examine organisational attempts to transcend professional boundaries, jurisdictions, and career paths for professions in search of economies and innovation, and the enduring barriers posed by professional identity. This chapter adds to understandings of boundary work by considering boundary work in terms of interactions and not as a simple 'mix' of different modes. In taking this approach we are able to demonstrate how forms of competitive boundary work can be mirrored across professionals to create solidarity and enable collaboration and integration achieved through the reiteration of boundaries rather than the breaking down of them.

In the following sections, we examine policy driving the integration of health and care and discuss the way in which boundary work has been conceptualised and studied, with particular focus on the fields of health and care.

D. Hodgson
Sheffield University Management School, Sheffield, UK
e-mail: d.hodgson@sheffield.ac.uk

The Drive to Integrate Health and Care

An 'integrated' approach to health and social care has been advocated as a model which can harness new forms of collaboration and connectivity to better respond to the needs of contemporary societies by politicians and some professionals. Integration, it is asserted at a policy level, is a means to enhance patient-centred care, reduce admissions to hospital care, facilitate faster and effective discharge from hospital, and in doing so, reduce costs while improving quality (Briggs et al., 2020). 'Integration' remains a health and care policy cornerstone driven in England through various initiatives including the Integrated Care Pioneers Programme, the Better Care Fund, Integrated Care Systems (ICSs), and, most recently, the formation of Sustainability and Transformation Partnerships (STPs) across England (Briggs et al., 2020). Strategic policy initiatives such as the NHS Five Year Forward View (NHS England, 2014) have brought new emphasis to breaking down barriers between 'family doctors and hospitals, between physical and mental health, between health and social care' in England (Shortell et al., 2015). This represents a significant move in the English context where health and social care services have historically existed in separate systems since the divide created by the 1948 creation of the NHS. Health and care have different budgets and administration, are accessed in different ways, and are managed separately with different resources, governance structures, statutory responsibilities, and service delivery boundaries. In addition, the professions that make up the health and social care work forces have been educated and socialised in very different ways, impacting on work conduct, ideology, and necessarily informing relationships between professions (Finn et al., 2010; Exworthy, 2015).

This policy direction has endured despite claims that the evidence to back up many of these assertions is often tenuous (Cameron et al., 2014; Cameron, 2016; Humphries, 2015; Lewis et al., 2013). Indeed, even the definition of integration in this context is subject to extended debate. There are multiple ways to classify models of integrated care, looking at breadth, type, process and focus of integration, and definitions alternate between outcome-based (patient/service user perspective and person-centred coordinated care) or process-based (health system adaptations to deliver complex care) understandings (Stokes et al., 2016). It has also been observed that the integration of care can be understood to take place at different levels, such as team, service, profession, or organisation (Robertson, 2011). Other researchers distinguish approaches to integration in terms of their focus and form, differentiating between structural, functional, normative, interpersonal, and process integration (Singer et al., 2018).

Integration is thus multifaceted but by definition it implies changes to the boundaries of work in health and social care. It may therefore be argued that the resilience of professional boundaries and identities presents the most substantial obstacle to such integration initiatives (Martin et al., 2009). Understanding integration demands a close interrogation of professional boundaries and the kinds of boundary and identity work which takes place when organisational change disrupts such boundaries.

Professions and Boundary Work

The definition of a profession predominantly refers to established occupations that are recognised as experts within a given jurisdiction, often requiring a specific qualification (Abbott, 1988; Freidson, 2001). Through institutionalisation, such professionals are permitted to regulate themselves and their field of practice, generating professional autonomy alongside professional responsibility and discipline (Muzio et al., 2008; Muzio & Kirkpatrick, 2011; Adams, 2015). Anteby et al. (2016) suggest that occupations and professions can be understood through lenses of 'becoming', 'doing', and 'relating'—that is by looking at 'how occupational members learn to be part of the collective, what activities they engage in, and how they relate to others outside their group' (188). Key to understanding professionalism, then, is a consideration of jurisdiction, in terms of the boundaries of professional identity and practice, the relationship of the profession to those outside of it, and thus the boundary work which professionals engage in on a day-to-day basis.

Boundaries serve to distinguish categories and regulate the interactions between them (Lamont & Molnár, 2002; Zietsma & Lawrence, 2010;

Bucher et al., 2016), and professional boundaries distinguish professions from each other, typically on the basis of the jurisdiction of expert knowledge and practice. Boundaries are important for identity formation but also because they define a profession's access to material and non-material resources such as power, status, and remuneration. Significantly, professional boundaries are not static but continuously evolving and require ongoing identity and boundary work in order for their parameters to be maintained, changed, and defended (Abbott, 1988; Bucher et al., 2016; Lam, 2019).

Boundary work, then, encompasses the strategies used by individuals and collectives to 'influence the social, symbolic, material or temporal boundaries, demarcations and distinctions affecting groups, occupations and organizations' (Langley et al., 2019: 3). Different forms of boundary work have been identified and theorised in the literature on this topic (Gieryn, 1996; Bucher et al., 2016; Langley et al., 2019). These categorisations have tended to focus on the purpose of boundary. Gieryn (1996), for example, identifies three forms of boundary work: *expulsion* (attempts to exclude others), *expansion* (trying to control a new area), and *protection* of a given autonomy (defensive moves to protect existing boundaries).

Similarly, Langley et al. (2019) in a review of boundary work literature identify three main forms of boundary work, each with three subcategories: *competitive* (how people defend, contest, and create boundaries to distinguish themselves from others to achieve some kind of advantage); *collaborative* (inter-occupational or inter-organisational practices of negotiation and accommodation 'where groups cannot achieve collective goals alone'); and *configurational* (where 'managers, institutional entrepreneurs, or leaders work to reshape the boundary landscape of others to orient emerging patterns of competition and collaboration, often combining elements of both') (Langley et al., 2019). Policy initiatives to integrate health and social care may be seen to represent instances of configurational boundary work, with boundary changes being reshaped from above to meet policy demands through changes to existing jurisdictional boundaries for those working in each sector, and thus imply both competitive and collaborative boundary work by professionals.

Understanding whether collaborative or competitive boundary work takes place requires a consideration of how such negotiations are framed.

Bucher et al. (2016) identify four framing foci used when professions discursively negotiate their boundary claims: framing the issue of interprofessional collaboration, framing of justifications for favoured solutions, framing the profession's own identity, and framing other professions' identities. Importantly, these four foci are employed differently depending on power relations, defined they argue by field position, centrality, and status within the profession—reflecting earlier work which suggests, for example, that higher-status professions are more likely to defend existing boundaries while lower-status professions strive to change them (Abbott, 1988; Battilana, 2011). Allen (2000) found this, for example, when examining nurse managers attempt to accommodate jurisdictional change to medical-nursing and nursing support worker interfaces with doctors in hospital settings. Similarly, Burri (2008), when looking at how radiologists reacted to the introduction of new technology, found attempts to maintain existing jurisdiction and regain professional authority alongside attempts to improve professional status by this group. Thus status and inter-/intra-professional power relations influence the strategies adopted in boundary work and outcomes. Recognising the range of possible boundary work is therefore critical for an understanding of how professions change and evolve in interaction with other professions.

Boundary Work in the Field of Health

The significance of boundary work in healthcare settings has long been acknowledged (Liberati, 2017; Powell & Davies, 2012), healthcare being a sector where professional demarcations are well established, with medical professionals enjoying dominance (Currie et al., 2009), but where numerous professions are constantly working to maintain or extend jurisdictions (Abbott, 1988; Finn, 2008; Bucher et al., 2016; Bach et al., 2012; Hazgui & Gendron, 2015). Focusing on operating theatres, Finn (2008) for example examined the ongoing boundary and relationship work between surgeons, anaesthetics, nurses, and operating department practitioners during team work—noting the significance of professional hierarchies in this setting. Similarly Bucher et al. (2016) explored how the existing boundaries and position of five health professions (Physicians, Registered Nurses and Psychologists together with their junior professions of Registered Practical Nurses and Psychological Associates) in Ontario, Canada, responded to a new government initiative.

Research on professional competition in healthcare has primarily focused on relationships within the medical hierarchy (Liberati et al., 2016) or between the medical profession and management/employers/regulators (Bryce et al., 2018). Such research has shown the significance of professional identity for how those in different health professions behave in organisations and how they conduct themselves in relation to other professions and occupations, shaping the way in which work is carried out (Hall, 2005; Nancarrow & Borthwick, 2005; Currie et al., 2008, 2009; Martin et al., 2009; Finn et al., 2010). Relative professional status impacts on who is able to voice opinions within team work and speak out and the distribution of tasks for example (Satterstrom et al., 2020; Finn & Waring, 2006; Atwal & Caldwell, 2005; Glendinning, 2003). These hierarchical relationships are shown to potentially make team work harder and impact on patient safety and care. Indeed, multidisciplinary work has been found in some cases to reinforce professional boundaries rather than break them down (Finn et al., 2010; Liberati et al., 2016).

Policy initiatives to integrate health and care are not the only efforts to overcome professional boundaries and introduce greater collaboration in healthcare bureaucracies. Other initiatives include the encouragement of non-hierarchical collaboration (typically through networks) (Ferlie et al., 2012) and the creation of hybrid roles (Spyridonidis et al., 2015). Work in these areas have typically focused on individual boundaries in isolation (clinician-manager, for instance, or doctor-nurse) but have rarely compared different organisational responses to the same boundary changes. Advances in our understanding of boundary work (Langley et al., 2019; Singer et al., 2018; Bucher et al., 2016) present the opportunity to explore the intersection of different kinds of boundaries, including jurisdictional boundaries over tasks and knowledge, and the relationship between different professions and occupations as well as multiple group negotiations around boundaries in the context of policy-driven configurational boundary work.

In this chapter we draw on the existing theoretical literature to inform our analysis of the integration of health and social care in an English city. We seek to identify the different kinds of boundary work generated by top-down efforts to integrate health and social care, the implications for professional identities and collaboration, and explore the implications for the viability of such efforts to integrate health and social care.

Methodology

In this case study, the integration of health and social care was attempted via the establishment of a local care partnership which was tasked with ensuring the co-location of two main providers, community health and social care services, to form 12 community 'neighbourhood teams', 4 in each of the 3 localities that the city in question had been divided into (Mitchell et al., 2020). Each of these teams would include social care and nursing professionals as well as a team leader, with additional collaboration with GP and third sector partnerships. Staff however continued to be employed by either the council or their NHS trust, which means a lack of parity in employment conditions. This approach to integration could be understood as process based (Stokes et al., 2016), taking place at the multiple levels—notably at an organisation and service delivery level (Robertson, 2011) and in form structural and interpersonal (Singer et al., 2018).

Face-to-face semi-structured interviews were conducted with 24 practitioners involved in the integration of health and social care across a range of levels. Six interviewees were at a strategic level and eighteen in operational roles, including team leader, managers, frontline health clinicians, and social care staff. Equal numbers of health and social care professionals were interviewed covering all three localities. Interviews are thus classified by sector (health/care) and level (strategic/operational). We used a combination of purposive and snowball sampling for maximum variation and balance. All interviews were carried out in 2018 by a combination of three experienced qualitative researchers. Most interviews were carried out by a single interviewer, with a small number being carried out in pairs. The interviews lasted between 45 minutes and 1 hour 30 minutes, with most being approximately 1 hour long.[1]

[1] This study was approved by the Alliance Manchester Business School Panel (reference: 2017–2979-4620) and by the Health Research Authority (IRAS 238256, REC reference: 18/HRA/1267). Informed consent was given by all participants via written agreement.

Data collection was informed by a rapid scoping review of the literature on the integration of health and social care, as well as policy and planning documents and grey literature related to integration (Munn et al., 2018; Tricco et al., 2016). The search terms 'integrated health and social care', 'multidisciplinary teams', and 'interdisciplinary teams' were used for this scoping review. We focused on studies conducted in the UK and published in English between 2000 and 2018. Additional snowball searching was also conducted with bibliography searches of articles found and recommendations from colleagues with expert knowledge on the topic. In total 116 texts were deemed suitable for inclusion. Further methodological details of this study can be found in the project report (Mitchell et al., 2019).

The interviews focused on the context in which integration was taking place, factors affecting the implementation of integration and the impact of integration on service delivery and care provided. All interviews were recorded, transcribed verbatim, anonymised, organised in NVivo 11, and subjected to thematic analysis. The research team developed an initial coding framework through team discussion, trial, and revision based on our collective interpretation of the data. We used NVivo 11 to enable blind coding and verification of code application to check consistency of analysis. Coding and interpretations were discussed at regular intervals throughout the analysis phase of the study. As well as the established initial codes (e.g. clinical, informational, organisational, financial, and administrative) we added further codes (e.g. boundaries, relationships, identity, and leadership) to the framework inductively as appropriate through an iterative process and then coded across all transcripts (for a previous example see Fereday and Muir-Cochrane, 2006). We focused our analysis on the analytical framework, moving between the data and the literature in order to refine and situate our findings in relation to integration within wider discussions about shifts in professional and organisational identities and boundaries—this is in line with Braun and Clarke (2006).

Our methodological choices meant that we accessed the experiences of people working at strategic and operational levels within the integrated partnership but recognise the views of these 24 participants are in a specific location and context. This study did not capture service user experiences or views, nor did it utilise observational data which could potentially have provided another dimension of understanding such changes in practice; these are a limitation of the current study and would be of interest in future research.

Findings

The integration of health and social care within this case study was found to have resulted in extensive and varied boundary work by those involved across professions, organisations, and geography. Different forms of competitive, collaborative, and configurational boundary work were all present across a multiplicity of interconnected boundaries. In this section the forms and strategies of boundary work undertaken are considered alongside an examination of the multiplicity of boundaries.

Motivations for Boundary Work

The integration of health and social care services was described as a 'top-down' initiative by interviewees. They perceived limited efforts to consult or engage. Although many seemed to agree with the direction of travel (towards greater integration), several described experiencing disempowerment and some frustration as a result of this.

> No one really seems to be asking us how do we think it should work… decisions have been made around how things are going to be and how things will work, and that our voices aren't really going to be listened to … feeling helpless in the process, really, feeling insignificant in the process is obviously very negative and it is frustrating. (Interviewee 13 social care/ operational)

The integration of health and social care services occurred then as a result of a 'configurational' boundary shift (Langley et al., 2019), based on a regional policy initiative.

While the change itself was described as enforced, the practical boundary work needed to make such a significant shift work was described as being left up to those on the front line, with an expectation that those affected would work collaboratively to achieve the aims of integration, with a strong reliance on local 'champions' and local 'adaptation'.

> There will be people who will do something that makes a team feel like a team… I think some of it is around your champion … But then it's also then, being able to replicate something similar, in other parts of the city. So while I've got a natural champion in X in locality 3, it's then trying to find the equivalent of X in locality 3, in locality 5 and locality 4, to make that happen (…) So it's really important that it comes from those who are doing it, really, on the frontline. (Interviewee 1 social care/strategic)

Many described integration as a threat to their professional identity, heightened by the strategically driven nature of reorganisation. There was concern among many neighbourhood team-members that team leads could be from another profession. Framing their opposition, individuals frequently began from a position of being personally against such a move, then highlighted that this was shared not only by their fellow professionals but by the 'other' professionals, and cemented this argument by discussing the difficulty of overcoming professional boundaries in the abstract, as exemplified in the following quote from a health professional:

> There's a very rose-tinted view of how important people feel their professional registration is, and I would be an example of that. Because as a neighbourhood lead, there was no requirement to have a professional qualification. But (...) I have been very clear, as have my social work colleagues, there are a couple of social work colleagues who have got professional registrations, and they feel exactly the same way as I do. There is absolutely no way I would give up my professional qualification and identity, and that's how the people within these integrated teams will feel … I think the vision is, we can sit them all down, and they'll all be really friendly, and they'll go, 'oh yeah, let's do that together'. But, those professional boundaries, will be really, really difficult to overcome. (Interviewee 20 healthcare/operational)

Competitive boundary work here is reinforced by the expectation that 'competing' professions will also fight to defend professional boundaries—ironically, generating a kind of perceived solidarity between competing professionals, that both health and care professionals would want to maintain professional boundaries.

Despite this, some collaboration did, however, take place. Collaboration was found to occur most frequently and successfully when existing professional boundaries were reconfirmed and a process of arbitrage was agreed.

> We set the stall out that these are the roles, and this is what I can do, and this is outside of my scope of practice … So triage is predominantly undertaken by a health or a social care colleague and once those staff were familiar with some of the health components and the health staff were familiar with the care components, there's now only one person, as opposed to two. (Interviewee 19 social care/operational)

Here, then, it was the respect of established boundaries that enabled collaborative boundary work.

Framing of Boundary Work

Multiple existing jurisdictional boundaries were defended, often on the basis of professional identity, specialist knowledge, and the regulatory requirements of a given profession. The assumption by senior managers that professional boundaries would be easily broken down to enable integration and collaboration was seen as unrealistic by many professionals. This drive to break down professional boundaries was framed by some as not only challenging but also dangerous.

There was a concern from operational staff on both sides that changes to boundaries might result in additional work without additional support or resources. Both health and social care staff asserted that their 'side' would be most likely to carry the burden of the extra work. At the same time, it was argued by staff (on both sides) that an expectation for the workforce to work across professional boundaries would leave them and those they care for at risk.

> All this conflict between the social workers in my areas that are coming through, and the medical model and the health professional, there will always be a conflict ... It's like me, a social worker, and a district nurse come and report to me about a dressing and the wound that she's done. I haven't got a clue, I don't know. (Interviewee 22 social care/operational)

Both health and care professionals identified a lack of inter-professional understanding on the part of their counterpart professionals—healthcare professionals believing that 'social care' could not understand healthcare, and social care professionals believing the same of healthcare. For example, the importance of technical knowledge (and regulation) was repeatedly stated as being needed for safe and effective working, and something which was held by those only within a given profession:

> It's a bit ludicrous ... that 'you don't need to be a social worker to manage social workers'. Well, I kind of disagree with that a little bit 'cause you're not going to have a lot of respect if you haven't done the job ...you know if I said, you don't have to be a nurse to manage nurses, how far would that get you? Or a brain surgeon to manage brain surgeons. You'd just be laughed out of the place, wouldn't you? ... what you end up with is the technical knowledge is all based at the bottom and then above it you're asking people to make decisions about things they have absolutely no knowledge about. (Interviewee 18 social care/operational)

The importance of support and supervision from those within one's own profession, at peer and management levels, was asserted to ensure both career progression and appropriate advice on care and conduct.

> I'm quite worried about, you know, the idea of being managed either long-arm, by somebody who's not based where I'm based, either that, or be managed by somebody who's not a social work professional, somebody who's maybe a health professional or something. And there are issues around professional identity, supervision ...the important stuff really. So the informal supervision and the kind of daily chats and checking in and bouncing ideas ... we do have differing priorities and different agendas. We do have very different kind of ideologies. (Interviewee 13 social care/operational)

This perceived lack of understanding on the part of others pertained not just about the specifics of role remit and specialist knowledge but also in regard to legal requirements and philosophical approaches to care.

> You're bringing those professions together, and expecting them to have a mutual appreciation of what's important to each. And actually, their core values are completely different. (Interviewee 20 healthcare/operational)

Such arguments suggested that the values and approaches of health and social care were not just different but at times in conflict.

Multiple Boundaries

It was also clear that multiple boundaries co-existed, and were in fact inter-related, with work on one boundary impacting others. A hierarchy of boundaries was evident, with certain boundaries situated as more important or requiring more defence or establishment than others.

Unsurprisingly the boundary between health and social care featured strongly, reinforced by historical feelings in social care that their sector was under-resourced and neglected.

> Health is kind of like the big brother and we're the kind of the poor relation (…) everything's around Health and the conversations that have taken place … the Health budget is bigger, they've got more of the pie, they've got more of the work, so they are the kind of the main part of it, but that doesn't mean that the Adult Social Care stuff isn't important. (Interviewee 13 social care/operational)

Competitive boundary work between health and care was however not the only line of tension; the boundary between professionals based in the community and those based in the acute hospital was often invoked frequently.

> I think what's played out is that my opinion is that systems, the community health services as less important than acute staff. They're always a bit second-rate, really. And I think there's a great lack of understanding in

> acute-centric circles and hospitals around actually what a difference an investment in community services could make, and that's just a personal view. (Interviewee 6 health/strategic)

Both health and social care workers saw the inequity between hospital and out-of-hospital funding as more problematic for resource access, and most felt that those professionals in hospitals had even less of an understanding of their role, irrespective of profession.

> Over time in area 2 what's happened is the scale is weighted much more at the high end of acute care, mental health and in physical health. So we've got to balance those scales with some transformation money and over time try and put some of the balance back into primary care community services that are very much more joined up with social care so that we get the neighbourhoods to function very effectively from a provision of service perspective. (Interviewee 3 social care/strategic)

Beyond the shared suspicion of hospital services, health and care professionals in the neighbourhood teams were also unified in their shared commitment to professionalism of any kind, particularly given the prospect of supervision by non-professionals, So, for instance, while nurses felt it was important to be supervised by a fellow nurse, and social workers by fellow social workers, both groups agreed that supervision by any kind of professional was preferable to supervision by a non-professional:

> The neighbourhood leads will be a mix, so it could be that it's a voluntary (sector) person sat in this seat, managing one of those services, yeah … It sends a shiver down my spine … And as one organisation, as a nurse, I feel that that's dangerous. (Interviewee 20 healthcare/operational)

Discussion: Mirrored Boundary Work and Inter-Professional Solidarity

The integration of health and social care presents considerable challenge to existing professional practices in both fields, institutionalised as they are around enduring and hierarchical boundaries of professional expertise and practice. Integration represents a significant change to previous ways of working, working remit, and intra-professional collaboration, and exploring the dynamics of boundary work reveals various dimensions of tension, but also solidarity and grounds for collaboration.

The original drive for integration was top-down, driven by decisions at the policy and strategic levels, representing a case of configurational boundary work as described by Langley et al. (2019), involving the coalescing of boundaries. This integration initiative used policy change, resource allocation, and restructuring of organisations at the level of teams, including the appointment of leads for integrated neighbourhood teams, that is, a formal set of change levers acting on those professionals in operational positions. However, the practical boundary work needed to bring together separate domains and deliver new ways of working relied on the willingness of the operational workforce in both health and social care to engage in collaborative, rather than competitive, boundary work.

Given the long history of tension and direct/indirect competition between the health and social care sectors and professions in England, it is unsurprising that the response to this integration initiative was a significant amount of competitive boundary work, intensified by national and regional policy drives towards integration, and reflecting previous work (Allen, 2000; Bach et al., 2012; Burri, 2008; Hazgui & Gendron, 2015). The competitive boundary work was a defensive reaction to policy change that altered their roles and remit (as also seen in the work of Allen, 2000; Martin et al., 2009).

Notably, each profession mirrored the other in the kind of boundary work they undertook: framing the issue as one of inter-professional collaboration but making references to the importance of effective regulation and the obligations of legal duty and safe care to justify maintaining boundaries and asserting their own profession identity and remit (Bucher et al., 2016). Both professions agreed on the problem, adopted the same tactics, and both were more concerned about non-professionals encroaching on their remit than the challenge from other professional groups—generating a consistency in opposition, particularly to the notion of being managed by someone outside their own profession. There was little evidence that the experience of working together was dissolving the boundaries between health professionals and care professionals (at this point), or replacing competing professional identities with, for instance, a place-based concept of identity; instead, the proximity of working appeared to be clarifying inter-professional differences.

While most research into boundaries still focuses on competition, recent research has begun to identify forms of collaborative boundary work, where competition is downplayed and boundaries are dismantled in pursuit of mutual gain (Barrett et al., 2012; Liberati, 2017; Rodriquez, 2015). And indeed, despite the competitive stance described above, collaborative work did occur in this case. Much of this was around the practical need to get work done on a day-to-day basis. A substantial degree of collaborative work relied on individuals embodying boundaries, being individual champions of the cause, with this work occurring in different silos in different forms across the city (Langley et al., 2019; Azambuja & Islam, 2019). Notably, and in contrast to much of the aforementioned work which has identified collaboration, much of the 'successful' collaborative work started by reaffirming existing boundaries, specifically recognising existing profession identities and remits.

A degree of inter-professional solidarity also emerged due to collective resentment of other parts of the sector, such as secondary care or indeed non-professionals. The process of integration generated a renewed focus on other professional and sector boundaries, such as the boundary between in hospital and out-of-hospital care, and the difficulties health and care professionals sometimes encountered working with non-professionals. This opened up shared space between health and social care to collaborate based on shared challenges—the shared concern about the prospect of non-professionals assuming managerial positions within integrated teams, and the broader tension between professionals working in neighbourhoods and the historically prioritised acute sector. This, and the shared foundational belief that in some way, integration in principle is the correct way forward, maintained the prospect of a degree of effective collaboration based on a mutual recognition of professional commitments and identities.

Conclusion

In this chapter we have examined the different kinds of boundary work generated by a top-down initiative to integrate health and social care in a major city in the north of England and examined the implications for professional identities in health and social care.

Drawing on Langley et al.'s (2019) typology, we have interpreted the integration initiative studied here as a form of configurational boundary work, and in keeping with other research in this field, we witnessed this top-down approach increasing competitive boundary work between health and care professionals, each deploying markedly similar but opposing arguments to frame their respective defence of boundaries. We also found evidence of a degree of collaborative boundary work, in response to day-to-day pressures of work and shaped in places by local leadership.

This was not, however, a simple 'mix' of modes of boundary work and the study suggested a more complex relationship between these modes. So, as noted, a more surprising result of integration and the imposed boundary changes was how the response of both health and social care professionals mirrored each other, and their shared resistance to the principle of being supervised by someone outside their profession,—or, worse, a non-professional—generated a degree of solidarity. In a similar manner, shared resentment of the dominance of the hospital sector over primary and community health and care offered another source of unity against common perceived threats. Furthermore, where collaboration was identified, this was not the result of a blurring, ignoring, or breaking down of boundaries but rather collaboration was facilitated through a reiteration and acknowledgement of them. In practice, then, our findings question the value, and the feasibility, of 'breaking down' professional boundaries. Instead, we suggest that a more viable route for 'integration' may be to protect professional boundaries and, potentially, look to supersede these divisions by invoking commonalities between professionals and importantly shared challenges and threats.

This study thus highlights how modes of boundary work need to be considered in terms of their interaction, such that competitive boundary work may paradoxically support collaboration in the longer term as professional boundaries are reaffirmed and recognised, turning attention of shared challenges—here, the potential infringement of non-professional leadership and the dominance of (professionals within) the acute sector. For researchers of health and care, we would therefore seek to underline the need to attend to multiple and inter-related boundaries in analyses of integration and inter-professional work.

References

Abbott, A. (1988). *The system of professions. An essay on the division of expert labor.* University of Chicago Press.

Adams, T. L. (2015). Sociology of professions: International divergences and research directions. Work. *Employment and Society, 29*(1), 154–165.

Allen, D. (2000). Doing occupational demarcation: The "boundary-work" of nurse managers in a district general hospital. *Journal of Contemporary Ethnography, 29*(3), 326–356.

Anteby, M., Chan, C. K., & DiBenigno, J. (2016). Three lenses on occupations and professions in organizations: Becoming, doing, and relating. *Academy of Management Annals, 10*(1), 183–244.

Atwal, A., & Caldwell, K. (2005). Do all health and social care professionals interact equally: A study of interactions in multidisciplinary teams in the United Kingdom. *Scandinavian Journal of Caring Sciences, 19*(3), 268–273.

Azambuja, R., & Islam, G. (2019). Working at the boundaries: Middle managerial work as a source of emancipation and alienation. *Human Relations, 72*(3), 534–564.

Bach, S., Kessler, I., & Heron, P. (2012). Nursing a grievance? The role of healthcare assistants in a modernized national health service. *Gender, Work and Organization, 19*(2), 205–224.

Barrett, M., Oborn, E., Orlikowski, J., & Yates, J. (2012). Reconfiguring boundary relations: Robotic innovations in pharmacy work. *Organization Science, 23*(5), 1448–1466.

Battilana, J. (2011). The enabling role of social position in diverging from the institutional status quo: Evidence from the UK National Health Service. *Organization Science, 22*(4), 817–834.

Bucher, S. V., Chreim, S., Langley, A., & Reay, T. (2016). Contestation about collaboration: Discursive boundary work among professions. *Organization Studies, 37*(4), 497–522.

Burri, R. V. (2008). Doing distinctions: Boundary work and symbolic capital in radiology. *Social Studies of Science, 38*(1), 35–62.

Braun, V., & Clarke, V. (2006). Using thematic analysis in psychology. *Qualitative Research in Psychology, 3*(2), 77–101.

Briggs, A. D. M., Göpfert, A., Thorlby, R., Allwood, D., & Alderwick, H. (2020). Integrated health and care systems in England: Can they help prevent disease? *Integrated Healthcare Journal, 2*(1), e000013.

Bryce, M., Luscombe, K., Boyd, A., Tazzyman, A., Tredinnick-Rowe, J., Walshe, K., & Archer, J. (2018). Policing the profession? Regulatory reform, restratification and the emergence of responsible officers as a new locus of power in UK medicine. *Social Science & Medicine, 213*, 98–105.

Cameron, A. (2016). What have we learnt about joint working between health and social care? *Public Money & Management, 36*(1), 7–14.

Cameron, A., Lart, R., Bostock, L., & Coomber, C. (2014). Factors that promote and hinder joint and integrated working between health and social care services: A review of research literature. *Health & Social Care in the Community, 22*(3), 225–233.

Currie, G., Finn, R., & Martin, G. (2008). Accounting for the `dark Side' of new organizational forms: The case of healthcare professionals. *Human Relations, 61*(4), 539–564.

Currie, G., Finn, R., & Martin, G. (2009). Professional competition and modernizing the clinical workforce in the NHS. Work. *Employment and Society, 23*(2), 267–284.

Dixon-Woods, M., Yeung, K., & Bosk, C. L. (2011). Why is UK medicine no longer a self-regulating profession? The role of scandals involving "bad apple" doctors. *Social Science & Medicine, 73*(10), 1452–1459.

Exworthy, M. (2015). Iron cage and the gaze: Medical control in the English health system. *Professions and Professionalism, 5*, 1.

Fereday, J., & Muir-Cochrane, E. (2006). Demonstrating rigor using thematic analysis: A hybrid approach of inductive and deductive coding and theme development. *International journal of Qualitative Methods, 5*(1), 80–92.

Ferlie, E., McGivern, G., & FitzGerald, L. (2012). A new mode of organizing in health care? Governmentality and managed networks in cancer services in England. *Social Science & Medicine, 74*(3), 340–347.

Finn, R. (2008). The language of teamwork: Reproducing professional divisions in the operating room. *Human Relations, 61*(1), 103–130.

Finn, R., Learmonth, M., & Reedy, P. (2010). Some unintended effects of teamwork in healthcare. *Social Science & Medicine, 70*(8), 1148–1154.

Finn, R., & Waring, J. (2006). Organizational barriers to architectural knowledge and teamwork in operating theatres. *Public Money and Management, 26*(2), 117–124.

Freidson, E. (2001). *Professionalism: The third logic*. Polity Press.

Gieryn, F. (1996). Policing STS: A boundary-work souvenir from the Smithsonian exhibition on "science in American life". *Science, technology, & human values, 21*(1), 100–115.

Glendinning, C. (2003). Breaking down barriers: Integrating health and care services for older people in England. *Health Policy, 65*(2), 139–151.

Hall, P. (2005). Interprofessional teamwork: Professional cultures as barriers. *Journal of Interprofessional Care, 19*(supp 1), 188–196.

Hazgui, M., & Gendron, Y. (2015). Blurred roles and elusive boundaries: On contemporary forms of oversight surrounding professional work. *Accounting, Auditing & Accountability Journal, 28*(8), 1234–1262.

Humphries, R. (2015). Integrated health and social care in England–progress and prospects. *Health Policy, 119*(7), 856–859.

Lam, A. (2019). Hybrids, identity and knowledge boundaries: Creative artists between academic and practitioner communities. Human Relations, 0018726719846259.

Lamont, M., & Molnár, V. (2002). The study of boundaries in the social sciences. *Annual Review of Sociology, 28*, 167–195.

Langley, A., Lindberg, K., Mørk, B. E., Nicolini, D., Raviola, E., & Walter, L. (2019). Boundary work among groups, occupations and organizations: From cartography to process. *Academy of Management Annals, 13*(2), 704–736.

Lewis, G., Vaithianathan, R., Wright, L., Brice, M., Lovell, P., Rankin, S., & Bardsley, M. (2013). Integrating care for high-risk patients in England using the virtual ward model: Lessons in the process of care integration from three case sites. *International Journal of Integrated Care, 13*, 4.

Liberati, E. G., Gorli, M., & Scaratti, G. (2016). Invisible walls within multidisciplinary teams: Disciplinary boundaries and their effects on integrated care. *Social Science & Medicine, 150*, 31–39.

Liberati, E. G. (2017). Separating, replacing, intersecting: The influence of context on the construction of the medical-nursing boundary. *Social Science & Medicine, 172*, 135–143.

Martin, G. P., Currie, G., & Finn, R. (2009). Reconfiguring or reproducing intra-professional boundaries? Specialist expertise, generalist knowledge and the 'modernization' of the medical workforce. *Social Science & Medicine, 68*(7), 1191–1198.

Mitchell, C., Hodgson, D., Tazzyman, A., & Howard, S. (2019). Understanding and supporting the integration of health and social care at a neighbourhood level in the city of Manchester – Report part A: A rapid scoping review. CLAHRC, University of Manchester. https://www.arc-gm.nihr.ac.uk/media/Resources/OHC/CLAHRC%20GM%20Manchester%20Integration%20report%20Part%20A%20final.pdf

Mitchell, C., Tazzyman, A., Howard, S. J., & Hodgson, D. (2020). More that unites us than divides us? A qualitative study of integration of community health and social care services. *BMC Family Practice, 21*(1), 1–10.

Munn, Z., Peters, M. D., Stern, C., Tufanaru, C., McArthur, A., & Aromataris, E. (2018). Systematic review or scoping review? Guidance for authors when choosing between a systematic or scoping review approach. *BMC Medical Research Methodology, 18*(1), 143.

Muzio, D., Ackroyd, S., & Chanlat, J. F. (2008). *Re-directions in the studies of expert labour: Established professions and new expert occupations*. Palgrave Macmillan.

Muzio, D., & Kirkpatrick, I. (2011). Introduction: Professions and organizations-a conceptual framework. *Current Sociology, 59*(4), 389–405.

Nancarrow, S. A., & Borthwick, A. M. (2005). Dynamic professional boundaries in the healthcare workforce. *Sociology of Health & Illness, 27*(7), 897–919.

NHS England. Five Year Forward View. (2014). Retrieved September 18, 2020, from https://www.england.nhs.uk/wp-content/uploads/2014/10/5yfv-web.pdf

Powell, A. E., & Davies, H. T. O. (2012). The struggle to improve patient care in the face of professional boundaries. *Social Science & Medicine, 75*(5), 807–814.

Robertson, H. (2011). Integration of health and social care: A review of literature and models. Implications for Scotland. Royal College of Nursing Scotland.

Rodriquez, J. (2015). Who is on the medical team?: Shifting the boundaries of belonging on the ICU. *Social Science & Medicine, 144*, 112–118.

Shortell, S. M., Addicott, R., Walsh, N., & Ham, C. (2015). The NHS five year forward view: Lessons from the United States in developing new care models. *British Medical Journal, 350*, h2005.

Singer, S. J., Kerrissey, M., Friedberg, M., & Phillips, R. (2018). A Comprehensive Theory of Integration. Medical Care Research and Review, p.1077558718767000.

Spyridonidis, D., Hendy, J., & Barlow, J. (2015). Understanding hybrid roles: The role of identity processes among physicians. *Public Administration, 93*(2), 395–411. https://doi.org/10.1111/padm.12114

Satterstrom, P., Kerrissey, M., & DiBenigno, J. (2020). The Voice Cultivation Process: How Team Members Can Help Upward Voice Live on to Implementation. Administrative Science Quarterly. https://doi.org/10.1177/0001839220962795.

Stokes, J., Checkland, K., & Kristensen, S. R. (2016). Integrated care: Theory to practice. *Journal of Health Services Research & Policy, 21*(4), 282–285.

Tricco, A. C., Lillie, E., Zarin, W., O'Brien, K., Colquhoun, H., Kastner, M., Levac, D., Ng, C., Sharpe, J. P., Wilson, K., & Kenny, M. (2016). A scoping review on the conduct and reporting of scoping reviews. *BMC Medical Research Methodology, 16*, 15.

Zietsma, C., & Lawrence, T. B. (2010). Institutional work in the transformation of an organizational field: The interplay of boundary work and practice work. *Administrative Science Quarterly, 55*, 189–221.

9

The Rights and Wrongs, Ups and Downs, and Ins and Outs of Organisational Cultures in Australian Public Hospitals

Kate Churruca, Chiara Pomare, Louise A. Ellis, Janet C. Long, and Jeffrey Braithwaite

Introduction: Exploring Organisational Culture in Healthcare

For many scholars, organisational culture centrally involves the shared behaviours, values, and attitudes of meso and macro work groups (e.g., Schein, 2004). Over the past three decades, interest in organisational cultures in healthcare has flourished (Davies et al., 2000; Braithwaite et al., 2010c), and it is increasingly recognised as an important mediating influence on quality improvement and patient outcomes (Mannion & Davies, 2018). A recent systematic review showed that among 62 studies, 74%

K. Churruca (✉) • C. Pomare • L. A. Ellis • J. C. Long • J. Braithwaite
Centre for Healthcare Resilience and Implementation Science, Australian Institute of Health Innovation, Macquarie University, Sydney, NSW, Australia
e-mail: kate.churruca@mq.edu.au; chiara.pomare@mq.edu.au; louise.ellis@mq.edu.au; janet.long@mq.edu.au; jeffrey.braithwaite@mq.edu.au

R. Kislov et al. (eds.), *Managing Healthcare Organisations in Challenging Policy Contexts*, Organizational Behaviour in Healthcare,
https://doi.org/10.1007/978-3-030-81093-1_9

reported a consistent positive association between organisational and workplace cultures and patient outcomes (Braithwaite et al., 2017). For example, an organisational culture characterised as more supportive, trusting, and inclusive is likely to be associated with increased patient satisfaction and lower mortality rates (Braithwaite et al., 2017). Another review found evidence that hospitals with lower hospital-acquired infection rates tended to have a positive safety culture, generative leadership styles, embraced innovation, engaged and empowered staff, and enhanced collaboration and communication (van Buijtene & Foster, 2019).

These reviews broadly reflect a view of organisational culture as something a hospital *has,* but even when treated as something an organisation *does,* its important role in patient outcomes is still clear. For example, Weick and Sutcliffe's (2003) analysis of the Bristol Royal Infirmary disaster demonstrated how 'small actions can enact a social structure that keeps the organisation entrapped in cycles of behavior that preclude improvement' (p. 74), and which ultimately contributed to the deaths of multiple babies. Staff at the hospital engaged in behavioural commitment, rationalising the poor performance of the paediatric cardiac surgery unit as a result of case severity rather than any failings on their part.

There are many methods to assess organisational cultures; however, self-report surveys are by far the most common in healthcare, particularly those focusing on the assessment of safety culture as a subset of organisational culture (Jung et al., 2009; Halligan & Zecevic, 2011). Surveys have the advantage of being cost-effective, quick, and straightforward to administer at scale (Tucker et al., 1990), making them highly suited for use in large hospitals. Quantitative data obtained from surveys can be aggregated to look at the attitudes of staff or subsets of them across a whole health system, or used to compare different organisations, professional groups, or wards within a hospital, and provide insights into where differences may lie (Yauch & Steudel, 2003). In that way, survey data can give an indication of how fragmented, differentiated or integrated the culture of an organisation or system is (Davies et al., 2000; Martin, 2001; Martin, 1992). Collecting data over time also enables the tracking of improvements and measuring the effectiveness of culture change interventions (Nieva & Sorra, 2003; Morello et al., 2013). The Agency for Healthcare Research and Quality (AHRQ), as an example, developed the

Hospital Survey on Patient Safety Culture and runs a comparative database where hospitals in the United States can deposit their survey data and receive a report in return that compares their data to the entire database, providing both cross-sectional, snapshot information and trend data over time (AHRQ, 2019).

Theoretically, in attempting to understand and study organisational culture in healthcare, researchers often make a distinction between organisational *culture* and organisational *climate* (Braithwaite et al., 2010c). The latter is thought to involve peoples' *perceptions* of their organisation (i.e., its procedures, practices, and the kinds of behaviour that are tolerated or rewarded), whereas culture is considered by many scholars to operate on a deeper, more enduring level, representing the underlying, sometimes unconscious, beliefs and values enmeshed within an organisation (Flin et al., 2006). However, others in the field use the terms 'culture' and 'climate' interchangeably (Cox & Flin, 1998). Van den Berg and Wilderom (2004) argue that these variations in nomenclature reflect different research paradigms with organisational culture having more sociological, qualitative, and social constructionist origins, while climate hails from a psychological and quantitative tradition, and hence aligns more with survey research. We appreciate that using organisational *climate* provides an additional layer of extrapolation, acknowledging that methodologically surveys provide a snapshot or window into an organisation's culture at a particular time (Scott et al., 2003; Colla et al., 2005; Ginsburg et al., 2013; Mearns & Flin, 1999), while qualitative approaches (interviews, focus groups, observations, and particularly ethnography) are more suited to examining culture in richer, drawn-out detail (Laflamme et al., 2019; Nakrem, 2015; Nugus, 2019). Here, for simplicity we employ the word *culture* to acknowledge that surveys, while having limitations, attempt to examine some of the same core issues, processes, and features as methods like ethnography (Braithwaite et al., 2010b).

When governments, policymakers, or hospital leadership carry out any sort of survey of organisational cultures—something which they do frequently in countries such as the United Kingdom, Canada, and Australia (Mannion et al., 2009; Bishop & Fleming, 2014; Simpson et al., 2019)—they are (assumedly) most interested in the results of that investigation.

However, the contents of the tool(s) used to collect that data are also revealing about the cultures of that organisation, government body, health system or nation, and about the kind of things valued, prioritised, and expected of those working within it. As such, it is worth examining these instruments and the purposes for which they are used. In this chapter, we take up this task, focusing on the measurement of organisational culture across the Australian public hospital system. We first examine the context of the Australian healthcare and public sector systems, both of which require assessment of culture. We then present an analysis of the surveys most widely used to assess organisational culture in Australian public hospitals, focusing on their contents and what the data collected is used for. We conclude the chapter with a consideration of the implications of this analysis and reflections on how use of large-scale organisational culture surveys could be improved.

Organisational Surveys in the Australian Political and Policy Context

Australian Healthcare: A Complex, Federated System

Healthcare systems worldwide increasingly recognise the importance of understanding and assessing organisational cultures within their services, particularly with regard to their impact on safety (Halligan & Zecevic, 2011). Australia provides a particularly useful context for examining the large-scale assessment of organisational culture in hospitals because the country's size, geographical and demographical diversity, and mix of local, state, and federal funding and governance arrangements have contributed to a public hospital system that is complex and highly fragmented (Hall, 2015). This translates to a multitude of different stakeholder groups and levels, as well as approaches through which culture might be examined in Australian hospitals. Indeed, a brief scoping of grey and academic literature (Table 9.1) identified numerous assessments of organisational culture and safety culture using different approaches and targeted at varying organisational levels in hospital in Australia (see also

Table 9.1 Examples of organisational culture measurement in Australian hospitals and the healthcare system

Organisation	Level	Assessment tool
Department of Health and Human Services (TAS)	State	Competing Values Framework (Goodman et al., 2001; Shannon et al., 2012)
Bundaberg hospital (QLD)	Hospital	Retrospective public inquiry (Morris, 2005; Casali & Day, 2010)
Local Health districts (NSW)	Region	Hospital Survey on Patient Safety Culture (Piper et al., 2018; Sorra & Dyer, 2010)
St Vincent's hospital (VIC)	Hospital in a public/ private network	Patient Safety Culture Survey, a modified version of the Safety Attitudes Questionnaire by Sexton et al. (2006) (St Vincent's Hospital Melbourne, 2018)

Hogden et al., 2017). The purposes of these assessments (e.g., understanding), and what was ultimately done as a result of collecting this information (e.g., quality improvement, organisational change), varied and were not always clear. Similar issues have been identified in England, with recent research finding an extensive range of tools used to assess and understand cultures in National Health Service (NHS) Trusts; these included surveys specifically intended for that purpose, as well as other measures (e.g., of patient satisfaction) and indicators of safety and quality, with users having varying levels of satisfaction with these tools (Simpson et al., 2019).

The quality standards of the Australian healthcare system, which are evaluated based on accreditation methodology (Braithwaite et al., 2010a; Hinchcliff et al., 2012; Greenfield & Braithwaite, 2008), require hospitals to 'develop a culture of safety and quality improvement' (Australian Commission on Safety and Quality in Health Care, 2017, p. 6). This includes as a key task ensuring 'that systems are in place to regularly survey and report on organisational culture' (Australian Commission on Safety and Quality in Health Care, 2019a). However, there is currently no explicit guidance on how Australian hospitals should go about meeting the standards, such as what type of culture assessment to use, how regularly to collect this data, and what to do with it, although delivery of this advice is in the planning phases (Australian Commission on Safety and Quality in Health Care, 2019b; Australian Institute of Health and Welfare, 2016).

While Australia's accreditation standards are set nationally, publicly funded health services are operated by state governments through shared funding responsibilities with the national government. Management of hospitals is largely devolved to smaller, geographically bounded regions akin to the United Kingdom's NHS Trusts (known as Local Health Districts in New South Wales (NSW), Hospital and Health Services in Queensland). At the lower levels are localised layers of management, quality improvement units, and clinical microsystems operating *within* each hospital. As Hall (2015) indicates, the result of these sorts of arrangements 'is a complex set of overlapping and fragmented responsibilities' where 'no single level of government has all the policy levers needed to ensure a cohesive health system' (p. 495).

The Public Sector Policy Landscape and Organisational Culture Surveys in Australian Hospitals

In addition to the national healthcare standards, public sector policy in Australia emphasises routine collection of data which acts as a further window into organisational cultures in hospitals. The *Public Sector Management Act 1994*, Section 21, denotes the Public Sector Commissioner's role in monitoring and assisting agencies to comply with public sector standards (Australian Capital Territory, 1994). Surveys are thereby used to monitor what goes on in Australian public organisations, including public hospitals. The stated reasons for collecting these data are to: (a) determine the extent employees' view behaviour in their organisation as consistent with good human resource practice, ethical practice, and diversity and inclusion principles; (b) assess employees' job satisfaction; and (c) examine their perceptions regarding leadership, management, and administration in their organisation (Australian Capital Territory, 1994).

While originally positioned as tools to examine non-compliance, such public sector employee surveys are increasingly used by state departments of health to measure organisational cultures (Public Sector Commission,

2018). A justification for conducting these surveys is to contribute to continually improving workplace culture including strengthening the values of collaboration, openness, respect, and empowerment (NSW Health, 2018). Australian states and territories routinely conduct their own versions of these surveys. In Victoria, the *People Matter Survey* is administered to all public sector employees (Victorian Public Sector Commission, 2019), with a similarly named survey used in the Northern Territory (Northern Territory Government , 2019) and also now in NSW (NSW Government Public Service Commission, 2019). The *NSW People Matter Employee Survey* was previously (i.e., pre-2015) termed *Your Say Workplace Culture Survey.* Other states and territories have distinguishable but broadly comparable surveys (Government of South Australia, 2019; Tasmanian Government, 2019), with variations to the names of the instruments over the years (Department of Health, 2019). As the survey names have changed, so too has the focus of some questions. That is, while core questions may be held constant, aspects of the surveys have altered over time to address new concerns and priorities in public and healthcare policy. For example, cognitive testing of the *NSW People Matter Workplace Culture Survey* led to the implementation of new questions in the 2018 survey related to physical harm, sexual harassment, and abuse (NSW Government, 2018).

We know that assessments of culture, and particularly safety culture, happen at more localised levels in the Australian healthcare system (see Table 9.1 and Hogden et al., 2017), but these surveys represent the most widely used and closest approximations of a national- or state-level consistent assessment of organisational culture within the otherwise fragmented public hospital system. Despite consistency in the use of these surveys across the different states and territories, and the fact that some states use some of the same survey items, no research has examined the propensity for overlap in the content of these tools. Nor has there been an attempt to examine and compare how the results from these surveys are used between the different states. This would highlight potential similarities, differences, and priorities in the conceptualisation and measurement of organisational cultures in healthcare across Australia. These insights will be useful to those working in other health systems such as the United Kingdom and Canada that also routinely conduct large-scale assessments of organisational cultures using a range of tools (Mannion et al., 2009; Bishop & Fleming, 2014) and particularly annual staff surveys (Simpson et al., 2019).

Method

Organisational culture surveys used in the Australian public hospital sector were examined. These surveys were identified through searches of state government and department of health websites. Where possible, the most recent year for which the full survey form was available was used. We also examined associated public reporting of the results of these surveys, comparing between states and identifying whether and how results were used within hospitals (e.g., monitoring, quality improvement).

Survey Item Mapping

All items, excluding demographic data, were extracted from the organisational culture surveys and formatted into an Excel spreadsheet for purposes of thematic analysis. We also extracted the topic themes or headers used within each survey form to group items. These topic themes were used as the starting point for codes; we first inspected the headers and read through the items listed under them to familiarise ourselves with intended themes. By grouping together common or conceptually related topic themes from across surveys, a draft framework was derived, and codes subsequently defined. This framework was then used to code each survey item, a process that was completed independently but simultaneously by two authors (KC, LAE), who discussed the code assigned for each item and managed any discrepancies before proceeding to the next. Items were assigned to 18 different codes (see below in Results, Table 9.3).

Items that did not adequately fit under any of the codes or were coded inconsistently were reviewed a second time, leading to minor modifications (e.g., changes to the definition or title), or development of new codes to cover emergent issues (inductive coding). Two new codes were 'safety culture related' and 'initiative and autonomy'. All coded items were then reviewed a final time to ensure they adequately fit under their assigned code.

Thematically associated codes were then organised together to highlight broader themes among the items. The starting point for this was the distinction between items that asked about individual perceptions, evaluations, and experiences, compared with those focused on more collective, interpersonal, or external factors. From there four themes were developed: (1) individual feelings and experiences at work, (2) social issues at work, (3) leadership and supervision, and (4) organisational and workplace factors.

Reporting and Using Results from Public Sector Culture Surveys in Healthcare

A scoping review of the grey literature was conducted to examine how the findings from the Australian public sector surveys, specific to healthcare, are reported and used. This included examining the websites of state departments of health and looking for reports or uses of the surveys by regional health units (e.g., local health districts in NSW) using Google Search function. The most recent reports were identified for each state (2018 or 2019) and data were extracted regarding how findings were reported and any detail on how the findings would be used (e.g., improvement). Extracted data were tabulated to enable comparison across states and territories.

Strengths and Limitations of the Method

The coding framework used to classify items was, for the most part, based on pre-existing approaches. In coding these items, though, it became clear that many constructs are closely related. For example, it was difficult to separate 'job satisfaction' from 'engagement'. Having two coders to complete this task (analyst triangulation, Patton, 1999), creating explicit coding rules and discussing codes until consensus was reached, overcame most of the difficulties and led to a more rigorous analysis.

Another limitation was that only seven surveys used in Australian public hospitals were examined, with the Australian Capital Territory (ACT) survey missing. Furthermore, it was not always possible to compare the same surveys in the same years for all states. This reflects the fragmentation in the use of these surveys by states; not all complete them annually, and not all states make survey forms available for all years.

Results

Survey Item Mapping

Seven surveys used in the public sector for six Australian states (NSW, Queensland [QLD], South Australia [SA], Tasmania [TAS], Victoria [VIC], Western Australia [WA]) and the Northern Territory (NT) were identified. These surveys are outlined in Table 9.2.

A total of 597 survey items across the seven surveys were examined. There was considerable similarity among these survey items but very few identical items; for example, among the items assessing job satisfaction there were: 'I would recommend my workplace as a good place to work' (NSW), 'I would recommend the Tasmanian State Service as a good place to work' (TAS), 'I would recommend my organisation as a good place to work' (QLD, VIC, WA), and 'I would recommend my agency as a good place to work' (SA, NT). Although it is worth noting this overlap, in the analysis each item from every survey was treated as independent.

Of the 18 codes identified (see Table 9.3), the most common were 'organisational values and behaviours' (n = 68), 'discrimination or

Table 9.2 List of organisational culture surveys

State/territory	Name of survey
NSW	2015 NSW Health your say workplace culture survey
NT	2014 People matter survey
QLD	2017 Working for Queensland
SA	2018 I WORK FOR SA—Your voice survey
TAS	2017 People matter survey
VIC	2017 People matter survey (Health edition)
WA	2019 Minister for Health engagement survey

Table 9.3 Number of items mapped to survey constructs

Theme	Construct	NSW	QLD	SA	TAS	VIC	WA	NT	Total no. of items
Individual feelings and experiences at work	Burnout, health, and wellbeing	1	4	2	1	0	1	1	10
	Job satisfaction	2	12	10	11	9	2	10	56
	Engagement	4	2	10	3	2	4	6	31
	Personal plans around employment	0	5	3	2	1	0	1	12
	Role and fitting in with the organisation	3	3	3	3	4	5	3	24
	Initiative and autonomy	5	3	4	3	1	4	1	21
Social issues at work	Discrimination or tolerance	5	9	2	5	31	2	8	62
	Bullying and sexual harassment	10	10	0	3	2	0	7	32
	Domestic and family violence	0	6	0	0	0	0	0	6
Leadership and supervision	Performance assessment and development	3	10	4	7	6	5	8	43
	Line manager	5	13	10	12	0	2	13	55
	Senior management	6	10	8	5	4	3	3	39
Organisational and workplace factors	Workgroup/team values and behaviours	5	13	6	10	8	3	3	48
	Workplace environment	1	3	3	1	1	2	0	11
	Organisational values and behaviours	10	12	5	7	13	6	15	68
	Organisational processes, policies	8	3	3	13	12	4	7	50
	Organisational change and improvement	3	3	4	2	0	1	5	18
	Safety culture related	1	0	0	1	6	3	0	11
Total		72	121	77	89	100	47	91	597

tolerance' (n = 62), 'job satisfaction' (n = 56), and 'line manager' (n = 55). The codes represented by the least number of items were 'domestic and family violence' (n = 6) and 'burnout, health and wellbeing' (n = 10). Between states, there was differential coverage of some coded constructs; for example, 'performance assessment and development' and 'senior management' items were present in every survey, but only four had 'safety culture related' items and only one state had items mapped to 'domestic and family violence'. No survey included items related to all 18 constructs.

In addition to a range of individual issues (e.g., job satisfaction, burnout), the surveys broadly assessed staff's perceptions of the shared behaviours, values, and attitudes of their work group and leadership and, in that sense, would seem to focus on aspects of organisational culture. In terms of organisational values, many items were concerned with idealistic qualities such as openness ('My organisation is open to new ideas'), inclusion ('My input is adequately sought and considered about decisions that directly affect me'), fairness ('People are treated fairly and consistently in my workplace'), justice ('If I raised a complaint, I feel confident that it would be taken seriously'), and improvement ('My manager encourages people in my workgroup to monitor and improve the quality of what we do'). Taken as a whole, these questions were somewhat superficial and arguably normative, setting a standard for how public hospital staff *should* behave and what they should value, rather than attempting to characterise what makes them tick in the first place. Few items focused on patient care or healthcare issues explicitly though (e.g., 'In my workplace patient safety is at the centre of all decision making'), likely because these surveys were developed for a general workforce of public sector employees.

Reporting and Using Results from Public Sector Culture Surveys in Healthcare

We scoped state government and department of health websites followed by searches of Google for other reports or uses for the results of the different state organisational culture surveys. These results are displayed in Table 9.4.

Table 9.4 Differences in how state surveys of organisational culture are used

State	How are staff survey results disseminated specific to health sector?	What was the data used for?
NSW	NSW Health reports at **state level** and by **department and agencies**, including by local health districts (but not individual hospitals).	Reports suggest areas for improvement but not how the data will be practically used.
NT	NT people matter survey results reported at the **state level for the whole public sector**.	The state-level report indicates areas for improvement and encourages local entities to take action by providing a worksheet. However, there were no specific ideas for how the data will be used.
QLD	Findings are reported at the **state level** and broken down by **departments, public sector offices and government entities, and health agencies**.	Reports suggest areas for improvement but not how the data will be practically used.
SA	SA survey findings reported at **state level for the whole public sector**.	State-level reports encourage local entities to take action by providing a worksheet, although no specific ideas for how the data will be used.
TAS	Survey findings from Tasmania only reported at the **state level for the whole public sector**. It is up to heads of agencies (e.g., Tasmanian Health service) to decide how their results will be made available to employees. No evidence found that Tasmanian Health service publicly releases this data.	The report identified areas that need to be improved at state level (e.g., management/leadership) but not how the data will be used for change.

(*continued*)

Table 9.4 (continued)

State	How are staff survey results disseminated specific to health sector?	What was the data used for?
VIC	High level survey results are reported publicly **at state level for the whole public sector**, with some data broken down by health. Results are apparently privately fed back to organisations. Individual reports are issued by **some regions**.	The reports suggest results will assist organisations to understand employee engagement and job satisfaction, and encourage local entities to then work out how to improve the working environment. Some regions report and provide insights into what changes they are making because of it. For example, introducing more opportunities for regular discussion and feedback, including monthly organisation-wide staff meetings (Kerang District Health, 2016)
WA	Survey results reported at the **state level**. Findings are compared across health services (e.g., Department of Health, Health support services), but not reported in detail specific to regions.	The state-level report indicates areas for improvement and encourages local entities to take action by providing a worksheet, although no specific ideas for how the data will be used.

This analysis revealed that there is inconsistency even in describing these surveys as measures of organisational cultures. For example, the *Working for Queensland Survey* was badged as a measurement of employees' perceptions of their work, manager, team, and organisation (Queensland Government, 2019). This description makes no mention of organisational culture, although some of its items made explicit reference to culture: 'My workplace has an inclusive culture where diversity is valued and respected'. Alternatively, the 2015 *NSW Health Your Say Workplace Culture Survey* was described as a workplace culture survey (NSW Government, 2019).

States and territories differed in how they publicly distributed their survey findings, or indeed whether they distributed them at all. Some states reported on the region level, while others only reported results on the state level for the whole of the public sector. QLD and NSW had public reports of their organisational culture survey findings available at various levels (e.g., state, department, agency). States also had limited information on *how* the findings would be practically used for improvement within the hospitals involved. Where survey results were available, they supported the idea that little improvement was made based on the results of the previous years' survey findings. For example, a few of the items coded to 'Organisational change and improvement' specifically asked about the extent of changes made in one's organisation since the previous years' survey (QLD). A majority of the responses from participants at most of the healthcare organisations examined disagreed that changes had been made in light of previous findings.[1] The fact that most states did not report all their data by at least the healthcare sector, or use the same wording of items or response ranges even when questions were extremely similar, precluded comparisons between states and territories. Hence, it was not possible to aggregate organisational culture survey data to draw conclusions nationally for Australia or make comparisons by state.

The fragmentary nature of the Australian healthcare system likely contributed to the inconsistent reporting of findings and limited discussion of actions taken to improve working conditions. To the latter, reports from many states indicated that the responsibility for making improvements based on the surveys would be handled by the relevant regional authority, and some provided generic tools to help with this (e.g., SA, WA). While consideration of local context is important when trying to improve healthcare organisations (Churruca et al., 2019), in this instance it means local authorities must take ownership of the end stage of a process that they had limited control of, including in terms of the survey contents.

Discussion: What Value Do Annual Staff Surveys Have in Understanding Organisational Cultures in Hospitals?

Our examination of the annual surveys specifically or ostensibly used to assess organisational cultures in Australian public hospitals identified the most common themes and highlighted differences in the constructs

[1] Average across all health agencies in Queensland was 62.3%=NO; a further 15.8% reported having worked in the organisation for <12 months.

covered by different states. States also differed in reporting results of these surveys and made varying claims about the uses of the data.

Survey Contents

If we take these surveys as a window into the culture of hospitals, or at least the priorities when it comes to measurement of that culture, the variability among states suggests that there are overlaps but no overarching perspective on cultures in Australian hospitals. The constructs most consistently identified also bore similarity to those in the annual NHS staff survey, including morale; equality, diversity, and inclusion; health and wellbeing; and bullying and harassment; however, the NHS survey includes an explicit focus on safety culture (NHS England, 2020).

In our study, the job satisfaction items were among the most common. Although individual-focused, literature supports a strong association between culture and job satisfaction (Sempane et al., 2002). Engagement items were also common, with studies from England associating this variable with higher-quality ratings in NHS acute Trusts (Wake & Green, 2019). Other items endeavoured to assess general aspects of culture—good leadership, collaboration, and a supportive environment—that have been found to have an association with the quality and safety of patient care (Braithwaite et al., 2017; van Buijtene & Foster, 2019). However, in our study only a few items were healthcare specific or focused on safety culture, despite the priority these receive in the Australian national standards (Australian Commission on Safety and Quality in Health Care, 2017). Furthermore, no items captured the more complex aspects of healthcare delivery such as when two organisational priorities (e.g., efficiency, patient-centredness) are in conflict with one another (Hollnagel et al., 2013).

Because they are updated yearly, these surveys also responded to contemporaneous social concerns. For example, the QLD survey included items related to domestic violence, a prominent issue that has received increased national public attention over the last five years (Keane & Slessor, 2018; A. Piper & Stevenson, 2019).

Purpose and Use of Surveys

If the original purpose of these surveys, as stated in public sector policy, is not assessment of organisational cultures per se, but monitoring employee experiences and evaluations of their workplace; we find they fulfil that brief. However, questions must be asked then about what value there is in conducting them, often yearly at considerable time and expense, when there is limited evidence of change based on the data. This is perhaps because surveys are designed and analysed at one level (state), but in many instances results must be interpreted and actioned at another, lower level.

The organisational culture surveys used in the Australian public hospital sector are also curated and 'marketed' for the political climate of the time. For example, the newest iteration of a WA survey, which ran for the first time in 2019, was represented as a state election promise where the survey findings would be used to improve the WA health system, enhancing its prospect as an employer of choice (Department of Health, 2019). Findings were distributed via media statements, arguably, to boost political agendas, without providing details of how the government would improve or make changes to the health system (Government of Western Australia, 2019b). For example, an Employment Engagement Index of 62%[2] was reported in press releases, and compared favourably with the results of surveys from other Australian states (Government of Western Australia, 2019b). These media statements made no mention of the fact the response rate was only 33% (Government of Western Australia, 2019a), nor that the people most likely to fill in such a survey are also likely to be the most engaged.

All of this suggests that the use and reporting of results from these surveys may serve political purposes, while the practical applications of findings remain opaque. At the extreme, it could be argued that culture surveys—taking place at the state level on an annual basis—are mostly a bureaucratic exercise; they have vague substantive goals and do not often lead to real improvements in individual hospitals. While the federated and fragmentary nature of the Australian healthcare system may have

[2] Unclear how this index was scored, but likely based on engagement and job satisfaction items.

contributed to poor and inconsistent reporting and utilisation of results, other research suggests that the use of performance data—or lack thereof—is a widespread problem in public sector management (Moynihan & Pandey, 2010).

Implications for Hospital Managers and Policymakers

How well do these surveys do in assessing organisational culture across Australian public hospitals? In terms of consistency, there were many overlaps but few direct comparisons in the items used in the surveys across states. From these overlaps a picture begins to emerge of an idealised workplace and the employee within it: fair and equitable treatment, ability to report issues, a focus on improvement. Undoubtedly, these features play a role in the capacity for hospital staff to provide safe and high-quality care (Braithwaite et al., 2017; van Buijtene & Foster, 2019). Overall, though, items lacked the healthcare focus and nuanced complexity required to understand organisational culture at a level useful for providing insights into patient care. In terms of meeting national standards, then, some hospitals might use a survey like this as *one component* of the system 'to regularly survey and report on organisational culture' (Australian Commission on Safety and Quality in Health Care, 2019a), but it should not be the only one. However, we did not study whether the staff responsible for quality management and improvement within hospitals use these surveys for this purpose. In England, a similarly focused annual staff survey is used within some hospitals to understand their culture, and in fact receives a relatively high satisfaction score for this purpose; however, that survey has much greater coverage of safety culture than the ones we examined here (NHS England, 2020; Simpson et al., 2019).

Of course, critique of these particular surveys in many respects only echoes the criticisms levelled at all culture surveys, that in isolation they are not ideal for exploring the underlying assumptions at the heart of an organisation's culture (Schein, 2006). In Australian hospitals, the other limitation of these surveys relates to their typically poor response rates. For example, the *2018 I WORK FOR SA—Your Voice Survey*, yielded a response rate of only 22% (Government of South Australia, 2019). Many academic studies stress the importance of achieving a high response rate (>60%) to gain a fair representation of the sample and draw inferences about culture (see Pronovost & Sexton, 2005).

Moving forward, our analysis points to the limited utility of large-scale organisational culture surveys in meaningfully understanding organisational culture within any one hospital, and particularly in relation to quality and safety. Nevertheless, hospital management may find value in the results of the surveys in pointing to areas of concern, particularly if there is a pattern of extreme responses among related items. However, in order to trust the integrity of such results, a hospital must achieve a high enough response rate in the first place. This would require not only local support for the survey by hospital management when it is rolled out, but also for employees to see some value in filling it in. And this is less likely to happen unless results are fed back, and changes or improvements made in light of the findings. For policymakers, then, rather than treating these surveys as purely an annual process of monitoring—simply because that is what the original public sector policy outlined—greater consideration to what goes into these surveys, and what substantive uses they can be put towards, is required.

Conclusion

The measurement of organisational culture can be useful in managing hospitals, influencing the delivery of healthcare, and is mandated by Australian national standards for healthcare organisations. However, policy does not provide guidance on appropriate tools, strategies for use, and analysis and results feedback. State-based public sector surveys represent the closest approximation of large-scale attempts at organisational culture measurement in hospitals in Australia. In reviewing these surveys, we identified items covering 18 different constructs. In conjunction with examining the reports on the results of these surveys, we see that these surveys are as much a window into the ideal public sector employee, and social and political context, as a hospital's culture. Indeed, despite the extensive resources that go into running and promoting the regular roll-out of these surveys, their substantive value to healthcare organisations appears to be limited. Greater consideration of what goes into these surveys, and what should come out of them, is required for them to truly have value in hospitals.

References

AHRQ. (2019). SOPS Hospital Database. https://www.ahrq.gov/sops/databases/hospital/index.html

Australian Capital Territory. (1994). Public sector management act 1994. In ACT Parliamentary Counsel (Ed.), (Vol. A1994–37). Canberra.

Australian Commission on Safety and Quality in Health Care. (2017). *National safety and quality health service standards* (2nd ed.). ACSQHC.

Australian Commission on Safety and Quality in Health Care. (2019a). Action 1.1 Governance, leadership and culture. Retrieved September 10, 2020, from https://www.safetyandquality.gov.au/standards/national-safety-and-quality-health-service-nsqhs-standards/clinical-governance-standard/governance-leadership-and-culture/action-11

Australian Commission on Safety and Quality in Health Care. (2019b). *The state of patient safety and quality in Australian hospitals 2019*. ACSQHC.

Australian Institute of Health and Welfare. (2016). *Australia's health 2016*. AIHW.

Bishop, A., & Fleming, M. (2014). Patient safety and engagement at the front-lines of healthcare. *Healthcare Quarterly, 17*, 36–40.

Braithwaite, J., Greenfield, D., Westbrook, J., Pawsey, M., Westbrook, M., Gibberd, R., et al. (2010a). Health service accreditation as a predictor of clinical and organisational performance: A blinded, random, stratified study. *Quality and Safety in Health Care, 19*(1), 14–21. https://doi.org/10.1136/qshc.2009.033928

Braithwaite, J., Greenfield, D., & Westbrook, M. T. (2010b). Converging and diverging concepts in culture and climate research: Cultate or climure? In J. Braithwaite, P. Hyde, & C. Pope (Eds.), *Culture and climate in health care organizations* (pp. 7–18). Palgrave Macmillan.

Braithwaite, J., Hyde, P., & Pope, C. (2010c). *Culture and climate in health care organizations*. Palgrave Macmillan.

Braithwaite, J., Herkes, J., Ludlow, K., Testa, L., & Lamprell, G. (2017). Association between organisational and workplace cultures, and patient outcomes: Systematic review. *BMJ Open, 7*(11), e017708.

van Buijtene, A., & Foster, D. (2019). Does a hospital culture influence adherence to infection prevention and control and rates of healthcare associated infection? A literature review. *Journal of Infection Prevention, 20*(1), 5–17.

Casali, G. L., & Day, G. E. (2010). Treating an unhealthy organisational culture: The implications of the Bundaberg hospital inquiry for managerial ethical decision making. *Australian Health Review, 34*(1), 73–79.

Churruca, K., Ludlow, K., Taylor, N., Long, J. C., Best, S., & Braithwaite, J. (2019). The time has come: Embedded implementation research for health care improvement. *Journal of Evaluation in Clinical Practice, 25*(3), 373–380. https://doi.org/10.1111/jep.13100

Colla, J., Bracken, A., Kinney, L., & Weeks, W. (2005). Measuring patient safety climate: A review of surveys. *BMJ Quality & Safety, 14*(5), 364–366.

Cox, S., & Flin, R. (1998). Safety culture: Philosopher's stone or man of straw? *Work & Stress, 12*(3), 189–201. https://doi.org/10.1080/02678379808256861

Davies, H. T. O., Nutley, S. M., & Mannion, R. (2000). Organisational culture and quality of health care. *Quality and Safety in Health Care, 9*(2), 111–119. https://doi.org/10.1136/qhc.9.2.111

Department of Health. (2019). Minister for Health Engagement Survey 2019. Retrieved January 15, 2021, from https://ww2.health.wa.gov.au/Reports-and-publications/Minister-staff-survey

Flin, R., Burns, C., Mearns, K., Yule, S., & Robertson, E. (2006). Measuring safety climate in health care. *Quality and Safety in Health Care, 15*(2), 109–115.

Ginsburg, L. R., Tregunno, D., Norton, P. G., Mitchell, J. I., & Howley, H. (2013). 'Not another safety culture survey': Using the Canadian patient safety climate survey (can-PSCS) to measure provider perceptions of PSC across health settings. *BMJ Quality & Safety*, bmjqs-2013-002220.

Goodman, E. A., Zammuto, R. F., & Gifford, B. D. (2001). The competing values framework: Understanding the impact of organizational culture on the quality of work life. *Organization Development Journal, 19*(3), 58–68.

Government of South Australia. (2019). *I WORK FOR SA—Your Voice Survey.* https://publicsector.sa.gov.au/about/office-for-the-public-sector/iworkforsa-yourvoicesurvey/

Government of Western Australia. (2019a). *Your Voice in Health—Minister for Health Engagement Survey 2019: WA health system results report* (pp. 103). Government of Western Australia.

Government of Western Australia (2019b). Your Voice in Health staff survey finds engaged and dedicated workers. https://www.mediastatements.wa.gov.au/Pages/McGowan/2019/07/Your-Voice-in-Health-staff-survey-finds-engaged-and-dedicated-workers.aspx

Greenfield, D., & Braithwaite, J. (2008). Health sector accreditation research: A systematic review. *International Journal for Quality in Health Care, 20*(3), 172–183. https://doi.org/10.1093/intqhc/mzn005

Hall, J. (2015). Australian health care—The challenge of reform in a fragmented system. *New England Journal of Medicine, 373*(6), 493–497.

Halligan, M., & Zecevic, A. (2011). Safety culture in healthcare: A review of concepts, dimensions, measures and progress. *BMJ Quality & Safety, 20*(4), 338–343. https://doi.org/10.1136/bmjqs.2010.040964

Hinchcliff, R., Greenfield, D., Moldovan, M., Westbrook, J. I., Pawsey, M., Mumford, V., et al. (2012). Narrative synthesis of health service accreditation literature. *BMJ Quality & Safety, 21*(12), 979–991. https://doi.org/10.1136/bmjqs-2012-000852

Hogden, A., Ellis, L., Churruca, K., & Bierbaum, M. (2017). *Safety culture assessment in health care: A review of the literature on safety culture assessment modes*. Macquarie University.

Hollnagel, E., Braithwaite, J., & Wears, R. L. (2013). *Resilient health care*. CRC Press.

Jung, T., Scott, T., Davies, H. T., Bower, P., Whalley, D., McNally, R., et al. (2009). Instruments for exploring organizational culture: A review of the literature. *Public Administration Review, 69*(6), 1087–1096.

Keane, D., & Slessor, C. (2018). New domestic violence campaign to focus on 'boys being boys' attitude in society. https://www.abc.net.au/news/2018-10-03/prevention-campaign-for-violence-against-women-to-launch/10330696

Kerang District Health. (2016). You said. We did. Outcomes from the 2016 People Matter Survey. http://www.kerangdistricthealth.com.au/about-us/publications/KDH%20You%20said%20we%20did%20report%202017.pdf

Laflamme, K., Leibing, A., & Lavoie-Tremblay, M. (2019). Operating room culture and Interprofessional relations: Impact on nurse's retention. *The Health Care Manager, 38*(4).

Mannion, R., & Davies, H. (2018). Understanding organisational culture for healthcare quality improvement. *BMJ, 363*, k4907. https://doi.org/10.1136/bmj.k4907

Mannion, R., Konteh, F., & Davies, H. (2009). Assessing organisational culture for quality and safety improvement: A national survey of tools and tool use. *BMJ Quality & Safety, 18*(2), 153–156.

Martin, J. (1992). *Cultures in organizations: Three perspectives*. Oxford University Press.

Martin, J. (2001). *Organizational culture: Mapping the terrain*. Sage Publications.
Mearns, K. J., & Flin, R. (1999). Assessing the state of organizational safety—Culture or climate? *Current Psychology, 18*(1), 5–17. https://doi.org/10.1007/s12144-999-1013-3
Morello, R. T., Lowthian, J. A., Barker, A. L., McGinnes, R., Dunt, D., & Brand, C. (2013). Strategies for improving patient safety culture in hospitals: A systematic review. *BMJ Quality & Safety, 22*(1), 11–18. https://doi.org/10.1136/bmjqs-2011-000582
Morris, A. J. H. (2005). Bundaberg Hospital Commission of Inquiry Interim Report. https://quackwatch.org/wp-content/uploads/sites/33/quackwatch/casewatch/foreign/patel/interimreport.pdf
Moynihan, D. P., & Pandey, S. K. (2010). The big question for performance management: Why do managers use performance information? *Journal of Public Administration Research and Theory, 20*(4), 849–866. https://doi.org/10.1093/jopart/muq004
Nakrem, S. (2015). Understanding organizational and cultural premises for quality of care in nursing homes: An ethnographic study. *BMC Health Services Research, 15*(1), 508. https://doi.org/10.1186/s12913-015-1171-y
NHS England. (2020). *NHS staff survey 2019: National Results Briefing* (pp. 42). Survey Coordination Centre.
Nieva, V., & Sorra, J. (2003). Safety culture assessment: A tool for improving patient safety in healthcare organizations. *BMJ Quality & Safety, 12*(suppl 2), ii17–ii23.
Northern Territory Government, O. o. t. C. f. P. E. (2019). People Matter Survey. https://ocpe.nt.gov.au/nt-public-sector-employment/people-matter-survey
NSW Government. (2018). People Matter Employee Survey. https://www.psc.nsw.gov.au/reports%2D%2D-data/state-of-the-sector/people-matter-employee-survey
NSW Government. (2019). 2015 YourSay Workplace Culture Survey results. https://www.health.nsw.gov.au/workforce/yoursay/2015/Pages/default.aspx
NSW Government Public Service Commission. (2019). People Matter Employee Survey. https://www.psc.nsw.gov.au/reports%2D%2D-data/people-matter-employee-survey
NSW Health. (2018). Workplace culture. https://www.health.nsw.gov.au/workforce/culture/Pages/default.aspx
Nugus, P. (2019). Re-structuring the negotiated order of the hospital. *Sociology of Health & Illness, 41*(2), 378–394. https://doi.org/10.1111/1467-9566.12838

Patton, M. Q. (1999). Enhancing the quality and credibility of qualitative analysis. *Health Services Research, 34*(5 Pt 2), 1189.

Piper, A., & Stevenson, A. (2019). The long history of gender violence in Australia, and why it matters today. https://theconversation.com/the-long-history-of-gender-violence-in-australia-and-why-it-matters-today-119927

Piper, D., Lea, J., Woods, C., & Parker, V. (2018). The impact of patient safety culture on handover in rural health facilities. *BMC Health Services Research, 18*(1), 889.

Pronovost, P., & Sexton, B. (2005). Assessing safety culture: Guidelines and recommendations. *Quality and Safety in Health Care, 14*, 231–233.

Public Sector Commission. (2018). 2018 Employee Perception Survey explained. https://publicsector.wa.gov.au/sites/default/files/documents/2018_eps_explained.pdf

Queensland Government. (2019). Working for Queensland survey. https://www.forgov.qld.gov.au/working-queensland-survey

Schein, E. H. (2004). *Organizational culture and leadership*. Jossey-Bass.

Schein, E. H. (2006). So how can you assess your corporate culture. In J. V. Gallos (Ed.), *Organization development: A Jossey-Bass reader* (pp. 614–633). Jossey-Bass.

Scott, T., Mannion, R., Davies, H., & Marshall, M. (2003). The quantitative measurement of organizational culture in health care: A review of the available instruments. *Health Services Research, 38*(3), 923–945.

Sempane, M. E., Rieger, H. S., & Roodt, G. (2002). Job satisfaction in relation to Organisational culture. *The Journal of Individual Psychology, 28*(2), 23–30. https://doi.org/10.4102/sajip.v28i2.49

Sexton, J. B., Helmreich, R. L., Neilands, T. B., Rowan, K., Vella, K., Boyden, J., et al. (2006). The safety attitudes questionnaire: Psychometric properties, benchmarking data, and emerging research. *BMC Health Services Research, 6*(1), 44.

Shannon, E., Holden, J., & Van Dam, P. (2012). Implementing national health reform—Is organisational culture the key? In R. Eccleston, N. Safeman, & F. Gray (Eds.), *Australian political studies association conference, School of Government, University of Tasmania, 2012* (pp. 883–896). Australian Political Studies Association.

Simpson, D., Hamilton, S., McSherry, R., & McIntosh, R. (2019). Measuring and assessing healthcare Organisational culture in the England's National Health Service: A snapshot of current tools and tool use. *Healthcare, 7*(4). https://doi.org/10.3390/healthcare7040127

Sorra, J. S., & Dyer, N. (2010). Multilevel psychometric properties of the AHRQ hospital survey on patient safety culture. *BMC Health Services Research, 10*(1), 199.

St Vincent's Hospital Melbourne. (2018). St Vincent's Quality Account 2018.

Tasmanian Government. (2019). Employee Surveys. http://www.dpac.tas.gov.au/divisions/ssmo/Employee_Surveys

Tucker, R. W., McCoy, W. J., & Evans, L. C. (1990). Can questionnaires objectively assess organisational culture? *Journal of Managerial Psychology, 5*(4), 4–11.

Van den Berg, P. T., & Wilderom, C. P. (2004). Defining, measuring, and comparing organisational cultures. *Applied Psychology, 53*(4), 570–582.

Victorian Public Sector Commission. (2019). People Matter Survey. https://vpsc.vic.gov.au/data-and-research/people-matter-survey/

Wake, M., & Green, W. (2019). Relationship between employee engagement scores and service quality ratings: Analysis of the National Health Service staff survey across 97 acute NHS trusts in England and concurrent care quality commission outcomes (2012–2016). *BMJ Open, 9*(7), e026472. https://doi.org/10.1136/bmjopen-2018-026472

Weick, K. E., & Sutcliffe, K. M. (2003). Hospitals as cultures of entrapment: A re-analysis of the Bristol Royal Infirmary. *California Management Review, 45*(2), 73–84.

Yauch, C. A., & Steudel, H. J. (2003). Complementary use of qualitative and quantitative cultural assessment methods. *Organizational Research Methods, 6*(4), 465–481.

Part III

Organisational Leadership in Challenging Policy Contexts

10

Personal and Organisational Ambidexterity During Policy Turbulence: The Case of Long-Serving Chief Executives in the National Health Service in England

Naomi Chambers and Mark Exworthy

Background

Chief Executive Officers (CEOs) represent a unique category at the apex of the organisational hierarchy. There is a body of evidence about their work in the health sector (Blackler, 2006; Dargie, 1998, 2000; Learmonth, 2001). Dargie (2000), for example, points to evidence of how NHS CEOs are not able to monopolise control and have to flex their role to

N. Chambers
Alliance Manchester Business School, The University of Manchester, Manchester, UK
e-mail: naomi.chambers@manchester.ac.uk

M. Exworthy (✉)
Health Services Management Centre, University of Birmingham, Birmingham, UK
e-mail: m.exworthy@bham.ac.uk

R. Kislov et al. (eds.), *Managing Healthcare Organisations in Challenging Policy Contexts*, Organizational Behaviour in Healthcare,
https://doi.org/10.1007/978-3-030-81093-1_10

take into account particular configurations of influence and competing medical, political and managerial groups. Blackler (2006) found that these NHS leaders felt undermined and demoralised by the extent of 'interference' in their jobs. Learmonth (2001), by contrast, ironically analyses their narratives as conquering heroes. However, relatively little is known about the CEO paradox as it affects the minority of health care CEOs who are long-serving. The gap in evidence about this sub-sample of CEOs is especially pertinent in publicly funded health care systems where new public management (NPM) regimes have put increasing strain on staff through performance management and decentralisation (Hyde & Exworthy, 2016).

The era of NPM was premised on organisations becoming disaggregated from larger bureaucracies and the individual managers assuming greater autonomy in their roles. Organisations become 'free' to be managed and to compete, whilst managerial cadres were responsible for driving organisational performance and being held to account for it (Hyde & Exworthy, 2016). Throughout the chapter, we reflect on this dual perspective of organisations and individuals.

Moreover, CEOs can become vulnerable as the focal point for failings within organisations, especially those which are subject to media scrutiny. In the National Health Service (NHS) in England, although central records are not kept, the median tenure for substantive chief executives is reported to be three years and the mean is four years (Anandaciva et al., 2018). This rapid turnover then prompts the question: what keeps a small minority of CEOs in post for much longer than this? How does this subgroup of CEOs exercise their agency and manage the challenging policy imperatives?

Why Might Longevity in Management Be an Issue?

This chapter explores, for the first time, NHS CEOs who have held long periods of tenure. We frame the chapter in terms of the evolution of NPM and the anomaly that long-serving CEOs present. In addition, we consider organisational behaviours and strategic competencies on the one hand and CEOs' personal traits and actions on the other. We examine these concepts by drawing on data from an interview study of ten long-serving CEOs in the English NHS. We have chosen to separate the organisation and personal lens in this study to shine a light on, first, CEOs in context, and, second, their personal agency, and how these intersect.

Organisational Lens

Accounts of the evolution of NPM are numerous and detailed, with much attention devoted to managerial implications. However, there has been less on the apex of the organisation—the CEO. (Some NHS CEOs have written their own accounts; for example, Dunn, 2019; Rodrigues, 2018.)

Recent iterations of NPM have emphasised notions such as post-bureaucracy and decentred governance, among others. Pollitt (2009) argued that organisations were increasingly shedding their bureaucratic form and function in favour of post-bureaucracy:

> Post-bureaucratic organizations are supposed to be faster, more efficient, more flexible, more committed and more outward-looking. (p. 200)

This was associated with an increasingly rapid turnover of (senior) staff, a greater fluidity of organisational boundaries and a loss of organisational memory. In terms of workforce, the NPM policy of short-term contracts allied to performance management was intensified. CEOs of organisations newly formed from restructuring (another characteristic of NPM) often had little connection with the area that the organisation served or the organisational networks therein. Lack of organisational memory is problematic for strategic competence; here, taken as 'the ability of organisations … to acquire, store, recall, interpret and act upon information of relevance to the longer-term survival and well-being of the organisation' (Hodgkinson & Sparrow, 2002, pp. xiv–xv). Rapid turnover of managers and CEOs hampers such competence.

The implementation of NPM ideologies and policies has subsequently decentred the governance of organisations, internally and externally (Bevir & Waring, 2020). To balance competing imperatives, CEOs increasingly seek to flex their leadership behaviours. A repertoire for board-level roles has been proposed, including acting as conscience, sensor, diplomat, coach and shock absorber for the organisation. Senior leaders thus need to demonstrate behaviours which exhibit a mix of stewardship (service improvement), agency (holding to account), stakeholder (staff and patient engagement) and resource dependency (building and nurturing external relationships) (Chambers et al., 2019). Externally, organisations are increasingly operating within decentred networks, relying on mutuality and reciprocity to achieve individual and collective aims (Ferlie et al., 2013). In the English NHS, these have taken the form of clinical networks and, more recently, Sustainable and Transformation Plans/Partnerships/Programmes (STPs), Integrated Care Systems (ICSs) and Primary Care Networks (PCNs). (Voluntary organisations and community groups could also be added to the list.) The decentred networks have precipitated a plethora of organisations, some of which lack legislative foundation, not only adding to the existing array of inter-organisational relations but equally confusing and obfuscating lines of accountability (Checkland et al., 2013).

We argue that the multiple uncertainties brought about by recent incarnations of NPM shape and are shaped by CEOs behaviours and actions. However, there is little empirical evidence how, using an organisational *and* a personal lens, they go about this work. We now turn to focus on the personal lens.

Personal Lens

Whilst managerial cadres were present throughout the organisation, the CEO came to symbolise the NPM approach. The logic of NPM policy and practice entailed that senior staff would not remain in post indefinitely if performance dipped below acceptable levels. It, therefore, became commonplace in NHS organisations that CEOs would have time-limited contracts with specific performance indicators to meet (Kirkpatrick et al., 2017; Macfarlane et al., 2011). This promoted a short-term perspective to organisational change (Pettigrew et al., 1992). In England, the apogee of this regime was captured in the term 'targets and terror' (Bevan & Hood, 2006).

Hodgkinson and Sparrow (2002) make the case for strategic competence in the utilisation of information but also the balancing of analysis with creativity, intuition and flexibility. They also argue for leaders to exhibit a strong (though not excessive) internal locus of control, an attribute which Chambers et al. (2018) found to be the case in senior leaders in English hospitals. They were likely to have a greater quality and innovation outcomes orientation than those with an external locus of control, who attribute the fortunes of their organisation more to external agencies. This sense of an internal locus of control resonates with managers' political astuteness in terms of the skills, judgements and capabilities of leaders to understand and influence their informal 'political' environment, especially in the context of NPM policies. It also encompasses the ability to build coalitions, and bargain with other agents to achieve joint goals (Hartley et al., 2015; Clarke et al., 2021). Such astuteness is critical if CEOs are to maintain the balance between internal and external imperatives, and in order to perform and survive.

Practising leadership with such astuteness is possible only when leaders experience a sense of self-efficacy and feel able to deploy their personal discretionary effort. In healthcare organisations, this resilient leadership includes the ability to deliver emotionally responsive, patient-centred services, in the face of multi-level pressures (Arond-Thomas, 2004). Evidence from the NHS suggests that organisations which enjoy stability of leadership also demonstrate better performance; conversely, organisations in difficulty find it relatively more difficult to attract and retain suitably experienced CEOs. Furthermore, the 'CEO paradox' contrasts the need for stability (which longevity engenders) with the lack of conditions to create it, as generated by the dominant NPM paradigm. Longer tenure itself is not the goal *per se*, but it can be an enabler of more effective boards and organisations, notwithstanding the potential for the 'dark side of resilience' (Chamorro-Premuzic & Lusk, 2017) presenting itself as a consequence of strong leadership.

Given that longevity of CEOs in the English NHS runs counter to the dominant NPM narrative, we pose two main research questions. The first adopts an organisational lens: how do long-serving CEOs manage internal and external interests? The second adopts a personal lens: what contributes to the 'staying power' of these CEOs?

Methods

A maximum variety sample of NHS CEOs was identified from NHS websites and researchers' own networks. Our primary defining criterion was the definition of long-serving; here, taken to be ten years or longer (Table 10.1).

Table 10.1 CEO sample

Gender	Female	5
	Male	5
Clinical background	Clinical	2
	Non-clinical	8
Length of time as CEO (average of all 10 CEOs was 17 years)	10–15 years	1
	>15 years	9
Career as CEO	Single organisation	5
	Multiple organisation	5
Current organisation	Acute	6
	Community/mental health	2
	Joint acute/community	2
Care Quality Commission inspection rating (at the time of interview) of the organisation led by the CEO	Inadequate	0
	Requires improvement	2
	Good	5
	Outstanding	3

Having secured the appropriate research ethics exemptions and approval,[1] we wrote by email or letter, inviting 12 CEOs to take part and 10 accepted. A mutually convenient time and place for the interview was agreed. All took place in the CEO's office, except one which was undertaken by telephone. Interviews took place in spring 2019 and lasted between 60 and 100 minutes. We sought to maintain confidentiality and protected participants' identities by the use of pseudonyms.

Our interest in CEO careers and roles pointed towards a methodological approach which resembled the Wengraf's (2001) biographical life narrative interview method. Such interviews are detailed accounts of participants' career. As our interest was not simply their career, we also explored relevant behaviours and attitudes of the CEOs. Attention was also given to personal and organisational factors shaping their career and current role as well as any self-defined 'failure' or 'setbacks' (Macfarlane et al., 2011) resulting in an interview schedule, which covered career choices, talent pipelines, roles and relationships, and organisation and personal horizon scanning.

Interviews were audio-recorded in eight of the ten interviews; in one case, the recorder failed and for one phone interview, extensive contemporaneous notes were taken. All audio-recorded interviews were transcribed. Both researchers read all transcripts and contemporaneous notes repeatedly to achieve immersion in the data. The transcripts were analysed to identify issues and patterns, in relation to the organisation and the personal lens, and in connection to the two main research questions. These issues and patterns were then charted using the framework approach to develop interim themes across the ten interviews. The coherence of themes was checked and refined in the course of revisiting the transcripts. Differences between transcripts were discussed to refine the theme or to retain as a counter example. As interviews took place over a couple of months, we were able to partially undertake a process of abduction whereby initial analysis of transcripts revealed contradictions and

[1] Ethical approval for this study was granted by the University of Manchester Research Ethics Committee on 24/03/2019. Such approval concerned, for example, participant consent and anonymity in publications.

paradoxes which could be explored in subsequent interviews (Korica & Nicolini, 2016).

The method of a series of single interview carries limitations. First, there was no corroboration. As a small, unfunded study, it was not possible to triangulate the CEOs' accounts with other stakeholders and/or public documents. Interviewer experience and knowledge enabled some critical questioning but this was always likely to be partial. Second, some CEOs were adept at presenting specifically public accounts. Interviewing technique and longer interviews did start to reveal some private accounts but CEO availability limited the interview time in some cases. Moreover, Chatterjee and Hambrick (2007) suggest that narcissistic CEOs have particular influences upon organisational strategies. The sample of CEOs was, by definition, an elite group. For all these reasons, we were aware that a non-standard interview might be required. Dexter (2012) suggests that elite interviews need to allow 'space' for interviewees to reflect and to 'teach' the researcher what the problems, situations or solutions are. With limited time for reflection, such interviews can thus be cathartic for the interviewee.

Findings

We present the findings using two contrasting lens: the organisational and the personal. These lens intersect but, in doing so, cast light on different ways to understand and explain CEOs' longevity.

Organisational Lens

Our first research question concerned how these CEOs had managed to develop their organisation over a long period and establish a balance between the interest of their own institution and that of the wider system.

Phases

A consistent theme across all interviews was the evolution of the CEO's long tenure in terms of identifiable phases, that is time periods during their career in which different personal and professional priorities dominated. As long-serving CEOs, they had experienced a number of such phases. This was a key finding around CEO longevity of service. Sally divided her tenure into three-year periods: 'first you need to be listening and learning. Then you start doing'; these periods were followed by a merger with a neighbouring organisation. However, these phases prompted her to ask if she had something to offer for the next term. This also linked to phases in her personal development: heads down phase/imposter phase, 'normal' CEO phase and then 'people seeking your advice' phase.

These phases often coincided with the expansion of the organisation (in terms of staff and budgets). This growth meant that the initial span of control of the CEO was no longer possible; for example, services were now being delivered in multiple locations and contracts were held with numerous commissioners. One CEO explained her role initially combined another executive role too but now her organisation was multi-divisional:

> Each of those [three] divisions is the size of a small Trust—each is £200 million and two to three thousand staff … So each of those divisional teams is run by three people—a managing director, a nurse director and a medical director. (Christine)

These phases coincided with an expectation (espoused by senior NHS staff) that CEO tenure would last for only a limited period or that they should move to another post to gain experience of larger organisations. Many of our sample resisted this because they grew 'attached' to the organisation and each phase entailed new policy and organisational challenges.

> So there's definitely a link between my leadership and the organisation … it seems that I've found a link and it found a link with me, and I haven't really wanted to break it. (Sally)

> I thought I'd be here about five years, do a good job in a medium sized Trust… and then I'd go and be a chief exec in a London teaching hospital … you are made to feel that you are not making the right contribution if you stay too long. (Catriona)

A related consequence of longevity (and their age) was that some CEOs were less worried about their future career prospects. Some were close to retirement; some had children who had left home and were less of a financial responsibility. The intersection of personal and organisational lens was notable in the data.

> You couldn't do me much damage. The mortgage was paid off, the kids had got their property—that's my parenting days financially finished. (Don)

Board Relations

CEOs commonly spoke of the stability of their executive teams, upon which CEOs claimed to rely. CEOs' position, it seemed, required stability (and competency) of (at least some of) the executive team, as it underpinned CEOs' external activities. These seemed to be more important to the performance of the organisation than relations with their Chairs and Non-Executive Directors, which were occasionally fractious (Exworthy & Robinson, 2001). As Oscar put it:

> A diverse yet cohesive leadership unit is quite important. The diverse bit is important so that you can reduce the concept of groupthink, and you can get alternative views and opinions going. The cohesive bit is, [because] as a leadership group, we cast a shadow, and I don't mean shadow in a negative way, but people watch and observe what we do.

These tensions between diversity and cohesion and between stability and new executives were a common preoccupation for this sample. There was also a widespread recognition that stability of the executive team was vital to the effectiveness of the CEO:

> You can't do anything, you know, if the executive team's short term... and if you keep turning over executive teams, you get nowhere. (Don)

Yet, some also pointed to the need for renewed purpose associated with new appointments:

> If you've got a long-standing chief exec, some change at exec level is a good thing. So I've always enjoyed having a blend of long serving with new fresh ideas. (Catriona)

A strong theme of relations with executive directors was the role of the deputy CEO. Deputies were important given the growing size of many of these organisations. With many long-serving staff in this group, there was a high level of experience and competency which meant that many tasks could be delegated. The deputy was thus seen as a natural successor to the CEO.

> My deputy—it'll be 10 years in a couple of months' time ... I've needed a deputy who can step up, so he is like a first among equals. (Sally)
>
> So we've worked through a process that my deputy—it's a big role and he gets a sizeable pay hike because of ... that it part of the succession. (Felicity).

The effectiveness of this deputy role was evident during a period of absence by Felicity when the organisation continued to run smoothly.

External Relations

CEOs recognised the networked nature of their external role, as Oscar explained in his focus on making common cause:

> A key theme, certainly in my tenure as being a chief executive, has been about collaboration both inside and outside the organisation.

By contrast, Sally described her role 'to put up an umbrella over the organisation'. External relations comprised a significant part of the CEO whilst internal affairs were often the remit of the Deputy, Chief Operating Officer or similar. All CEOs recognised that managing local networks took significant efforts and the task was often problematic.

> I think some of the hardest challenges are political relationships and dispersed power challenges. (Christine)

Many CEOs have complained that they invariably looked 'upwards' to central authorities (NHS England and the Department of Health) (Exworthy et al., 2002). According to this atypical sample, these power relations were less threatening because they had learnt how to cope with such pressures and/or had high levels of political astuteness.

> I've only been able to deploy the organisation to best effect in more recent, probably the last five years. So the first ten years felt… we were fighting all the time to tick boxes. (Felicity)

> Nobody bothers me … because our performance is really good. (Don)

However, some (including those managing less well-performing organisations) emphasised the importance of maintaining positive and courteous relationships with the regulatory bodies.

A consequence of their longevity was that several interviewees had been invited to play national roles in shaping policy reform or leading wider organisational change. Some of our sample was thus seen as 'safe pairs of hands' to lead these national programmes, in the knowledge that their 'host' organisation was already well managed and could tolerate their absence for an extended period (as much as 50% of their time for three years). Their justification for taking the role was precisely because they too had stability among their executive colleagues.

> And the reason I could take on my national role as well as the chief exec role is precisely because not only have I got a really longstanding and rather excellent set of executive directors. (Christine)

Some had taken up national roles earlier in their career and felt that this had been of huge benefit in preparing them for their subsequent and current CEO positions:

> Doing both national and local really enhances the CEO role. The ability to pick up the phone—a live line for steering and influencing. (Jane)

Oscar sounded a warning note, however, about circumstances when the national role can take over to the detriment of the day job:

> There are some colleagues that I've seen, where being on that national stage has become their job. Whereas I would always comment that everything that I would do nationally, I would always want to be able to relate that back to an individual that lives in the catchment area that I serve, or a member of the group of colleagues that I work with.

Personal Lens

Our second research question was concerned with the agency of CEOS in revealing how these CEOs developed and maintained their personal 'staying power' to carry on. All CEOs demonstrated the ability to reinvent themselves, in order 'to adapt to change, to different environments, different contexts' (Oscar).

CEO Identification with Organisation and the NHS

The CEOs' backgrounds were varied, including managers with clinical qualifications (2), those who had been graduate management trainees (3), those who had previous careers outside the NHS (3) and those who had come up from the first rung of the organisation (2).

Some, but not all, described strong ideological motivations at the start of their careers to work in the public or welfare sector, a continuing close identification with the mission of the NHS, and later, a love of their own organisation. For example, Miles was 'hell bent on wanting to change the world'. Matthew's story also illustrates this well:

> Because I was motivated, in those days I was quite left wing, and therefore I wanted to work in the public sector.

Matthew goes on to describe a continuing intoxication, over 30 years since he first joined the NHS, coupled with an intense dissatisfaction with the current situation: 'I am part of lots of rubbish decisions'.

The identification between the individual and organisation was frequently strong. Christine confessed that she would find it hard to leave her post:

> I've been here 20 years so it's almost perhaps painful to think of not being here … I'm so happy here that they could carry me out in a box.

Likewise, Sally talked about being 'the head of a family … it's a big thing to try and pick another family and will that group of people allow you to be the head of their family?' These statements are of strong, intimate relations between the person and the organisation. Clearly, these are positive expressions which need to be contrasted with possible malign effects of longevity and their accounts of career setbacks.

The CEO's mission was also expressed in ways which reflected their longevity and the embodiment of their role as strategic leaders. For example, Miles discussed the importance of setting long-term goals that resonated with staff and patients, and not to be too distracted by operational matters. Each had a distinct guiding leadership philosophy, as Matthew, who had moved a number of times as CEO, explained:

> I do not believe in the heroic leadership model … And when I came here [as CEO 3 years ago] … I met with about 30-odd staff, on a one-to-one, asking them what they thought my priorities should be. Everybody mentioned culture.

Oscar described how his leadership style had evolved over time:

> I've evolved, I think, I've got a much more natural and broader passion for people. You know, if you were describing me in those days [early days of being a CEO], I think I might have had a concept of the sort of heroic

> leadership model, and I think today I would class myself more as the servant leader type model.

These CEOs had distinctive leadership styles but in common was a belief in collective leadership. Whilst this was also highlighted by the reliance on senior managers, this was not restricted to board members.

Personal Resilience

In some respects, the sample of CEOs displayed a *de facto* level of resilience by virtue of their longevity. Their tenure was marked by tortuous changes in government health policy and the recent period of economic austerity.

Most of the interviewees referred to having high levels of energy:

> I'm high energy, I've always worked hard … from a good working class stock … but they are punishing hours. (Christine)

> One of my strengths is that I'm hugely resilient and I get a buzz from the direct impact on people of my hospital job. (Catriona)

Personal resilience became a touchstone during periods of rapid organisational and policy change:

> I think at any one time in the organisation, there's a great deal of flux and change. So I feel it's my job to offer some anchor points without becoming stale, an old fossil. (Christine)

Similarly, several spoke to the relatively rapid turnover of their CEO colleagues elsewhere and yet, they could offer long-term commitment to the organisation. This was sometimes compared with senior doctors who might work in the same organisations for 30 or 40 years.

> If you take this organisation, the majority of people work here a lifetime… the people that you need to lead, you know, in the main, in the consultant body, they will come and give their life to a career. And if you've got Chief

> Executives [coming and going], that's what they see … they're not committed to us, they're not committed to what we're trying to do, why should I trust them? (Sally)

Some, but not all, interviewees were guarded about sharing stories of managing setbacks and failures. Matthew was candid and sanguine in mentioning that at times in his current job that he has been 'extremely anxious'.

> I have been fortunate, because I've applied for [tens of] jobs and not been given them, and so that's been good because I've always ended up in jobs that seem to have gone well for me. So, one of the questions, I think, is you know, have I had any sticky patches in my career?

Unable to obtain a 'unit general manager' job in an acute hospital, Matthew ended up taking the equivalent post in a mental health organisation. He subsequently had over two decades as a CEO working in mental health and learning disability services. By contrast, Jane described how she has grown and developed in her CEO role, and shared her personal mantra for tackling successive setbacks:

> I've lightened up. I was very intense. I was very ambitious. I have fun now. I went through pain barriers. I can be who I am. Fake it 'til you make it, until you convince yourself it's not about me, and moving on.

Regrets did not largely feature, although one (Sally) said that they wished they could turn the clock back and 'do' an organisational merger differently. Another gave the following piece of advice for a new CEO, which was drawn from personal experience:

> If you find yourself setting the alarm earlier and earlier, not sleeping, and obsessing, you know it's time to talk to a trusted colleague. (Christine)

Oscar described the feelings of being in the 'eye of the storm', during a crisis:

> There's a real importance that you, first of all, understand how you're feeling about something, and not being afraid to talk to others about how you're feeling.

Good luck as well as good judgement was mentioned in how, sometimes, the CEOs came through the difficult times; the terms 'luck' or 'lucky' were mentioned 28 times across the ten interviews. James, for example, mentioned how 'the storm [i.e. the specific problematic incident that nearly cost him his job] had moved on'. Also, Miles mentioned the importance of not taking failures personally, and instead enquiring and reflecting on the causes of the setbacks. Yet, while citing 'luck' may be self-effacing of our interviewees, Weber reminds us that 'good fortune' also needs to be seen as legitimate and deserved (Whimster, 2004).

The CEOs recognised their own personal emotional reactions to problematic moments in their tenure, and the importance of moving from unproductive ruminating to problem-solving. They often managed this with the help of a wider, external network of colleagues and mentors. Clearly, a 'selective' long-term memory about the more negative experiences could be a form of *post hoc* rationalisation.

Personal Development

Half of our interviewees had stayed at the same trust and the other half had been CEOs elsewhere:

> I move because of variety in terms of culture, learning, finances and ways of learning. I like new challenges and variety of the politics. (Jane)

A few of the interviewees had attended senior leadership programmes or obtained higher degrees in later life (e.g. MBA or doctorate) in pursuit of formal learning. Others talked about learning from others and from extensive private reading. A final group said that the job itself provided the opportunity for continuous personal development and learning.

The CEOs frequently cited their need for and use of coaching and mentoring. Coaching was mentioned 20 times (by 7 of the 10 interviews) and mentoring 33 times (by 8 CEOs).

> I have a long term coach and I feel very safe with [them]. (Felicity)
>
> I had a close relationship with a chief executive, which actually has been important throughout my career in having a mentor who's been able to teach me. (Catriona)

There was a good deal of reciprocity for these CEOs in being the mentor for others in the NHS; sometimes, these were other (newer) CEOs, but often they were middle managers.

For those CEOs who did not have a coach, they had, nonetheless, on occasion, engaged a mentor or senior experienced colleagues during a crisis. For example, although Christine claimed that she was 'not a great one for mentoring or coaching personally', she did, however, recognise its contribution:

> There were things that we did then that still influence me now. It was great. But I think as Chief Exec, doing the job has mainly been my development. We so never stood still. That to be honest, it does just feel like I've never stopped learning. (Christine)

Many (but not all) were members of institution-based networks, such as the Cavendish Square Group and Shelford Group. A smaller number remarked that they were not natural networkers, although they learnt from particular mentors, sometimes from outside the NHS.

Discussion

The interviewees revealed various ways in which these CEOs developed and maintained their personal resilience and development. Underpinning their various strategies was a consciousness of needing to attend to 'preventive maintenance' of their leadership—an appreciation of fostering their own identity, skills, career and also personal well-being. This inward-looking reflexivity was mirrored by the strategic competence they articulated in working as a leader of systems and networks as well as a leader of their own institution. The findings add to the literature on CEOs by shining a spotlight on leadership practices (which contribute to CEO survival) and the contemporary praxis of post-NPM/post-bureaucracy.

Organisational Lens

It was notable that three out of the five CEOs who had remained long-serving in the same organisation had presided over significant growth over time through mergers and acquisitions. The other two CEOs who had stayed in the same place had invested in their organisations by building the global 'brand' of their very specialist service or by improving the fortunes of a district general hospital. Their behaviours reflect the managerialisation of the NHS through the NPM tenets of performance management and improvement, and more recently, decentred governance.

Amongst these CEOs, there were many examples of the repertoire of roles of board-level leaders (Chambers et al., 2019), including conscience (close alignment with the mission of patient care), coach (restless for quality improvement), ambassador (building the 'brand'), sensor (knowing the organisation's performance from board to ward) and shock absorber ('putting an umbrella up') for the organisation. By contrast, a stated focus on efficiencies, value for money and cost control was generally absent from the discourse.

The CEOs viewed the NHS as a decentred networked system within the shadow of a strong central hierarchy (Heritier & Lehmkuhl, 2008); this balanced policy imperatives with a (sometimes fierce) loyalty to their own organisation. This was evident, for example, in taking on external (often, national) roles or managing the external environment compared to the internal focus on their deputy. Thus, CEOs embodied the tenets of NPM at the apex of the organisations, sometimes blurring the boundary between person and the organisation. Despite some delegation to their deputies, they were also the repositories of the organisational memory (either of their organisation or of the NHS collectively), seemingly contrary to aspects of post-bureaucratic narrative. In this respect, they were anomalies in the NHS. The stability of some of their senior managers and the emergent emphasis on health systems supported this notion. However, repeated re-organisations (internally and externally) counteracted this.

Personal Lens

The dominant themes included a high level of reflexivity amongst CEOs, implying their ability to examine their feelings, motives and subsequent actions. There was also generally a positive mind-set; significant setbacks were seen either as opportunities or as problems to be solved, rather than worrisome. There was a consciousness of the value of support from senior trusted colleagues, from peer networks and from continuously learning. Underpinning this was a level of self-confidence from having over many years carved out a distinctive personal leadership model, a way of being, acting and performing as the CEO.

The leadership approach of these CEOs resonated with notions of decentred governance; namely, their espoused behaviours exhibited a mix of stewardship (service improvement), agency (holding to account), stakeholder (staff and patient engagement) and resource dependency (building and nurturing external relationships) (Denis & Van Gestel, 2015). They demonstrated behaviours that combined strategic competence and political astuteness (Clarke et al., 2021). They displayed a high internal locus of control whilst signalling respecting their position vis-à-vis national and local stakeholders. We argue that this equates to an advanced form of organisation ambidexterity, in which the ability to balance current and future personal needs intersects with the internal and external risks associated with the organisation. This also speaks to Hodgkinson and Sparrow's (2002) view of the need to generate knowledge through innovation, creativity and exploitation of available information.

Regarding political astuteness, we noted the adroitness with which all the CEOs had shaped their personal narrative, seemingly as much for their own personal sense-making, as for our benefit as researchers (Parry,

2003). This burnishing of their story into a coherent, credible and compelling narrative inevitably meant the foregrounding, to themselves and to others, of some elements and the omission of others. This could potentially develop into a level of self-belief, self-confidence and complacency that connects with the darker side of resilience. Coupled with a love of the job that could turn addictive, these are some warning signs to which some CEOs themselves alluded.

Implications for Healthcare Managers and Leaders

Whilst this study does not resolve the CEO paradox, it does offer new perspectives which help elaborate it in the contemporary NHS. The NPM-style conditions which have perhaps undermined the likelihood of long-term CEOs may have transformed into a more decentred, networked form, while some of the centralising tendencies remain. Clearly, this atypical sample has navigated a career as a CEO which has balanced organisational imperatives with personal competencies and motivations. To explain this, we argue NHS CEOs with longevity may be able to enact an advanced form of personal and organisation ambidexterity, balancing personal resilience whilst addressing policy imperatives. On the former, the characteristics of this duality include having clear long-term organisational ambitions whilst maintaining managerial oversight within and beyond the walls of the institution. This balance was achieved with high levels of stability and appropriate changes in their management team, and building strong local and national relationships. These all contribute to advanced strategic competence and political astuteness, and support the conditions for maintaining personal resilience, which included high energy and continued enthusiasm for the job. Supporting new and not so new CEOs to develop organisational ambidexterity, personal resilience and strategic competence allied to effective system leadership would be a worthy priority for those with responsibility for nurturing and safeguarding top talent.

Our findings will remain pertinent for putative long-serving CEOs in healthcare, who will be operating in a policy climate which will be even more turbulent in the post-COVID-19 period. First, they need to retain a focus on patients, staff and communities, whilst navigating the external system and developing collegial relations with partners and stakeholders. Second, they need to establish a highly skilled and stable senior leadership team, with appropriate delegation to deputies. Third, they need to secure help and support, and especially when experiencing unhelpful levels of stress. Finally, they need to be self-reflexive, learning from setbacks. Such findings have implications for training, recruitment, career development, performance management and national policy.

The study also indicates that NHS system leaders would do well to resist the temptation to encourage successful CEOs to move necessarily on to new roles (whether or not the organisation is performing well), and where their personal inclination and preference is to stay put to shape and develop the services provided by their organisation in the long term.

Conclusions

This study explored how some CEOs in the NHS in England reinvented their organisation and themselves over their long tenure as CEO, using the conceptual lens of post-bureaucracy and decentred governance (among others). There were some unexpected features of this study which prompts a refinement of the conceptual lens. We were struck by the variety of their backgrounds and career trajectories. There was no one archetypal long-serving NHS CEO. We also considered what these CEOs chose not to discuss. On the organisation side, these included not much on current national health policies, nor cost control, value for money and efficiencies (cornerstones of NPM). This suggests to us that, to ensure their own survival, they had constructed their own personal accounts, which incorporated organisation ambidexterity, combined with a degree of personal policy entrepreneurship, which led to a feeling of not being overly constrained by others.

On the personal side, there was little mention of any mental health or family problems, experienced or overcome. There could be a number of reasons for this (in addition to the research interview conducted by a stranger). All were highly politically astute (unsurprising given an average of 17 years as CEO), highlighting their skill in negotiating and navigating internal and external exigencies. Given these strategic competences, it is remarkable that they also lived very 'in the moment', neither ruminating much about the past nor particularly focused on their personal future, say, over the next five years. This may be an important resilience mechanism for people doing these very difficult jobs.

This study can conclude that the CEO paradox, as applied here, was not so much about the conditions (precipitating short-termism) or even the need for stability, but rather about the intersection of organisational and personal trajectories. These trajectories thus shaped and were shaped by both organisational change and personal career paths. As such, they may not simply offer generalisation to *all* organisations and *all* CEOs, but may offer insights into the practice and impact of an increasingly post-bureaucratic and decentred NHS.

Future research should probe into the following areas: first, a more granular understanding of notions of organisation ambidexterity for CEOs in the healthcare setting, and framing that in relation to theorising about post-NPM and decentred governance; second, more detailed insights into the CEO as organisation coach, that is restless for change and improvement; third, exploration of the potentially more ruthless or dysfunctional aspects of being a longstanding CEO to understand better the continuum between staying power and hubristic behaviour; and, fourth, identification of an arc for leadership maturity by comparing the stories of experienced NHS CEOs with those who are new incumbents.

Acknowledgements We are extremely grateful to the Chief Executives who freely gave their time to be interviewed for this study. The study received no external funding.

References

Anandaciva, S., Ward, D., Randhawa, M., & Edge, R. (2018). *Leadership in today's NHS*. Kings Fund.

Arond-Thomas, M. (2004). Resilient leadership for challenging times. *Physician Executive, 30*(4), 18–21.

Bevan, G., & Hood, C. (2006). What's measured is what matters: Targets and gaming in the English public health care system. *Public Administration, 84*(3), 517–538.

Bevir, M., & Waring, J. (2020). *Decentring health and care networks: Re-shaping the organization and delivery of healthcare*. Palgrave Macmillan.

Blackler, F. (2006). Chief executives and the modernisation of the English National Health Service. *Leadership, 2*(1), 5–30.

Chambers, N., Proudlove, N., Smith, J., Thorlby, R., Kendrick, H., & Mannion, R. (2019). Roles and behaviours of diligent and dynamic healthcare boards. *Health Services Management Research*. https://doi.org/10.1177/0951484819887507

Chambers, N., Thorlby, R., Boyd, A., Smith, J., Proudlove, N., Kendrick, H., & Mannion, R. (2018). *Responses to Francis: Changes in board leadership and governance in acute hospitals in England since 2013*. Manchester: University of Manchester. http://www.research.mbs.ac.uk/hsrc/Portals/0/Docs/responses-to-francis-report.pdf

Chamorro-Premuzic, T., & Lusk, D. (2017, August 16). The dark side of resilience. *Harvard Business Review*. https://hbr.org/2017/08/the-dark-side-of-resilience

Chatterjee, A., & Hambrick, D. C. (2007). It's all about me: Narcissistic Chief Executive Officers and their effects on company strategy and performance. *Administrative Science Quarterly, 52*(3), 351–386.

Checkland, K., Allen, P., Coleman, A., et al. (2013). Accountable to whom, for what? An exploration of the early development of Clinical Commissioning Groups in the English NHS. *BMJ Open, 13*, 3. https://bmjopen.bmj.com/content/3/12/e003769.citation-tools

Clarke, J., Waring, J., Bishop, S., Hartley, J., Exworthy, M., Fulop, N., Ramsay, A., & Roe, B. (2021). The contribution of political skill to the implementation of health services change: A systematic narrative and narrative synthesis. *BMC Health Services Research, 21*, 260.

Dargie, C. (1998). The role of public sector chief executives. *Public Administration, 76*(1), 161–177.

Dargie, C. (2000). Observing chief executives: Analysing behaviour to explore cross-sectoral differences. *Public Money and Management, 20*(3), 39–44.

Denis, J. L., & Van Gestel, N. (2015). Leadership and innovation in healthcare governance. Chap. 72 in E. Kuhlmann, R. H. Blank, I. L. Bourgeault, & C. Wendt (Eds.), *The Palgrave international handbook of healthcare policy and governance* (pp. 425–440). Palgrave Macmillan.

Dexter, L. A. (2012). *Elite and specialized interviewing*. ECPR Press.

Dunn, S. (2019). *An NHS baptism of fire: My first years as an NHS chief executive*. E-book.

Exworthy, M., Berney, L., & Powell, M. (2002). 'How great expectations in Westminster may be dashed locally': The local implementation of national policy on health inequalities. *Policy and Politics, 30*(1), 79–96.

Exworthy, M., & Robinson, R. (2001). Two at the top: Relations between chairs and chief executives in the NHS. *Health Services Management Research, 14*, 82–91.

Ferlie, E., Fitzgerald, L., McGivern, G., Dopson, S., & Bennett, C. (2013). *Making wicked problems governable? The case of managed networks in health care*. Oxford University Press.

Hartley, J., Alford, J., Hughes, O., & Yates, S. (2015). Public value and political astuteness in the work of public managers: The art of the possible. *Public Administration, 93*(1), 195–211.

Heritier, A., & Lehmkuhl, D. (2008). The shadow of hierarchy and new modes of governance. *Journal of Public Policy, 28*, 1–17.

Hodgkinson, G., & Sparrow, P. (2002). *The Competent Organisation: A Psychological Analysis of the Strategic Management Process*. Milton Keynes: Open University Press.

Hyde, P., & Exworthy, M. (2016). Setting the workers free? Managers in the (once again) reformed NHS. Chap. 23 in M. Exworthy, R. Mannion, & M. Powell (Eds.), *Dismantling the NHS? Evaluating the impact of health reforms* (pp. 257–278). Policy Press.

Kirkpatrick, I., Vallascas, F., & Veronesi, G. (2017). Business experts on public sector boards: What do they contribute? *Public Administration Review, 77*(5), 754–765.

Korica, M., & Nicolini, D. (2016). Objects and monitoring practices: Understanding CEOs' information work as mundane accomplishment. In J. Swan, S. Newell, & D. Nicolini (Eds.), *Mobilising knowledge in healthcare: Challenges for management and organization* (pp. 41–60). Oxford University Press.

Learmonth, M. (2001). NHS Trust chief executives as heroes. *Health Care Analysis, 9*, 417–436.

Macfarlane, F., Exworthy, M., Greenhalgh, T., & Willmott, M. (2011). Plus ça change, plus c'est la même chose: Senior NHS managers' narratives of restructuring. *Sociology of Health and Illness, 33*(6), 914–929.

Parry, J. (2003). Making sense of executive sense-making: A phenomenological case study with methodological criticism. *Journal of Health Organisation and Management, 17*(4), 240–263.

Pettigrew, A., et al. (1992). *Shaping strategic change*. Sage.

Pollitt, C. (2009). Bureaucracies remember, post-bureaucratic organizations forget. *Public Administration, 87*(2), 198–218.

Rodrigues, L. (2018). *Being an NHS chief executive: What they never told me*. Laughton Press.

Wengraf, T. (2001). *Qualitative research interviewing: Biographic narrative and semi-structured methods*. Sage.

Whimster, S. (Ed.). (2004). *The essential Weber: A reader*. Routledge.

11

Reframing Healthcare Leadership: From Individualism to Leadership as Collective Practice

Katie Willocks and Simon Moralee

The Evolution of Leadership in Healthcare

The English National Health Service (NHS) has a long history of initiatives aimed at improving care delivery. Leadership is often considered one of the key ways in which such improvements occur. Traditional leadership models and theories have been dominated by the perspective that leadership is enacted by an individual leader who has a distinct set of traits and competencies (Pearce and Manz 2005). The GLOBE 'universal' definition of leadership (House et al. 2002, p.5) captures this as 'the ability to influence, motivate, and enable others to contribute towards the

K. Willocks
Manchester Metropolitan University, Manchester, UK
e-mail: k.willocks@mmu.ac.uk

S. Moralee (✉)
Alliance Manchester Business School, The University of Manchester, Manchester, UK
e-mail: simon.moralee@manchester.ac.uk

R. Kislov et al. (eds.), *Managing Healthcare Organisations in Challenging Policy Contexts*, Organizational Behaviour in Healthcare,
https://doi.org/10.1007/978-3-030-81093-1_11

effectiveness and success of the organization of which they are members'. This top-down understanding of leadership is frequently referred to as the tripod ontology, conceptualising leadership as being comprised of three distinct elements: leader(s), followers and a shared goal that they are working to accomplish together. The majority of leadership theory is built on this three-pronged approach (Drath et al. 2008).

However, within the field of leadership studies, over the last ten years there has been a significant shift in how leadership is conceptualised. As a consequence of growing concern with the tripod ontology and more 'individualistic' leadership approaches, there is an emerging movement towards seeing leadership as a collaborative process, one that is co-constructed by multiple organisational actors. This newer way of thinking about leadership has been termed 'post-heroic' and is used to depict leadership that is more collaborative, collective-in-nature and accomplished through shared practices, interactions and relationships (Crevani et al. 2010, Fletcher 2004, Uhl-Bien 2006). As a result, leadership development and training within the NHS has broadened from a focus on individuals to now encompass groups, teams, organisations and systems (West et al. 2015).[1]

This shift has also been enabled by a number of policy changes. Over the past decade, there have been a range of changes and initiatives that have influenced the way in which healthcare is organised. This includes a move towards more integrated care initiatives and partnership working between NHS organisations, local authorities and third sector organisations (NHS England 2014). Through these arrangements, hospitals are much more connected with community groups, GP practices and primary care organisations, in order to provide care that is focussed on the specific needs of a particular local population. Further policy drivers that are relevant for leadership have included the shift from competition to collaboration in order to meet the needs of increasingly complex, diverse and multifaceted patient needs, all broadly connected to the NHS Long

[1] Much of this has come about as a result of the Francis Inquiry (2013) into care at Mid Staffordshire NHS Foundation Trust, which placed importance on the need for better, more inclusive and effective leadership given its conclusion of 'a dangerous culture and weak leadership' (King's Fund 2013, p.3) at the Trust.

Term Plan (NHS England 2019), which talks about the integration of services and improvements to care quality (Alderwick et al. 2019).

In the context of such policy developments, models of leadership that place an emphasis on shared practices, collaboration and joint decision making are being taken much more seriously (West et al. 2015, Willcocks and Wibberley 2015). Current leadership development approaches in the NHS have also adopted a shared/collective leadership approach with work by Storey and Holti (2013), leading to the creation of a revised behavioural healthcare leadership model. In addition, to address anticipated failings in leadership highlighted by the now-published Francis Inquiry into Mid Staffordshire NHS Foundation Trust, the NHS established a leadership academy in 2012. It was tasked with transforming healthcare culture and services by professionalising leadership and creating a more strategic approach to the development of talent across the NHS (NHS Leadership Academy [NHSLA] 2012a). In doing so, leadership development would potentially be enhanced and embedded nationally through a combined individual-team-organisation-system approach (NHSLA 2012b).

In policy literature itself, there has been much discussion and reference to the importance of developing leadership capacity across the NHS for employees at all levels of the organisational hierarchy and not just those with managerial responsibilities (NHSLA 2012b). Willcocks and Wibberley (2015) explain that one notable policy shift here involves a move towards wider stakeholders, such as doctors, being involved in leadership regardless of position. Indeed, the latter half of the twentieth century saw the emergence of a number of policy initiatives aimed at involving doctors much more systematically in the management and leadership of health services (*Cogwheel Report*, Ministry of Health 1967, *Griffiths Report*, Department of Health and Social Security 1983).

This continued into the twenty-first century, with the profession's regulator, the General Medical Council (1993, 2003, 2009) (GMC), publishing various iterations of *Tomorrow's Doctors*, its framework for the requirements of the practising doctor, which outlined not only a requirement for knowledge and understanding of organisational, medico-legal, ethical and financial issues, but also guidance relating to more 'managerial' and leadership aspects of healthcare provision, such as risk management and quality improvement. Calls for increased clinical leadership continued to follow (Royal College of Physicians 2005, Department of Health 2008, Academy of Medical Royal Colleges [AoMRC] and NHS Institute for Innovation and Improvement [NHSI] 2010, NHSLA 2011, GMC 2012), supported by evidence that the level of engagement of an organisation with medical leaders correlated with improved outcome measures including organisational performance (National Institute for Health Research 2013, Veronesi et al. 2014, West et al. 2015).

Set against this wider context, our study explores the case for practices of healthcare leadership to shift from an individual to a collective focus through the following research question: *How do collective notions of leadership support the development of leadership practices in healthcare management and leadership?* In the following section we introduce one potentially useful approach for conceptualising such changes in terms of NHS leadership. The approach we introduce is referred to as 'leadership-as-practice' (LAP) (Carroll et al. 2008, Crevani et al. 2010, Raelin 2007).

Leadership-as-Practice

LAP has been described as a 'new movement' in leadership research and is concerned with the idea that leadership emerges in the ongoing flow of organisational practices (Crevani et al. 2010, Raelin 2017). LAP has its origins in social practice theory, which takes the view that social phenomena are constituted by practices, or practical orderings comprised of human, material and symbolic elements (Nicolini 2012, Reckwitz 2002, Schatzki et al. 2001). LAP theory targets leadership that emerges within the flow of those aforementioned social practices. The focus is not on the role and actions of an individual leader but on the 'unheroic work of ordinary strategic practitioners in their day-to-day routines' (Whittington 1996, p.734). In line with post-heroic ideals, LAP is typically collective-in-nature, having a strong discursive, interactional and relational component as practitioners connect with one another to accomplish leadership (Bolden et al. 2008, Chia and Holt 2006).

LAP scholars have also highlighted the important role of context and history in informing how leadership takes form in shared practices (Hunt and Dodge 2000, Kempster and Gregory 2017). LAP has been expounded as an especially useful ontology for conceptualising more collective and processual forms of leadership and is a fruitful area for future research (Carroll et al. 2008, Crevani et al. 2010, Kempster and Gregory 2017). At present, however, there are few documented empirical examples of leadership-as-practice, especially in healthcare work and there have been calls for more research that offers insight into leadership processes that unfold in the 'nitty-gritty' of everyday organisational life.

Our analysis builds upon a qualitative case study exploring a national policy initiative aiming to introduce change within UK medical curricula. Specifically, it offers insight into seven different leadership activities that comprise leadership-as-practice (Raelin 2016), which are outlined in Table 11.1. We show that whilst there are a multiplicity of examples of

Table 11.1 The seven co-constructed activities of leadership-as-practice (summarised from Raelin, 2016)

1. Scanning	Identifying resources, such as information or technology, that can contribute to new or existing programmes through simplification or sensemaking
2. Signalling	Mobilising and catalysing the attention of others to a programme or project through such means as imitating, building on, modifying, ordering or synthesising prior or existing elements
3. Weaving	Creating webs of interaction across existing and new networks by building trust between individuals and units or by creating shared meanings to particular views or cognitive frames
4. Stabilising	Offering feedback to converge activity and evaluate effectiveness, leading, in turn, to structural and behavioural changes and learning
5. Inviting	Encouraging those who have held back to participate through their ideas, their energy, and their humanity
6. Unleashing	Making sure that everyone who wishes to has had a chance to contribute, without fear of repercussion, even if their contribution might create discrepancy or ambiguity in the face of decision-making convergence
7. Reflecting	Triggering thoughtfulness within the self and with others to ponder the meaning of past, current, and future experience to learn how to meet mutual needs and interests

each of what Raelin termed the seven distinct 'activities',[2] at times the boundaries between these are somewhat blurred. Moreover, bringing to the fore the important role of context, culture and history in emergent collective leadership, our analysis reveals the messy, contradiction- and tension-imbued nature of such processes, which are bound up in the policy context described above.

Case and Method

This study explored micro-level practices in effecting change in UK medical education. In the 2000s, a national change initiative took place with the purpose of promoting greater leadership and management within multiple specialist medical curricula, with the ultimate aim of helping to create organisational cultures to improve services for patients across the UK (NHSI, 2010). This was intended to span all levels of medical training and was undertaken collaboratively by senior NHS stakeholders and representative organisations and associations of the medical profession.

Embracing a 'naturalistic design' (Lincoln and Guba 1985) as part of a qualitative research strategy and informed by Hiles' (1999) model of disciplined inquiry, an exploratory case study approach was adopted. Hartley (2004) considers such an approach informed 'to understand how the organizational and environmental context is having an impact on or influencing social processes' (Hartley 2004, p.325) supporting the relevance of its use in such a context.

The second author (SM) had previously explored leadership in healthcare as part of earlier research and through this gained access to the participants who conceived, designed, managed and oversaw the implementation and development of this national policy initiative.[3] We

[2] In much of the literature on practice approaches, different authors use the terms 'practice' and 'activity' interchangeably. In our study we use the term 'practice' when descripting an overall leadership approach or leadership in a more general sense. We align with Raelin's use of the term 'activity' to describe specific leadership undertakings within practice more generally.

[3] The study was bound by the Economic and Social Research Council (ESRC) Research Ethics Framework and received ethical approval from De Montfort University at the time of formal registration and acceptance onto the second author's doctoral programme in June 2011.

conducted semi-structured interviews (lasting approximately 60 minutes) with 22 members of the initiative's project team and steering group, including 13 managers and 9 doctors. By focussing on these two groups, accounts, stories and histories could be compared, notably around the impact of the project on how change was practised. Research participants were interviewed in 2012 after the project had ended and no longer had continuous ties to the initiative in question, although many did maintain existing links to the newly formed NHS Leadership Academy.[4] This study also employed analysis of historical documents. The use of documentation in case study research can offer rich, alternative insights into events that occurred as part of the case under examination (Hartley 2004). We analysed 906 pages of project plans, minutes and reports, which offered alternative explanations of the stories and narratives that arose from interviews to help in confirming or contrasting the various accounts of how the change was enacted.

However, one methodological limitation of our study is a lack of observational data, given access to the project and its participants came retrospectively. Whilst prospective data collection, allowing for observation to take place, can help strengthen any methodological approach, the diverse accounts collected via interviews, along with the documentary analysis undertaken, provided sufficient corroboration on their own, whilst acknowledging that any qualitative interpretive approach will only ever offer a version of the 'truth' (Bryman, 2008).

The case study employed thematic analysis, with interviews audio-recorded. Following transcription and entry into NVivo 10 (QSR International 2012), key concepts were identified and coded (Barbour 2008) by the second author (SM). 'Provisional coding' occurred, which involved an openness to new codes potentially emerging, in the context of evolving theoretical assumptions (Layder 1998, p. 55). The process of provisional and then open coding was abductive (Cunliffe, 2011), with

[4] Interviews covered the following topics: job role; self/others' involvement; people not involved/not invited; motivation for involvement; practices, actions, activities they undertook; approaches to role: self/others; role/position in relation to organisation's role; key relationships: people, organisations; typicality (or not) of groups; particular/notable/memorable incidents, for example tensions, agreements, tipping points; the resulting outcome; outcomes relevant to the participant/unofficial outcomes, that is, benefits, legacies, and so on; impact without participant/organisation's involvement; current developments/latest thoughts.

leadership and organisational theories, including notably Raelin's (2016) seven categories, the main source of a priori coding. As analysis of the transcripts progressed, in vivo/in situ codes were developed in response to the emerging themes to complement those developed from theory. For example, a concept that arose in vivo would be 'enthusiasm', which would become associated with the motivations individuals had for engaging with the initiative. In contrast, organisational and institutional theory literatures often discuss organisational 'cultures', but this manifests in different language in interviews, such as 'getting on with others' or 'the way we do things around here' and thus became a provisional code linked to an a priori concept. As Raelin's (2016) work encompasses 'actions' and 'behaviours', any data that spoke of mindsets, mental approaches, personalities, attributes and practices became provisional codes for those concepts.

In the following section we outline the findings from the case study, utilising Raelin's (2016) LAP framework, to elucidate how healthcare leadership embraces a collective approach.

Findings: Towards a Framework for Collective Leadership in Healthcare

Scanning

Scanning is the identification of resources, such as information or technology that can contribute to new or existing programmes through simplification or sensemaking (Raelin 2016). In the case study, project members identified resources such as previous healthcare leadership frameworks, including the NHS Leadership Qualities Framework (NHSI 2006) as well as the CanMEDS framework from Canada (Franks 2005). Furthermore, individuals drew on their understandings of the purpose of their roles, what could be considered practical interpretations of their job descriptions, to underpin their actions, for example:

I was bringing in that managerial and leadership Chief Exec experience ... doing the research on shared leadership and some of the focus groups with young doctors. I did a piece of work looking at the relationship between performance and doctor engagement. What I was able to demonstrate was that there was a link that was worth exploring between the highest performing organisations and the degree of engagement of doctors. [Jacqui,[5] manager, Project Team (PT)]

Moreover, practices were informed by seminal in-profession documents that acted as a catalyst for developing leadership within the medical curriculum:

The Royal College of Physicians developed "Doctors in Society: Medical Professionalism for a Changing World" and it really clearly stated that clinical leadership was absolutely essential if doctors were to maintain and develop their sense of professionalism ... [it] recognised the medical profession was in danger that if 'we don't do something about this, and actively demonstrate that we are making every effort to make sure we are professional, that we are safe clinically, that we're looking for good quality outcomes, that we can regulate ourselves, then the profession's going to be in a lot of strife'. So I guess that set the scene for a lot of what we did. [Kathryn, manager, PT]

By drawing on their job descriptions in a practical way, alongside relevant policy documents, participants were able to join these together to provide compelling motivation for the programme of work.

Signalling

Whilst scanning details the identification of resources, signalling concentrates on the mobilising and catalysing of others' attention to a programme or project through such means as imitating, building on, modifying, ordering or synthesising prior or existing elements (Raelin 2016). Within the case study, project members convened around an agreed purpose that the project was beneficial for the profession. Participants spoke of personal motivations, as well as a wider need for it,

[5] All of the participants' names have been replaced by pseudonyms.

to ensure the profession was able to best carry out its role as care givers *and* system leaders within the NHS. Working within a project infrastructure around that purpose, participants engaged others towards a possible future trajectory of action:

> *My actual contribution was getting the* [Royal] *Colleges and Academy* [of Medical Royal Colleges] *to embed these into the curricula, getting the GMC* [General Medical Council] *to make sure they have got them in the undergraduate curricula too. And increasing the discussions that occur in all sorts of fora about doctors and medical management and how they should be contributing more to that.* [Nathan, doctor, SG]

Far from being solely heroic 'entrepreneurs', these individuals worked in what Lawrence and Suddaby (2006) describe as intelligent, situated action, using discursive strategies to mobilise resources, acting more in a collective or distributed manner. Drawing on their professional interests, knowledge and mutual visions,[6] project members worked with participants in reference groups,[7] adopting various simultaneous practices: advocating, defining, educating, enabling, embedding and routinising the project's purpose through its mechanisms and practices, whilst also disassociating some of the moral foundations of arguments that had previously existed that doctors and leadership did not align (Lawrence and Suddaby 2006).

Part of this 'signalling' was to ensure that within the project itself, there were organisations and individuals who could act as influencers and enablers within the wider process of engagement:

> *We began to include one or two representatives of Colleges. There were a few occasions when other eminent people said they'd like to join the steering group and we'd have this discussion around, 'well, if [we] say yes to [X], then we really ought to be saying that to ten other people.' But at the same time, here's somebody who's got a lot of enthusiasm. And so the Vice-President of the Royal*

[6] Interests which encompassed clinical leadership; succession planning; career development; renewing the psychological contract between what was expected of doctors and the public.

[7] Groups of doctors at various career stages who were invited to comment on and develop the competency framework.

College of [organization] wanted to be involved, and we said, 'actually to get [specialty] inside the tent on this is really important.' [Joel, academic/senior manager, PT/SG]

Alongside this, members were able to connect the project to key events such as the consultation on the GMC's (2009) *Tomorrow's Doctors*, as a means of embedding leadership development within medical training. This is evident in project documents, such as steering group minutes, where it is noted that:

The consultation version of Tomorrow's Doctors will include a discussion paper on leadership … GMC are planning to talk with medical schools in summer around curriculum implementation. [Steering Group Meeting minutes, 24th November 2008]

By doing so, project members were undertaking 'scanning' as well as 'signalling', aligning project activities with the external timing norms of *Tomorrow's Doctors* and working with the profession towards future outcomes.

Weaving

According to Raelin (2016) 'weaving' describes practices or processes of creating webs of interaction across existing and new networks, by building trust between individuals and units and creating shared meanings to particular views. Our empirics demonstrated how individuals found ways to build that trust and reach shared understandings through their interactions, notably:

my world is very relational, so for me, leadership is about connecting and connectiveness and … what became clear was that the work [we] did in informing and forging relationships around leadership was starting to produce a slightly different view to challenge some of those kind of stereotypes [around doctors and management] *that had existed. So the more groundswell we could get, the broader the engagement, the more we could be having those conversations, and then finding people who could have their conversations and spread the word better.* [Ingrid, manager, PT]

This was also noted in project documentation, for example, the scoping study report of May 2006 (NHSI 2006, p.5):

Building relationships - The initial scoping phase of the project was specifically designed to provide time to build relationships with leaders of many of the medical professional and regulatory bodies. It also provided opportunities to meet a number of individuals with particular perspectives on, and interest and involvement in, medical management and leadership.

Furthermore, the way in which project members carried out their work was aligned to the 'prevailing conditions' (Moralee and Bailey, 2020) created by the existing policy context, for example *High Quality Care for All* (Department of Health, 2008), and the emerging workplace environment, for example *Doctors in Society* (Royal College of Physicians, 2005):

if we sit in our palace and don't work with the profession, understand the profession in its context, where it's being delivered, understand how it impacts on patients, understand the wider resource questions … [it's] about doctors doing their jobs professionally, in whatever healthcare setting they're working in or is created for them to work in. [Matthew, administrator, SG]

Like Raelin's (2016) notion of 'signalling', these ways of working are situated in existing sets and schemas of understanding as a way of easing in the passage of new practices and ideas. This juxtaposition of 'present' and 'emerging' makes the new ideas both understandable and acceptable and identifies the potential problems and shortcomings of past practices (Lawrence and Suddaby 2006):

there is no doubt, that's a leadership skill: listening to everybody, getting the ideas together and moving forward. That's more the leadership that everybody should be doing as opposed to the actual leaders of the organisations … it's embedding that type of thinking. [David, doctor, SG]

On the back of existing networks, trust between project members and other participants could be established and shared meanings created as a result.

Stabilising

The process of stabilising involves offering feedback to converge activity and evaluate effectiveness, leading to structural and behavioural changes and learning (Raelin 2016). Similar examples of shifting responsibilities away from the recognised experts (project members) and taking on board the views and perspectives of a more diverse group were evident, resulting in new learning:

> *[we were] very focused on what progress was being made, who we'd engaged with, what we should do with next steps ... we had away days, where we would brainstorm what the framework should look like, distilling all that feedback from focus groups and a whole range of formal partnership working and committees.* [Jacqui, senior manager, PT]

The project team did not consider this to be 'one-off' work, but iterative practices of receiving and responding to feedback:

> *we updated it* [the competency framework] *several times during the project to keep it current, using feedback that people were sending back to us to make sure that we were reflecting what was needed in the here and now and in the future.* [Kathryn, manager, PT]

In particular, some of the feedback that was received focussed on the creation of language and frameworks for learning:

> *we had had quite a bit of feedback on it* [the competency framework] *so ... gathering together all the different feedback and simulating that and working out 'we can take on board this, this isn't quite appropriate, that sort of thing', working out who we needed, who else we needed to consult with. And then working out what language we needed to get changed, go off for a plain English review, working with the publishers, the designers to get together and* [change] *the look and feel of it.* [Theresa, administrator, PT]

When looking at these practices more closely, it was clear that the participants coalesced around shared, collective understandings and use of words for the framework:

> *some of the feedback that we had was people were saying, 'well you know this is the first time we've ever had a common language to know what we're talking about, to be able to discuss leadership, because we just didn't know what it involved before'.* [Sarah, academic, PT]

It is noticeable from the excerpts above that an openness to receiving and acting on feedback helped to coalesce the various aspects of what ultimately became collective curriculum development, creating a tool with a shared language, which would ultimately lead to learning as well as structural and behavioural changes.

Inviting

Related to stabilising, inviting is the process of encouraging those who have held back to participate their ideas, energy and humanity (Raelin 2016). We found numerous examples of participation and inviting feedback, for example:

> *The consultation was through the reference groups … we'd present certain issues, where we'd got to and … they came back and commented on the scenarios, and made some really useful comments that, 'you need to emphasise this more and the patient more here'. So we went back and rewrote some of the scenarios with that in mind.* [Sarah, academic, PT]

This continuing participation and feedback from the reference group included ensuring individuals felt that their contribution was listened to and was worthwhile:

> *We had some of the junior doctors come to one of the later ones and one of them had just been on nights … the group were really good at listening and working it through, being really respectful of this poor person who had come along to this meeting, but obviously was too tired to really work out what they were say-*

ing … that again goes back to this shared leadership, so shared leadership is saying we can't do this without everybody contributing. [Philippa, senior manager, PT]

Despite the project team being full of senior professionals with high levels of experience and expertise, it was evident that they would actively seek out and invite ideas, challenge and pushback to progress the project, for example:

So those people varied because [we] needed to have different levels of knowledge … on the undergraduate work stream we needed medical school deans or people that were involved in the education of medical students. We had medical student representatives on there as well but we also had people from the service involved in that. Then at postgraduate level we needed to have people like postgraduate deans involved in that conversation. [Kathryn, manager, PT]

What is evident here is there was a role for project members to utilise their energy to create connections to and relationships with the wider profession, integrating their collective efforts to effect change.

Unleashing

Unleashing extends the concepts of stabilising and inviting further by ensuring that everyone who wishes to contribute has a chance to, even if their contribution might create discrepancy (Raelin 2016). Project members interacted with the medical profession, encouraging broader perspectives about the role of leadership within the profession and health service, such as:

the project itself was definitely wider than the CF [competency framework]. *It was more about encouraging a dialogue between doctors and managers and the system and making sure that doctors felt engaged and part of the service … recognising they had a part to play, it wasn't just seeing patients, as important as that is, they had other things they needed to be aware of and focused on.* [Theresa, project manager, PT]

This view is supported by aforementioned evidence (National Institute for Health Research 2013, Veronesi et al. 2014) that increased clinical involvement in management decision-making benefits the performance of services:

> *The evidence which has been accumulating over the last few years, and the gut feeling prior to that very much was, if doctors are close to the decision making processes, either making them or certainly buying into the decisions made by management structures, then you get a more efficient organisation, you get better morale amongst the staff and you get better patient outcomes at the end of the day. It's a win-win situation.* [Nathan, doctor, SG]

The involvement of doctors in management and leadership continues to be a contested area (Davies and Harrison, 2019), with differing views informing the developing of this field, and it is through processes such as unleashing, as indicated here, that strategy can be debated and informed and result in a better understanding of how leadership might be practised.

Reflecting

Finally, reflecting is the process of triggering thoughtfulness within self and others to ponder the meaning of past, current and future experiences and to learn how to meet mutual needs and interests (Raelin 2016). There were several examples of informal reflection processes that practitioners participated in:

> *usually it was quite pragmatic in terms of [having] further discussions about this, or another meeting. Sometimes it was just asking for advice, … but at the same time just trying to make links and understand, because maybe you had a conversation with somebody and they were working on something that was semi-related to one of the other workstreams. And sometimes that would only happen at the meeting because it was, 'oh you met with so and so, I met with so and so, oh they didn't mention they were meeting you.' So it was that sort of, more knowledge sharing I think, more than anything.* [Theresa, administrator, PT]

Furthermore, there were examples of how the approach to the change initiative had engendered wide reaching reflections about the purpose of the project:

> *this is much more about encouraging doctors to reflect on what they need to know about management and their leadership behaviours ... about the extent to which doctors need to understand the resource implications of their decisions ... [now], the focus of medicine is doing the best for your patient, almost irrespective of cost. But I, with my taxpayer hat on, perhaps question that.* [Matthew, administrator, SG]

Learning through collective reflection has been identified as a valuable form of learning at work, with reflective dialogue helping staff to function more effectively within their daily work practice. Research has also identified that staff value connecting and sharing knowledge with others, and that dialogue with more experienced colleagues and peers provides rich learning opportunities (Ipe 2003).

Leadership Development in Healthcare: Proposals for Practice and Research

Accomplishing Leadership Together

Our analysis offers insight into the practices of the seven co-constructed LAP activities (Raelin 2016). Considered holistically, we observe how in each of the LAP activities, participants from the study combined their knowledge and through their spontaneous collaboration and shared understandings accomplished leadership together (Gronn 2002).

We also see how many of the activities have a clear future focus, which is what depicts the practices as 'leadership' as opposed to organisational routines or simply 'organising'. In our case, the practitioners often had a shared purpose working towards a possible future trajectory of action (Drath et al., 2008). The seven activities facilitated a shared conception of what their work was aimed towards, subsequently mobilising a sense of collective intentionality, which Crevani et al. (2010, p.81) describe as 'co-construction of a sense of common direction in social interaction'.

Whilst the analysis offered above provides insight into each of the seven LAP activities separately, in the ongoing flux of daily practices, many of the practices interrelated. They were not discrete or distinct, but intricate, interconnected parts of a web of LAP. For example, when engaged in the practice of 'signalling', the practitioners in the case study also drew heavily on resources such as the competency framework ('scanning') in order to achieve the desired objectives.

Culture, Context and History

The emergence and unfolding of these interrelated practices were also informed by the culture, context and history of the empirical setting. The history of the division of work in healthcare, for example, traditionally impacts on the types of activities practitioners are 'invited' to participate in, as well as the themes of the 'reflective' conversations that the practitioners were involved in. Such historical factors are examples of 'antecedent influences' (Kempster and Parry, 2018) that act as a stimulus for leadership processes (Drath et al. 2008), yet within this case, we can begin to see an openness and 'levelling up' of hierarchies and voices. Moreover, the organisation and structure of the project, to hold multiple, diverse forums and meetings with individuals from all medical career grades, as well as the ways in which the project team, between themselves, and in their dialogue with the steering group, created a cultural and contextual norm, facilitated the LAP activity of 'reflection'.

Culture, context and history are often, however, the source of tensions and challenges within collective practice. In this respect, our analysis of the data revealed that whilst much of the activity of LAP was productive, constructive and purposeful, it was not without tension and conflict. When unpacking the practice of 'unleashing', for example, the data illustrated some of the power plays that pervade professional healthcare work, with some practitioners' involvement and contribution being thwarted. Critiques of LAP theory focus on its neglect of issues of power and asymmetry and how the idea of shared, collaborative and collective approaches to accomplishing leadership downplay embedded and inherent power relations that can arise as people 'do' leadership with others (Collinson

2018). In the NHS, professionals such as those discussed in this chapter are, in their practices, frequently navigating and negotiating complex and situated power dynamics, many of which are entrenched in longstanding professional ideology and expertise, as well as role- and boundary-related battles and tensions.

Future research needs to explore the subtle, yet pervasive, ways in which power impinges upon leadership-as-practice in healthcare work. Our research also highlights the interrelatedness of practices and their historical and contextual influences, thereby offering a more nuanced understanding of LAP in healthcare work. In this respect, future research could explore the subtle ways that context and history impinge upon contemporary leadership practices.

Implications for Leadership and Policy

This analysis questions the current conceptualisation and direction of travel. Traditional approaches to leadership development, such as in the NHS, focus largely on addressing the individual deficit in attributes/competencies which can be 'fixed' through leader development, such as the NHS Leadership Qualities Framework (2006), and subsequently the NHS Leadership Framework (2011). Such an 'understanding' comes from classic bureaucracies of the industrial age with ordered roles, compartmentalised functions and, still evident within the NHS, aforementioned hierarchical structures. Moreover, with leadership assumed to make a special, significant and positive contribution, leaders are therefore accorded the privilege of framing followers' reality, resulting in a romance and charisma of leadership which spreads the mythology of leader invincibility (Crevani et al. 2010, Raelin 2011, 2016). This further promulgates a pro-active and visionary archetype (akin to transformational leadership) of professional development for the 'heroic', individual leader.

Critics of this focus (MacGillivray 2018, O'Reilly and Reed 2011) describe how modern, complex work activity is organised around teams and groups within organisations and systems, not individuals, and provide a much-needed shift in discourse and rhetoric in policy literature away from the idea of leaders as heroes and leadership as an individual phenomenon. A typical focus on heroic/charismatic leaders can result in a lack of innovation and in professional service organisations, like healthcare, there is increasingly hybridisation of managerial and professional approaches. The policy discourse for public services uses a language of competition, survival, progress, as well as moral and intellectual pre-eminence, rather than the wisdom of the crowd and these approaches have failed to crystallise how public services may be transformed.

Our argument promotes leadership policy that accounts for practice and collective notions, which will help to create frameworks that foster more practice-based approaches. Such frameworks and models that are not individualistic in focus and do not just focus on individual qualities will emphasise how leadership is something that is enacted by multiple individuals and can be shared amongst people in a team at all levels of the organisational hierarchy.

Towards Shared and Collective Leadership in Practice

Indeed, concepts such as shared, collective and distributed leadership (Crevani et al. 2010, Storey and Holti 2013) have begun to reframe leadership in the delivery of healthcare services as more of a dynamic, situated, dialectic and negotiated activity (Raelin 2016) amongst multiple professional, as well as occupational, actors, which is supported by the examples in the case here. As Raelin (2016, p.7) attests, knowledge arises 'from a contested interaction among a community of inquirers [healthcare professionals] rather than a single source of expertise'. In their ongoing practices these individuals are collectively informing the routines, actions and habits of their teams, groups, departments or organisations. In view of this, there needs to be a much stronger policy movement towards shared, practice-based approaches if we are to see improvement in leadership within health services.

Leader and leadership development in the NHS needs to consider how to reframe and reinvigorate its approach towards flows of leadership practice in dynamic and situated activity, focussing more on existing strengths and skills and on 'problem identification' as a collective. This may include a greater emphasis on collective workplace-based learning and less on addressing individual weaknesses in terms of their leadership competency. Consideration of more critical leadership approaches and positions that focus on the problem, not the individual as a deficit to be corrected, may require policy makers to adopt a more patient- and person-centred approach, with greater emphasis on the specific local and national 'problems' within healthcare, rather than seeking to be seen to 'do something' through well-intended leader development solutions. With the creation of Primary Care Networks and Integrated Care Systems, policy has begun its journey to respond to these challenges (NHS England 2014).

In the context of scandals like Mid Staffordshire (Francis 2013) and Morecambe Bay (Kirkup 2015), both of which called for a change in culture due to a failure of leadership (Smith and Chambers 2019), shifting, or, in some cases, extending, investment to creating cultures, environments and spaces that foster collaboration, co-operation, shared reflection, working together and joint decision making—as espoused by the LAP activities highlighted in this case—could consign poor leadership cultures to the past, by enabling leadership training and development that enacts the rhetoric of valuing everyone's knowledge and input (including other less 'heroic' professional groups alongside patients).

For professional groups (who make up a large proportion of healthcare staff), this will require curriculum developers, heads of service and the professional groups themselves, as well as individual practitioners, to become versed with operating two potentially competing mental models: one that comes from innate, professional-scientific and individualised training *and* these alternative co-constructed leadership-as-practice activities. In doing so, there may need to be a shift away from a focus on 'biomedical' and technical models of training and development to more nuanced, situation-based, collective approaches.

References

Academy of Medical Royal Colleges and NHS Institute for Innovation and Improvement (2010). *Medical Leadership Competency Framework: Enhancing Engagement in Medical Leadership*, 3rd edition, July.

Barbour, R. (2008). *Introducing qualitative research: A Student's guide to the craft of doing qualitative research*. Sage.

Bolden, R., Petrov, G., & Gosling, J. (2008). *Developing collective leadership in higher education: Final report.* Leadership Foundation for Higher Education.
Bryman, A. (2008). *Social research methods* (3rd ed.). Oxford University Press.
Carroll, B., Levy, L., & Richmond, D. (2008). Leadership as practice: Challenging the competency paradigm. *Leadership, 4*(4), 363–379.
Chia, R., & Holt, R. (2006). Strategy as practical coping: A Heideggerian perspective. *Organization Studies, 27*(5), 635–655.
Collinson, M. (2018). So what is new about leadership-as-practice? *Leadership, 14*(3), 384–390.
Crevani, L., Lindgren, M., & Packendorff, J. (2010). Leadership, not leaders: On the study of leadership as practices and interactions. *Scandinavian Journal of Management, 26*, 77–86.
Cunliffe, A. L. (2011). Crafting qualitative research: Morgan and Smircich 30 years on. *Organizational Research Methods, 14*(4), 647–673.
Department of Health and Social Security. (1983). *NHS Management Inquiry (Griffiths report).* HMSO.
Department of Health. (2008). *High Quality Care for All: NHS Next Stage Review Final Report.* (Darzi Report), CM 7432, June. TSO: Norwich.
Drath, W. H., McCauley, C. D., Palus, C. J., Van Velsor, E., O'Connor, P. M., & McGuire, J. B. (2008). Direction, alignment, commitment: Toward a more integrative ontology of leadership. *The Leadership Quarterly, 19*(6), 635–653.
Fletcher, J. K. (2004). The paradox of post heroic leadership: An essay on gender, power, and transformational change. *The Leadership Quarterly, 15*, 647–661.
Francis, R. (2013). *Report of the Mid Staffordshire NHS Foundation Trust Public Inquiry.* HC 947, February, Norwich: TSO.
General Medical Council. (1993). *Tomorrow's doctors: Recommendations on undergraduate medical education.* General Medical Council.
General Medical Council. (2003). *Tomorrow's doctors.* General Medical Council.
General Medical Council. (2009). *Tomorrow's doctors.* General Medical Council.
Gronn, P. (2002). Distributed leadership as a unit of analysis. *The Leadership Quarterly, 13*(4), 423–451.
Hartley, J. (2004). Case study research. In C. Cassell & G. Symon (Eds.), *Essential guide to qualitative methods in organizational research* (pp. 323–333). Sage.
Hiles, D. (1999). Paradigms Lost – Paradigms Regained, a summary of the paper presented to the *18th International Human Science Research Conference*, Sheffield, UK, July 26–29.

House, R., Javidan, M., Hanges, P., & Dorfman, P. (2002). Understanding cultures and implicit leadership theories across the globe: An introduction to project GLOBE. *Journal of World Business, 37*, 3–10.

Hunt, J. G., & Dodge, G. E. (2000). Leadership déjà vu all over again. *The Leadership Quarterly, 11*(4), 435–458.

Ipe, M. (2003). Knowledge sharing in organizations: A conceptual framework. *Human Resource Development Review, 2*(4), 337–359.

Kempster, S., & Gregory, S. H. (2017). 'Should I stay or should I go?' Exploring leadership-as-practice in the middle management role. *Leadership, 13*(4), 496–515.

Kempster, S., & Parry, K. (2018). After leaders: A world of leading and leadership … with no leaders. In B. Carroll, J. Firth, & S. Wilson (Eds.), *After Leadership* (1st ed.). Routledge.

King's Fund. (2013). *Patient-centred leadership: Rediscovering our purpose.* King's Fund.

Kirkup, B. (2015). *The Report of the Morecambe Bay Investigation: An independent investigation into the management, delivery and outcomes of care provided by the maternity and neonatal services at the University Hospitals of Morecambe Bay NHS Foundation Trust from January 2004 to June 2013*. March.

Lawrence, T. B., & Suddaby, R. (2006). Institutions and institutional work. In S. R. Clegg, C. Hardy, T. B. Lawrence, & W. R. Nord (Eds.), *Handbook of organization studies* (2nd ed., pp. 215–254). Sage.

Layder, D. (1998). *Sociological practice: Linking theory and social research*. Sage.

Lincoln, Y. S., & Guba, E. G. (1985). *Naturalistic inquiry*. Sage.

MacGillivray, E. (2018). Leadership as practice meets knowledge as flow: Emerging perspectives for leaders in knowledge-intensive organizations. *Journal of Public Affairs, 18*, e1699.

Ministry of Health. (1967). *First report of the joint working party on the organisation of medical work in hospitals*. HMSO (Cogwheel Report).

Moralee, S., & Bailey, S. (2020). Beyond hybridity in organized professionalism: A case study of medical curriculum change. In P. Nugus et al. (Eds.), *Transitions and boundaries in the coordination and reform of health services: Building knowledge, strategy and leadership* (pp. 167–192). Palgrave Macmillan.

NHS England. (2014). *Five Year Forward View.* October.

NHS England. (2019). *Long Term Plan.* January.

National Institute for Health Research (2013). *New Evidence on Management and Leadership*. Health Services and Delivery Research Programme, December, Southampton: HS&DR Programme.

NHS Institute for Innovation and Improvement (2006). *Improving the effectiveness of health services: The importance of generating greater Medical Engagement in leadership*. May. Coventry: NHS Institute for Innovation and Improvement.
NHS Institute for Innovation and Improvement. (2010). *Enhancing engagement in medical leadership 2009/10 project plan*. NHS Institute for Innovation and Improvement.
NHS Leadership Academy. (2011). *Leadership framework: A summary*. NHS Institute for Innovation and Improvement.
NHS Leadership Academy. (2012a). *National centre of excellence for NHS leaders opens*.
NHS Leadership Academy. (2012b). *Introduction to the NHS Leadership Academy Core Programmes*.
Nicolini, D. (2012). *Practice theory, work and organization: An introduction*. Oxford University Press.
O'Reilly, D., & Reed, M. (2011). The grit in the oyster: Professionalism, managerialism and Leaderism as discourses of UK public services modernization. *Organization Studies, 32*(8), 1079–1101.
Pearce, C. L., & Manz, C. C. (2005). The new silver bullets of leadership. *Organizational Dynamics, 34*(2), 130–140.
Raelin, J. A. (2007). Towards an epistemology of practice. *Academy of Management Learning and Education, 6*(4), 495–519.
Raelin, J. (2011). From leadership-as-practice to leaderful practice. *Leadership, 7*(2), 195–211.
Raelin, J. A. (Ed.). (2016). *Leadership-as-practice: Theory and application*. Routledge.
Raelin, J. A. (2017). Leadership-as-practice: Theory and application - an editor's reflection. *Leadership, 13*(2), 215–221.
Reckwitz, A. (2002). Toward a theory of social practices: A development in culturalist theorizing. *European Journal of Social Theory, 5*(2), 243–263.
Royal College of Physicians. (2005). *Doctors in society: Medical professionalism in a changing world*. Report of a Working Party, December. London: RCP.
Schatzki, T. R., Knorr-Cetina, K., & von Savigny, E. (2001). *The practice turn in contemporary theory*. Routledge.
Smith, J., & Chambers, N. (2019). Mid Staffordshire: A case study of failed governance and leadership? *The Political Quarterly, 90*(2), 194–209.
Storey, J., & Holti, R. (2013). *Towards a New Model of Leadership for the NHS*. NHS Leadership Academy.

Uhl-Bien, M. (2006). Relational leadership theory: Exploring the social processes of leadership and organizing. *The Leadership Quarterly, 17*(6), 654–676.
Veronesi, G., Kirkpatrick, I., & Vallascas, F. (2014). Does clinical management improve efficiency? Evidence from the English National Health Service. *Public Money & Management, 34*(1), 35–42.
Whittington, R. (1996). Strategy as practice. *Long Range Planning, 29*(5), 731–735.
West, M., Loewenthal, L., Armit, K., Eckert, R., West, T., & Lee, A. (2015). *Leadership and leadership development in health care: The evidence base.* Faculty of Medical Leadership and Management.
Willcocks, S. G., & Wibberley, G. (2015). Exploring a shared leadership perspective for NHS doctors. *Leadership in Health Services, 28*(4), 345–355.

12

The Practice of Leadership in Healthcare Organisations: Interpretation, Authority, and Organisational Authorship

Giuseppe Scaratti, Mara Gorli, and Marta Piria

Introduction

Approaching leadership in context means acknowledging its reality as a fragmentation of meanings and practices (Alvesson & Jonsson, 2018). Instability and tumultuousness, evolving demands and regulations, and the uncertain availability of material and immaterial resources present a challenge in organisational contexts and disrupt professionals' daily activities. Professionals, especially those in leadership positions, deal with the challenge of fulfilling multiple roles in an effective way (Alvesson & Jonsson, 2018), keeping up with both organisational goals and concrete problems of everyday activities and acting in times of uncertainty and

G. Scaratti
University of Bergamo, Bergamo, Italy
e-mail: giuseppe.scaratti@unibg.it

M. Gorli • M. Piria (✉)
Catholic University of Milan, Milan, Italy
e-mail: mara.gorli@unicatt.it; marta.piria@unicatt.it

R. Kislov et al. (eds.), *Managing Healthcare Organisations in Challenging Policy Contexts*, Organizational Behaviour in Healthcare,
https://doi.org/10.1007/978-3-030-81093-1_12

ambiguity (Stacey, 2009). Leadership, in this view, is highly intertwined with sense-making, and this entanglement is especially interesting to analyse when it is coupled with systems of rules and mandates that are complex and can be interpreted in many ways.

Leadership in healthcare contexts involves enacting a boundary role (Williams, 2013; Kislov et al., 2016), with clinical leaders acting as tightrope walkers who must constantly fine-tune their position, balance, and direction in response to multiple internal and external tensions. Consequently, studying the intricacy of leadership is inseparable from exploring its manifestations in specific practices and contexts, whereby rigid models and general formulas are unlikely to be useful for identifying the patterns of meaning, influence, and action within the lived experiences of the leaders involved (Czarniawska, 2008; Fairhurst & Cooren, 2009; Hatch & Cunliffe, 2013; Alvesson et al., 2017; Crevani, 2018). To answer the question, "How do leaders do what they do?" we must address both the operative and subjective sides, exploring how interpretative and intersubjective meaning-making processes meet organisational roles and mandates.

A practical view of leadership, focusing on everyday practices, can be useful for producing relevant knowledge and enhancing a situated research approach (Scaratti et al., 2017; Gorli et al., 2015). This view contributes to building a community in which each member actively participates in the production of tacit knowledge, local meanings, negotiated understandings, and shared practices. This perspective, adopted here, bears a close connection to the leadership-as-practice approach (Raelin, 2011), with the main focus on the social interaction and social construction of processes that are embedded in contexts, spaces, and dialogues to create meaning and learning.

According to Pye (2005), leading is imbued with a notion of movement, progress, and transition from one place to another, both literally and metaphorically. Hence its derivation, leadership, is the process by which this movement is shaped and also a system of activities that must be managed in multiple ways to have an impact on practice. At stake is the possibility to assume *an itinerant and dynamic vision*, coping with a runaway work object in a constantly shifting organisational scenario. Clinical leaders are expected to move away from their previous professional identities, carving new professional hybrid trajectories (Currie &

Croft, 2015) and creating new approaches to problem-solving. Such evolution is not a given and can develop only through participation in multiple practices located at the intersection of interrelated social fields (Kislov et al., 2017; Omidvar & Kislov, 2014).

This chapter explores the emergent (Alvehus, 2018) unfolding of *practical leading*—always located in places, histories, and experiences—as exercised by clinical professionals who occupy leading roles in healthcare contexts. We offer a view of leadership as a continuous interaction incorporating subjectivity, intersubjectivity, interpretation, and meaning-making based on three intertwined perspectives:

1. The interpretation of one's organisational role
2. The exercise of authority and power
3. The development of organisational authorship, defined as a relational, embedded, and contextual activity leaving a mark on working activities and organisational roles

We draw our analysis from an ethnographic study on how head nurses act upon daily challenges and situations related to their leadership. Based on the data, we propose an overview of how role interpretation, authority, and authorship unfold. The chapter aims to highlight the value of a practice-based approach to leadership and to contribute to the understanding of its intersubjective and relational aspects. These insights could be helpful for healthcare leaders who seek to reflect on how they can actively play a leading role (and promote the leadership of others) in their organisations.

Connoting Leadership: Three Key Perspectives

Tackling real, complex problems requires people in leading positions to shift their perspective of issues and move between different interpretations of their own role, their exercise of authority, and their influence as authors reshaping the organisational world they inhabit. In this section, we describe how these three perspectives can help healthcare leaders to position themselves intersubjectively and practically and to acknowledge their individual stance critically.

Interpretation: The Playing and Shaping of the Roles

Organisations establish differences between roles mainly by defining them through norms and contractual agreements. Interpretation of the role requires, however, a mindful tuning of discretionary and compulsory aspects.

Examining the complex, dynamic interaction between the frontstage (the enactment of roles) and the backstage (the assumptions and expectations, often untold) enables us to shed light on the many masks and veils featured in daily interactions and situations in workplaces (Goffman, 1959). As in a theatrical screenplay, the same role can be interpreted in multiple ways. As the result of personal and social expectations, performance (Goffman, 1961) can range from actively engaging with the role, in which one experiences and expresses a good fit between the self and role (role embracement), to visibly distancing from the role and the self it implies (role distance).

Relations inside organisations are never merely inter-personal, but inter-roles; inhabiting roles involves interpreting and translating into practice the product of interdependency and the harmonisation of expectations, negotiations, and search for meanings.

Authority: The Managing of Dissymmetry in Power Dynamics

Interpreting a leading role calls into play the tacit assumptions on the nature of authority and power that directly affect how one approaches and exercises influence. In terms of power dynamics, authority involves negotiations, the creation of alliances and strategic moves, and dissymmetry, that is a sort of "violation" of symmetry concerning the organisational positions and expectations.

Power is not a possessed attribute but a result of relational processes that are developed through transactions, interactions, and mutually dependent movements (Friedberg, 1996; Crozier & Friedberg, 1980). Furthermore, authority generates and relies on unavoidable dissymmetric relations; effective leading means inhabiting dissymmetry to cross uncertain and complex situations while recognising the many parts at play—different investments, interests, stances, and narrations—and managing the double nature of authority as a resource and a possible threat to be both handled and participated.

Power refers to the authority and authorisation to "become" or to "let others become", and in this sense, it is connected to the key term *author*, from the Latin verb *augēre* = to nurture, to let grow. Exercising power as authority refers to letting others grow and become what they seek and want to be.

Organisational Authorship: The Reshaping of Organisational Realities

While organisational members in positions of power could have more direct access to decision processes (Clifton, 2014; Alvesson & Jonsson, 2018), all organisational members can influence their realities. Fairhurst and Cooren (2009) consider power and leadership as the effects of a collective action enacted by all kind of organisational actors, depending on their ability to make other actors present. Tourish (2014) has pointed out how power and agency, as constitutive elements of leadership, lie in the hands of both leaders and non-leaders, thus defining leadership as "networks of interaction between organisational actors" (p. 80). Thus leadership processes appear as a choral effort to interpret the life and culture of organisations taking place through exchanges, negotiations, and the creation of shared meaning.

Herein we refer to organisational authorship as a relational, embedded, and contextual activity that leaves a mark on working activities and organisational roles (Gorli et al., 2015). Those who hold leading roles must create conditions for enhancing both the awareness and the concrete influence that people can use for expressing their organisational authorship (Shotter, 1993; Cunliffe, 2014; Gorli et al., 2015; Benozzo et al., 2016). Fairhurst and Cooren (2009) propose how managers should commit to working on understanding "their role as reality framers" (p. 172), not only to truly grasp the role they play by being meaning makers but also to support other organisational members in being responsible authors (Shotter & Cunliffe, 2002).

Being an effective leading figure in a tumultuous reality requires one to be a "practical author" (Cunliffe, 2001; Shotter & Cunliffe, 2002), engaged with one's self and perceptions as well as with the surrounding reality. Authorship is not just a matter of unique contribution to shaping reality in everyday actions. Since human beings tend to be absorbed by the flow of daily experience, we must promote a more deliberate way of coping with one's activities (Yanow & Tsoukas, 2009). By reflexively taking into consideration the explicit and tacit and the theoretical and practical knowledge which circulates and is socially distributed, *authorship* processes can be enhanced to allow deeper levels of awareness and understanding of one's organisational influence (Gorli et al., 2015).

Zooming in: Leadership in Healthcare Contexts

In healthcare organisational literature (Kristiansen et al., 2016), leading roles are linked to issues and challenges that can be briefly summed up as follows:

1. An *intricacy of labyrinths* in terms of hierarchies, organisational levels, and depths that prove hard to reach, with the need to find strategies to cope with uncertainties and one's limited influence in the daily managing of organisational realities both locally and in a broader perspective, and
2. A *flow of entangled activities and movements* that link different stakeholders and different domains of organisational life, requiring efforts to keep up with a flurry of tasks and actions that can often interrupt and change one's working pace.

Our research project involved the professional group of head nurses engaged in coordinating systems of activities, relations, and decisions in healthcare organisations. Many reviews and studies have contributed to a depiction of skills and approaches used by head nurses to administer leadership daily (Kristiansen et al., 2016; Al-Dossary, 2017; Zampieron et al., 2013). Overall, two general dichotomies emerge:

1. That between the head nurse as an imaginative motivator who considers and encourages individuals and aims to inspire people (transformational and authentic leadership) while being a rational problem-solver who works to execute tasks quickly and efficiently (transactional leadership).
2. That between the head nurse as a high-status, commanding figure who centralises decisions and power (authoritative leadership) while helping the group build a shared vision of goals and practices, thus involving people in the decision-making process (authentic leadership) (Cummings et al., 2010; Lanzoni & Meirelles, 2011; Verschueren et al., 2013).

We concur with Willcocks (2012) that the articulation of these dichotomies is often accompanied by the authors' reflections on the complexity of the world of healthcare. Such complexity requires a kind of leadership that implements both tendencies: developing task completion and people engagement.

In the empirical study described below, we explore the subjective experiences of leadership by presenting contextualised accounts of head nurses, aiming to understand the interplay between interpretations, authority, and organisational authorship in leadership practices.

Methodology

As engaged researchers (Cunliffe & Scaratti, 2017), we profit by our involvement in numerous and extensive organisational projects, through which we were able to gain access to head nurses' experiences which were captured in the ethnographic data including narratives, field notes, and autoethnographic accounts.

We were contacted in 2018 by a hospital management board to develop a proposal aiming to improve the well-being of head nurses, a group that had been showing signs of fatigue and demotivation.[1] One hundred and twenty head nurses from four hospitals in a large region in Italy were invited to participate in five half-day reflexive sessions around the challenges of their role and organisational position. In each session, together with people from the same hospital, after a first introduction on the topic of leadership, the head nurses were divided into groups of eight to ten participants. Each of the authors of this chapter played the role of facilitator in these groups, enabling two different activities: a written "self-portrait" of the role, touching on more individual and biographical aspects, and a group discussion focused on the main issues and reflections that emerged from the work on the self-portrait.

Adopting principles of auto-ethnography (Sykes & Treleaven, 2009) and an at-home ethnography approach (Alvesson, 2009), the research solicited the emersion of personal diaries and written accounts that we analysed together with participants highlighting how they were interpreting their role. In this approach, the process of writing, narrating (Ellis, 2004; Gabriel, 2000), and portraying (by underlining some aspects of their own identity) is emphasised as a form of discovery which enables enquirers to learn more about themselves and their relationship with the research topic (Richardson & St.Pierre, 2005; Scaratti et al., 2018).

The written accounts and transcriptions of the recording for each group discussion were divided evenly between the authors to conduct a thematic analysis to identify the main themes and categories (Braun & Clarke, 2006). We met regularly to discuss emergent results, paying particular attention to the similarities and differences among groups.

The process ended for each hospital with a final meeting in October 2019 with head nurses, during which we shared and discussed the emerging data and reflections about role interpretation, authority and power, and authorship. Inputs from this process helped reconfiguring new courses of action and organisational attention that are still under development.

---

[1] The research was authorised by the Ethics Committee of Cerismas, Catholic University of Milan. It was conducted in full compliance with the Ethical Principles of Psychologists and Code of Conduct of the American Psychological Association (APA), integrated into the Associazione Italiana Psicologia (AIP) code of ethics. Furthermore, the study did not address any sensitive topics and was carried out via procedures for informed and consenting adults. Lastly, in accordance with Italian privacy law, the research ensured the anonymity and privacy of all participants.

Actor, Authority, Author: The Ethnographic Analysis of Three Perspectives

Head nurses configure repertoires that are constantly adapted and rewritten to sustain their activities and duties in a landscape of ambiguous policies and mandates. They also build interpretations and representations that silently impact the meaning they create for themselves as well as for those they manage. Role interpretation, authority, and authorship are crucial elements that we discuss herein one by one as emerging from our data, although they are always intertwined.

Interpretation: The Playing and Shaping of the Roles

The intricacy of healthcare organisations and activity flows are reflected in the role of head nurse. The existent job descriptions and organisational mandates are continuously interpreted by head nurses. Different responsibilities are implicitly and explicitly assigned to head nurses, as demonstrated in the following quotes:

> *There should be a project, an organisational vision given by higher spheres, but it lives only on paper.* (Informant 12, group discussion)

> *I see my role involving different aspects: the medical and nursing staff, the auxiliary personnel, the protection and prevention office, the quality office ... As a head nurse, you are the person in charge, responsible for managing all this.* (Informant 41, group discussion)

Head nurses manage duties or activities not directly connected to their job description:

> *Dealing with the hospital cleaning service is not a responsibility that comes with the role of head nurses. Since I was assigned to its supervision, though, I need to make sure the staff, both from outside and inside the hospital, are aware of certain criticalities and priorities.* (Informant 65, group discussion)

The playing out of the role comes to life in an environment that creates instability and fast-paced change. The need to address activities that, although requiring programming and scheduling, are heavily punctuated by daily disruptions is part of the challenge for the head nurse. There is a need for vigilant "*eyes and antennae*" (informant 25, group discussion) to be attuned to the situation and the work object. Head nurses can often be seen splitting their attention and resources over multiple issues concurrently, prioritising those they perceive as more urgent and working through daily disruptions as they emerge:

> *I need to send a fax, and while doing it the phone rings. When I get the call, the office phone starts ringing too, and I keep excusing myself with the persons I am talking with.* (Informant 12, written account)

> *You live day by day and deal with the impossibility to make defined plans as it was doable years ago because everything is unclear and uncertain.* (Informant 83, written account)

Furthermore, the organisational role of head nurse is also called into question by other organisational members. Our informants frequently highlighted the troubling nature of this "*border role*" (informant 71, written account) with a complex history that has not been fully acknowledged and integrated into practices and cultures inside healthcare facilities:

> *Documents and door plates featuring the term 'charge nurse' are widespread inside hospitals and health centres. Nobody calls you head nurse. Even my superior still refers to me as 'charge nurse'!* (Informant 32, group discussion)

Head nurses describe their role as one of "*a guide who looks beyond … who creates a common vision. That's what is expected from us*" (informant 3, group discussion), someone offering an element of fleeting stability to the staff immersed in an ever-changing organisational reality. This self-reported expectation can clash with the impression of being barely in control of the situation. The metaphors often used to describe their role painted a blurry picture, one in which head nurses see themselves as "*tightrope walkers*", as "*a factotum. I do head nurse work, [frontline] nurse work, I keep up with users and doctors*" (informant 22 and 106, written account), navigating an ocean of unfamiliar responsibilities and possibilities.

> *It's like running hurdles, you try jumping over them and when it's not doable, you have to accept some strong impositions … You're constantly looking for an escape from this labyrinth!* (Informant 88, group discussion)

The hectic and ambiguous nature of their role often leads head nurses to turn back to their roots in search of meaning and comfort. Being "*born a nurse*" (informant 50, group discussion) is strongly felt as the roots of their professional identity and the main lens through which head nurses still interpret their role, even if they are moving away from patient care towards operations management. They thereby risk feeling stripped of parts of their professional identity instead of bringing a richness of perspectives to put in action:

> *I'm now far away from the patients […] when you're born as a nurse, it's difficult to distance yourself from them.* (Informant 9, group discussion)

Authority: The Managing of Dissymmetry in Power Dynamics

Due to their position inside organisations, head nurses are highly involved in relational processes, seeking to oversee groups and activities. Their central role makes them key people in facilitating—or hindering—generative meaning-making processes.

Exercising authority in a context of blurred boundaries between health professionals roles and different expectations can lead to conflicts:

> *Your role is often questioned by others (nurses, doctors) who don't know what you deal with. We work on different parts of the patient journey, and it's often difficult to make them see and understand your contribution to the work.* (Informant 13, written account)

Furthermore, the exercise of power is often associated with loneliness:

> *We exchange opinions but, in the end, I am the one making decisions.* (Informant 6, written account)

> *I call my colleagues [other head nurses] sometimes, but I then basically spend the day by myself… everyone is in a group while you are left out.* (Informant 31, written account)

This individually connoted interpretation of authority is confronted with the necessity to operate in a complex net of roles and professional experiences, to find common ways of dealing with hectic daily flows and their disruptions.

Head nurses are in constant connection with their staff to keep a good hold of the unit's life. They exercise their influence in different ways according to the issue at hand, using different tools and channels to make themselves available, especially when they are not physically present. Dealing with this effectively requires them to know where one can and cannot go as well as the available pathways and shortcuts to move without wasting resources and energy:

> *This hospital is a big place, the pharmacy is on the opposite side of it, and by constantly coming and going the staff tire out … so I try to accumulate trips to reduce the number of times people need to walk there.* (Informant 17, written account)

> *I won't be present at today's meeting, since I have to work with the medical staff on a procedure. I'm calling the other unit's head nurse so that I can ask her to brush up on a few matters we wanted to bring up.* (Informant 112, written account)

According to the participants, contradictory sides emerge from head nurses' depiction of leadership and authority. They mention being the one lone person in command of the vessel ("*It's a unique role, there's only you and you can be very lonely*"—informant 8, written account), sometimes perceived as not truly invested with power ("*Sometimes I feel like I'm not really in charge here. It is very difficult to make yourself be heard*"—informant 11, group discussion), although invested with high levels of responsibility impacting the exercise of their authority ("*The line between making responsible decisions and causing a disaster is a fine one ... I feel like I am responsible for my staff and various groups of people, as a mother is for her children*"—informant 91, written account).

The head nurses have mentioned two main approaches to exercising authority. One approach is more "*authoritarian*", allowing "*little to no rebuttals*" (informant 79 and 119, written account) and used in the case of prescriptions being transgressed ("*I have to remind you of the procedure and consequences coming from not respecting it!*"—informant 15, written account). The other approach is described as "*authoritative*" (informant 7, written account), exercised through dialogue and openness towards a shared vision and action ("*Commanding without giving meaning is not useful and leads to dissonance and conflict*"—informant 52, group discussion).

Organisational Authorship: The Reshaping of Organisational Realities

Being an organisational author implies having an influential part in the storytelling and meaning-making activities we previously identified as crucial and powerful tools in the hands of organisational members. From our data, it appears that head nurses are often confronted by urgency and organisational requests that demand rapid thinking and decision-making. Descriptions of situations in which head nurses felt the necessity to "*distance oneself while being on the front line*" (informant 3, written account) have been brought up in their autoethnographic work, accompanied by feelings of "*frustration*", "*worry*", and of "*being a target*" (informant 45, 101 and 9, written account).

Head nurses revise practical strategies using "*trial and error*" as a way to manage what is not completely manageable; on the other hand, getting used to certain "*working rhythms and dynamics*" (informant 19 and 87, written account) is another solution applied by head nurses.

On some occasions, this process produces actual scripts that head nurses use to organise systems of activities:

> *I ask a set of questions on the phone: "You mentioned he seems disoriented, can you tell what caused it?"; "Are you keeping him sedated?"; "Do we need to restrain his movements?"; "So we give oxygen, don't we?"; "Anything else?" [...] They're not part of a protocol, I built them through time".* (Informant 37, group discussion)

Another situation, in which the head nurse recalled the previously mentioned episode of the broken door, shows a situation in which this head nurse took direct action before contacting technical support:

> *I took a wooden doorstop from a drawer, positioned it so that door stays open, and then contacted the technicians about this.* (Informant 4, written account)

Considering what is hidden "behind the scenes" and sharing it with other organisational members can foster paths of reflexivity and participation. These processes help develop an awareness of one's presence, stance, movement, and influence in one's organisation. To provide an example, a head nurse had a moment to share with her staff regarding a brief reflection on a delicate procedure:

> *A patient needed to be taken to Radiology for a scan. I told the physician I would take care of it myself if it was alright with her. Then, I brought along a young nurse in training and we pushed the patient's bed through many corridors, also taking an elevator to move to the Radiology floor. After leaving the patient, I asked the nurse if she thought we had conducted a safe transport [...] I explained that I had bypassed standard procedures because the patient was stable. I know how long it takes to complete the procedures ... they need to be contextually understood and applied with care, but also by using your brain and taking responsibility. The doctor agreed with me being in charge. Knowing procedures means also knowing when they're not useful.* (Informant 59, written account)

This case shows how re-elaborating with others contributes to the construction of new meanings or the reinforcement of cultural practices.

Authorship arises between constraints and discretion through a situated interpretation of own role and power to leave one's mark on organisational norms, routines, and practices. Interpreting a protocol or a procedure in this context creates a social and collective space for contextually meaningful actions.

The dialogical space opened between head nurses and researchers through group discussions and written accounts allowed the participants to put their representations, images, and meanings on a metaphorical table, to elaborate upon them with the help of external (questions) and internal (reactions/thoughts/feelings) cues. Head nurses reported in different moments the feeling of being involved in a generative moment:

> *Now that I'm talking with you, I'm realising a thing I wasn't expecting ... I'm finding more positivity than negativity in my work.* (Informant 42, group discussion)

> *This work is opening a few windows on things I take for granted.* (Informant 103, group discussion)

While reflecting on how their profession occasionally was not appreciated and recognised by their organisations, the participants have highlighted the opportunities their role afforded them to experience a sense of significance and possibilities to influence activities:

> *I can organise the space in a way that supports activities and let relatives be close to the patient without interfering with our work.* (Informant 12, group discussion)

> *I love creating things and sharing a sense of what we can create as a group. There are many things we can work on, so many.* (Informant 66, group discussion)

Sense-making is both an individual and a collective production. Head nurses must mediate between their own and others' points of view to construct a reading of the situation that can lead to action. This process can be especially hard when mandates and decisions coming from the management must be passed to the group by unconvinced head nurses. Nonetheless, the participants shared the following:

> *I had to create fantasies and positive views on the matter while disagreeing with them. But motivating the group is part of my role.* (Informant 114, written account)

> *There are issues you can't discuss, you have to say, 'It has to be done this way,' whether you like it or not … but I always try to mediate.* (Informant 5, written account)

Flexibility has been addressed by head nurses as crucial to the use of knowledge in an embodied and embedded way, integrating the experience gained through education and training in daily processes of building meaning and strategies to accomplish objectives. As informant 4 stated in a written account, "*I have a great deal of experience that supports me, studies and courses and experiences … I try to use them all to build what I build*". This has been associated with the idea of "*being always prepared*", explored by head nurses in many of the autoethnographic accounts through expressions like "*gathering data*", "*information*", and "*analysing*" as a way to be aware of the context and possible solutions to problems.

Concluding Thoughts

To answer the question, "How do leaders do what they do?" in healthcare contexts, we have analysed three different key perspectives: the *interpretation* of the role, the exercise of *authority*, and the practice of *organisational authorship*.

The first issue, interpreting a leading role, implies playing out an ambiguous script and coping with the troubling nature of an uncomfortable "*border role*". The metaphor of the "*tightrope walkers*" conveys the image of the troubled navigation through internal conflict (being close to the patient versus fulfilling a managerial/leadership role) and external pressures (requests, needs, activities, and relations with various stakeholders).

The second issue, exercising authority, refers to managing the dissymmetry and activities to facilitate the enhancement of the quality of care and nurture generative meaning-making processes. The portraits drawn by research participants vary from "*one lone person in command of the vessel*" to "*being a mother for her children*". Managing the practical processes of interaction and coordination means moving between opposite ends of a continuum. Head nurses must balance between setting strict rules and being a responsive point of reference that actively engage with the group's needs. Besides, they have to be attuned to the situation and manage people with care to facilitate practices and activities.

The third issue relates to the practice of organisational authorship and its impact on the flux of activities and discourses head nurses cross and inhabit. Moving between the metaphors of "*trial and error*" and "*working rhythms and dynamics*", the head nurses' organisational authorship develops through a situated interpretation of their role to enhance the organisational achievements while dealing with constraints and discretion. Authorship refers to the possibility to transform the place in a space (De Certeau, 1984); in such a *practised place*, the shaping of elements and their distribution and relations of coexistence are transformed by operations that orient it (direction), situate it (velocity), and temporalise it (time/history). From this perspective, head nurses' authorship opens paths for the unit staff not only to participate but rather to actively rewrite organisational processes and activities.

As witnessed in the field, leaders' problems are not grand revolutions to be heroically addressed but smaller struggles that unfold daily requiring constant tuning and direct and indirect acts of influence. Managing a role that inhabits borderlands in terms of responsibilities and role interpretation requires individuals to seek ways to negotiate boundaries with other members of the organisation through an intersubjective effort and process. There is no recipe for enacting the role, only different interpretations that interact to produce situated meaning and purpose. Head nurses are asked to create balance between urgency and routine, between moving themselves while moving others, and between sudden changes of pace during daily activities. Such effort requires interpretation, authority, and authorship to intertwine, combine, and jointly act for a reflective and critical experience of leadership.

The exploration of the leading experiences of head nurses highlighted how they perform in interpreting roles, therein exercising authority and assuming authorship in their daily practice. Drawing on Currie and Croft (2015), we can refer to these unfolding manifestations as different ways to enact a *hybrid role*. This process involves aspects of personal, professional, and social identity transition. As such, it features both a concrete (dealing with specific organisational spaces) and a metaphorical (dealing with an augmented social representation of one's own power) movement, specifically required from professionals occupying hybrid clinical-managerial positions. Compared to professionals (or leaders) in general, they have to cope with a far greater variety of objects and roles, constantly adjusting their leadership practices to multiple professional and organisational groups they aim to influence and thus operating as boundary spanners (Williams, 2013).

The portraits, metaphors, and repertoires we collected show these processes of role hybridisation in the form of shortcuts and maps for navigating and answering urgencies while creating stable routines. The role of head nurse crosses different professional aims and expressions—from nurse to manager, from patient care to process care—and the lack of well-affirmed mandates and identity often causes misunderstandings with other healthcare professionals.

The practice of leadership involves moving in a transformative trajectory, addressing inherent structural and agentic ambivalences, related to:

- The processes of *construction and production of knowledge*, starting from the recognition of existing problems in a situation and the attempt to construct answers (that are meaningful, valid, and adequate) for the people involved.
- *Transactions* (exchanges, conversations, speeches, and negotiations) developed between subjects/actors with roles configured by social labels (doctors, practitioners, nurses, operatives, health managers, patients, caregivers, and so forth).
- The dynamics of *legitimation and mutual recognition* necessary to build a sufficient level of trust to support the assumption of a leadership function and role.

- The provisional and progressively more stable *balances and compromises* configured between people, between individual interests and shared objectives, between material and intangible elements, and between tacit and codified knowledge.

As Raelin proposes (2011), the most fundamental characteristic of leadership in a leadership-as-practice orientation is the orchestration of the dialectical process of public reflection. People in leading positions need to learn through sharing mental models, images, inferences, and assumptions with others and about their behaviour and their own in practical situations. The leadership work is made "in the day-to-day discourse of human exchange" (Raelin, 2011, p. 200).

Post-heroic leadership is seen as the position of people interrogating themselves and the need to work reflexively on their way to initiate and manage organisational processes.

To this end, another key finding from our work is the need people in leading positions face to reflexively question their motivations (*Why am I doing this?*), to reflect on the object and boundaries of work (*Where shall I direct my intervention?*), and to position themselves in relation to their institutional context (*What is my mandate here?*). Addressing these questions can help head nurses use their hybrid trajectories and identities to enhance inter-professional, inter-organisational and inter-sectoral integration in health service delivery, ultimately increasing the quality of care provided to patients.

References

Al-Dossary, R. N. (2017). Leadership in nursing. In A. Alvininius (Ed.), *Contemporary leadership challenges* (pp. 251–264). InTech.

Alvehus, J. (2018). Emergent, distributed, and orchestrated: Understanding leadership through frame analysis. *Leadership Online First*, 1–20.

Alvesson, M. (2009). At-home ethnography: Struggling with closeness and closure. In S. Ybema, D. Yanow, H. Wels, & F. H. Kamsteeg (Eds.), *Organizational ethnography. Studying the complexities of everyday life* (pp. 156–174). Sage.

Alvesson, M., Blom, M., & Sveningsson, S. (2017). *Reflexive leadership: Organising in an imperfect world.* Sage.

Alvesson, M., & Jonsson, A. (2018). The bumpy road to exercising leadership: Fragmentations in meaning and practice. *Leadership, 14*(1), 40–57.

Benozzo, A., Koro-Ljungberg, M., & Carey, N. (2016). Post author/ship: Five or more IKEA customers in search of an author. *Qualitative Inquiry, 22*(7), 568–580.

Braun, V., & Clarke, V. (2006). Using thematic analysis in psychology. *Qualitative Research in Psychology, 3*(2), 77–101.

Clifton, J. (2014). Small stories, positioning, and the discursive construction of leader identity in business meetings. *Leadership, 10*(1), 99–117.

Crevani, L. (2018). Is there leadership in a fluid world? Exploring the ongoing production of direction in organizing. *Leadership, 14*(1), 83–109.

Crozier, M., & Friedberg, E. (1980). *Actors and systems. The politics of collective action.* The University of Chicago Press.

Cummings, G. G., MacGregor, T., Davey, M., Lee, H., Wong, C. A., et al. (2010). Leadership styles and outcome patterns for the nursing workforce and work environment: A systematic review. *International Journal of Nursing Studies, 47*(3), 363–385.

Cunliffe, A. L. (2001). Managers as practical authors: Reconstructing our understanding of management practice. *Journal of Management Studies, 38*(3), 351–371.

Cunliffe, A. L. (2014). *A very short, fairly interesting and reasonably cheap book about management.* Sage.

Cunliffe, A. L., & Scaratti, G. (2017). Embedding impact in engaged research: Developing socially useful knowledge through dialogical sensemaking: Embedding impact in engaged research. *British Journal of Management, 28*, 29–44.

Currie, G., & Croft, C. (2015). Examining hybrid nurse managers as a case of identity transition in healthcare: Developing a balanced research agenda. *Work, Employment and Society, 29*(5), 855–865.

Czarniawska, B. (2008). Organizing: How to study it and how to write about it. *Qualitative Research in Organizations and Management: An International Journal, 3*(1), 4–20.

De Certeau, M. (1984). *The practice of everyday life.* University of California Press.

Ellis, C. (2004). *The ethnographic I: A methodological novel about autoethnography.* AltaMira Press.

Fairhurst, G. T., & Cooren, F. (2009). Leadership as the hybrid production of presence(s). *Leadership, 5*(4), 469–490.

Friedberg, E. (1996). *Power and rules: The organizational dynamics of collective action*. Avebury.

Gabriel, Y. (2000). *Storytelling in organizations: Facts, fictions, fantasies*. Oxford University Press.

Goffman, E. (1959). *The presentation of self in everyday life*. Anchor Books.

Goffman, E. (1961). *Encounters: Two studies in the sociology of interaction*. Bobbs-Merrill.

Gorli, M., Nicolini, D., & ScarattI, G. (2015). Reflexivity in practice: Tools and conditions for developing organizational authorship. *Human Relations, 68*(8), 1347–1375.

Hatch, M. J., & Cunliffe, A. L. (2013). *Organization theory: Modern, symbolic, and postmodern perspectives* (3rd ed.). Oxford University Press.

Kislov, R., Hodgson, D., & Boaden, R. (2016). Professionals as knowledge brokers: The limits of authority in healthcare collaboration. *Public Administration, 94*(2), 472–489.

Kislov, R., Hyde, P., & McDonald, R. (2017). New game, old rules? Mechanisms and consequences of legitimation in boundary spanning activities. *Organization Studies, 38*(10), 1421–1444.

Kristiansen, M., Westeren, K. I., Obstfelder, A., & Lotherington, A. T. (2016). Coping with increased managerial tasks: Tensions and dilemmas in nursing leadership. *Journal of Research in Nursing, 21*(7), 492–502.

Lanzoni, G. M. M., & Meirelles, B. H. S. (2011). Leadership of the nurse: An integrative literature review. *Revista Latino-Americana de Enfermagem, 19*(3), 651–658.

Omidvar, O., & Kislov, R. (2014). The evolution of the communities of practice approach: Toward knowledgeability in a landscape of practice—An interview with Etienne Wenger-Trayner. *Journal of Management Inquiry, 23*(3), 266–275.

Pye, A. (2005). Leadership and organizing: Sensemaking in action. *Leadership, 1*(1), 31–49.

Raelin, J. (2011). From leadership-as-practice to leaderful practice. *Leadership, 7*(2), 195–211.

Richardson, L., & St.Pierre, E. A. (2005). Writing: A method of inquiry. In N. K. Denzin & Y. S. Lincoln (Eds.), *Handbook of qualitative research* (3rd ed., pp. 959–978). SAGE.

Scaratti, G., Galuppo, L., Gorli, M., Gozzoli, C., & Ripamonti, S. (2017). The social relevance and social impact of knowledge and knowing. *Management Learning, 48*, 57–64.

Scaratti, G., Gorli, M., & Heldal, F. (2018). Using narratives and portraits to foster reflexivity and learning from experience in health care organizations in Italy and Norway. In E. Antonacopulou & S. Taylor (Eds.), *Sensuous learning for practical judgement in professional practice* (Vol. 2, pp. 135–166). Palgrave Macmillan.

Shotter, J. (1993). *Conversational realities: Constructing life through language*. Sage.

Shotter, J., & Cunliffe, A. L. (2002). Managers as practical authors: Everyday conversations for action. In D. Holman & R. Thorpe (Eds.), *Management and language* (pp. 15–37). Sage.

Stacey, R. (2009). *Complexity and organizational reality: Uncertainty and the need to rethink management after the collapse of investment capitalism*. Routledge.

Sykes, C. S., & Treleaven, L. (2009). Critical action research and organizational ethnography. In S. Ybema, D. Yanow, H. Wels, & F. H. Kamsteeg (Eds.), *Organizational ethnography: Studying the complexities of everyday life* (pp. 215–230). SAGE.

Tourish, D. (2014). Leadership, more or less? A processual, communication perspective on the role of agency in leadership theory. *Leadership, 10*(1), 79–98.

Verschueren, M., Kips, J., & Euwema, M. (2013). A review on leadership of head nurses and patient safety and quality of care. *Advances in Health Care Management, 14*, 3–34.

Willcocks, S. G. (2012). Exploring leadership effectiveness: Nurses as clinical leaders in the NHS. *Leadership in Health Services, 25*(1), 8–19.

Williams, P. (2013). We are all boundary spanners now? *International Journal of Public Sector Management, 26*(1), 17–32.

Yanow, D., & Tsoukas, H. (2009). What is reflection-in-action? A phenomenological account. *Journal of Management Studies, 46*, 1339–1364.

Zampieron, A., Spanio, D., Bernardi, P., Milan, R., & Buja, A. (2013). Nurse managers' preferred and perceived leadership styles: A study at an Italian hospital. *Journal of Nursing Management, 21*(3), 521–528.

13

Considerations for Women's Leadership in Health Systems Through an Intersectional Lens

Zahra Zeinali, Kui Muraya, Sassy Molyneux, and Rosemary Morgan

Introduction

According to the World Health Organization (WHO), the proportion of women working in the health sector across the globe is, on average, higher than any other sector (WHO, 2016). In many countries, close to 70% of people working in the health sector are women (Boniol et al., 2019). Women have also been achieving near-parity in pre-service education, including in medical schools and other healthcare-related fields of academia (Economou, 2014). Nevertheless, the top levels of leadership in

Z. Zeinali (✉) • R. Morgan
Department of International Health, Johns Hopkins Bloomberg School of Public Health, Baltimore, MD, USA
e-mail: zzeinal1@alumni.jh.edu; Rosemary.Morgan@jhu.edu

K. Muraya
Kenya Medical Research Institute (KEMRI) – Wellcome Trust Research Programme, Nairobi, Kenya
e-mail: KMuraya@kemri-wellcome.org

R. Kislov et al. (eds.), *Managing Healthcare Organisations in Challenging Policy Contexts*, Organizational Behaviour in Healthcare,
https://doi.org/10.1007/978-3-030-81093-1_13

the health sector remain dominated by men, including in top global institutions of global policy and governance, in decision-making structures, governments, and across the public and private sectors.

Women, on the other hand, predominantly occupy lower-hierarchy positions such as nurses, midwives, and community health workers, which often represent lesser authority (*but not importance*) across the health sector (Dhatt et al., 2017; Hay et al., 2019). For example, in 2015 only 27% of ministers of health were women; in 2014, only 24% of directors of global health centers at the top 50 US medical schools were women; and at the 72nd World Health Assembly in 2019, only 22% of member state delegations had a woman as a chief delegate, down from 29% in the previous year (Dhatt et al., 2017; Women In Global Health, 2019). The Global Health 50/50 Reports, released since 2018, aim to shed some light on gender equality in 200 major organizations working in and/or influencing the field of global health. The reports note that decision-making power remains in the hands of men, comprising 68% and 80% of board chairs and 73% and 69% of executive directors in the organizations that were examined in 2020 and 2018, respectively (Global Health 50/50, 2018, 2020).

In a gender analysis of human resources for health (HRH) for the WHO, George (2007) notes that "*gender, among other power relations, plays a critical role in determining the structural location of women and men in the health labor force and their subjective experience of that location*" (p. 5). According to the WHO, gender biases in power, resources, entitlements, norms, and values are manifesting in the under-representation of women in leadership positions across health systems, the pay-gap, and physical and sexual violence and harassment (Commission on Social Determinants of Health, 2008; WHO, 2016). The *Lancet* series on Gender Equality, Norms, and Health (2019) further emphasize that

S. Molyneux
Kenya Medical Research Institute (KEMRI) – Wellcome Trust Research Programme, Nairobi, Kenya

Nuffield Department of Medicine, University of Oxford, Oxford, UK
e-mail: SMolyneux@kemri-wellcome.org

health systems contribute to gender inequalities in health by replicating and reinforcing restrictive gender norms and societal gender inequalities (Hay et al., 2019). It is for this reason that examining leadership in challenging policy contexts is not complete without exploring women's representation in health systems leadership. Moreover, it is necessary to examine how gender intersects with other social identifiers (such as age and race) and social stratifiers (such as socio-economic status and professional cadre); and how these are embedded within broader systems and structures of power to influence the career advancement of women. An intersectional approach enables us to do this.

Intersectionality, a concept first coined by Kimberlé Crenshaw in 1989, has emerged as a framework for explaining and addressing health inequities (Larson et al., 2016). Hankivsky (2014) has defined intersectionality as promoting

> *an understanding of human beings as shaped by the interaction of different social locations such as race/ethnicity, indigeneity, gender, class, sexuality, geography, age, disability/ability, migration status, religion. These interactions occur within a context of connected systems and structures of power including laws, policies, state governments and other political and economic unions, religious institutions and media. Through such processes, interdependent forms of privilege and oppression shaped by colonialism, imperialism, racism, homophobia, ableism and patriarchy are created.* (p. 2)

Within the literature there are examples of how inequity manifests in HRH. Thackwell et al. (2016), for example, describe the need for improved racial and gender diversity among healthcare providers to meet the needs of diverse societies such as South Africa. van Rensburg (2014) also points to the racial disparity present in the medical profession in South Africa. Filby et al. (2016) and Dhatt et al. (2017) examined cadre inequality in various settings which results in over-representation of certain healthcare professional categories, such as physicians, that are traditionally considered more "elite", in leadership positions. These so-called elite cadres are historically male dominated, which can potentially further exacerbate gender inequity in health leadership. Newman (2014) refers to this as horizontal occupational gender segregation—the idea that certain professions are more female/male dominated than others—noting that it contributes to lack of motivation and low morale, disempowerment, and maldistribution of the workforce.

The Third Global Forum on HRH produced the Recife Political Declaration on HRH (2013) committing to "*promote equal opportunities in education, development, management and career advancement for all health workers, with no form of discrimination based on gender, race, ethnicity or any other basis*" (p. 3). If this commitment is to be achieved, approaches are needed which seek to understand and address different manifestations of privilege, discrimination, and marginalization within HRH, including in health systems leadership.

This chapter examines the literature around leadership in the health sector with a focus on low- and middle-income countries (LMICs) and using an explicit intersectionality lens. The focus is narrowed down to LMICs to allow for a comprehensive examination of the literature, but global trends and statistics presented earlier show that this misrepresentation in leadership is not limited to LMICs but is rather a pervasive pattern everywhere.

Search Strategy

We conducted a systematized review of the literature on intersectionality in health systems leadership. A systematized review process models the systematic review process but lacks some features of a full systematic review, such as the quality assessment or two reviewers (Grant & Booth, 2009). We selected this approach because of the need for more flexibility in the review process, recognizing that there would likely be minimal articles published on this topic.

Literature for the systematized review was identified using five electronic databases. The search keywords and concepts included "leadership", "gender", "human resources for health", and "health systems", "intersectionality", and "low- and middle-income countries". The search was conducted in April 2018 and included articles starting from January 2000. We aimed to include studies that met all the following inclusion criteria: Primary research and literature reviews in English that had used an explicit intersectionality lens that incorporated at least two social stratifiers, focused on leadership in health systems and addressed gender (inequity). The electronic search yielded a total of 7701 titles/abstracts, which were further screened, and after taking the steps detailed in the PRISMA flowchart in Fig. 13.1 and applying the inclusion criteria, no articles were found that had used an explicit intersectionality lens to explore health systems leadership in LMICs. However, we identified 12 articles that discussed the role of multiple social stratifiers and experiences of health systems leadership, added five relevant studies they cited, as well as seven studies based on the recommendation of experts in the field to our review, resulting in a total of 24 articles. None of the final 24 papers included an explicit intersectionality lens but all touched on arguments relevant to this study.

Each of the final 24 articles was examined using an intersectionality lens. This was done through coding any social stratifiers mentioned in relation to barriers or enabling factors in achieving success or reaching leadership positions. If the social stratifier had been mentioned in the context of gender or there was a mention of how this stratifier intersects with gender to create an experience, this was also specifically coded. Similar codes were grouped together and gave rise to the emerging themes that have been included in the findings section of this study.

Gender and Leadership in Health Systems

In the initial steps of the search strategy we found that the intersectionality framework has mainly been used in the context of social determinants of health and understanding barriers to accessing healthcare in different settings. Much of the literature focusing on women's participation in the health sector focused on the broad categories of health professions rather than more specifically on leadership within those professions. In order to understand how gender intersects with other social stratifiers to influence women's experiences of, and opportunities for, leadership, it is important to first explore the role of gender and how gender inequity manifests within health systems leadership structures.

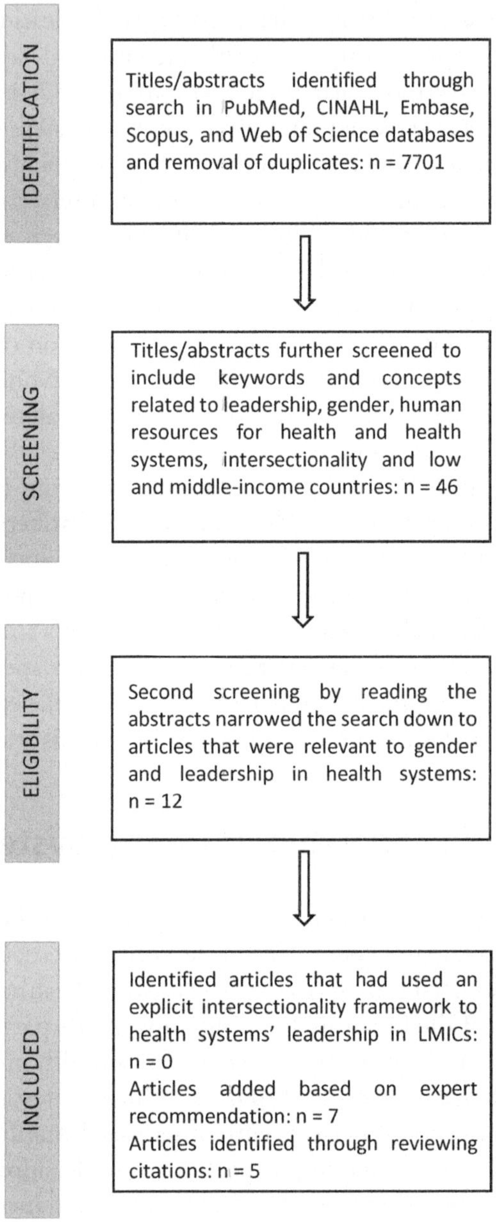

Fig. 13.1 PRISMA flowchart. (Source: Authors' conceptualization)

The gender-related barriers identified in this review were mainly focused on barriers women face and included: (1) women's relative lack of access to resources (social and financial) that improve career development; (2) women's relative lack of access to mentorship and sponsorship opportunities; (3) lack of value, recognition, and respect at work for women, and the attribution of success to feminine traits rather than professional competence, expertise, or hard work; (4) greater likelihood by women to take on dual burdens of professional work and childcare and domestic work; and (5) assumptions that women have leadership styles that are less effective for top management than men. It is notable that there was a dearth of discussion of how these barriers might manifest differently for women from different demographic groups including racial categories and professional cadre, which have been highlighted in literature as resulting in differential experiences for health workers (Muraya et al., 2019; Shung-King et al., 2018). Nonetheless, other social stratifiers were discussed to a limited extent within the studies, and these are further explored below.

When exploring leadership as a professional concept and related gendered experiences, Tominc et al. (2017) highlight that within a broad pattern of women getting fewer leadership opportunities than men, there is also an evolving recognition of a phenomenon of women being offered particularly challenging opportunities, referred to as the "*glass cliff*" opportunities. This term is used to describe a situation where women are offered leadership positions when uncertain and risky conditions decrease the likelihood of their success, and subsequently set them up them for failure and poor outcomes. This, in turn, can have adverse implications for external views about women's abilities as leaders and managers, as well as women's own internal view about their abilities, potentially discouraging them from taking up leadership positions (Tominc et al., 2017).

Gendered societal norms and expectations also have a significant influence on women's interest in, and ability to, participate in health leadership. A study in Cambodia demonstrated that managers who are men tended to emphasize that women's roles and priorities should be centered around their household responsibilities (Vong et al., 2019). Similarly, a study conducted with mid-level health managers in coastal Kenya found that women are perceived as having primary responsibility for child nurturing and domestic roles which in turn impacts on their willingness and ability to take up senior health management positions, and hinders their career progression (Muraya et al., 2019). Another study with health systems managers in South Africa describes a woman manager who aspired to be a surgeon alongside her husband, but decided to "*put her career on the back burner*" when they had children and "*allow her husband to follow his dreams*" (Shung-King et al., 2018).

A study on women in different professions in Sri Lanka noted that the current work norms of working long hours, stress, and competition promote a "*masculinization of management*" (Kodagoda, 2018). The general perception being that for women to be accepted as leaders they need to act like men, but in doing so, they risk losing their obligatory attributes of femininity. The study noted that if women try to take on leadership roles building on their feminine attributes, it would be viewed as challenging the right of men to hold positions of power. At the same time, women leaders using those same feminine attributes were at risk of being undermined for an apparent incapability to do the job (Kodagoda, 2018). The description of said feminine attributes was not elaborated on in the study.

Intersection of Gender with Other Social Stratifiers

Gender, Professional Cadre, and Race

Five studies addressed the intersection of gender, professional cadre, and race: George (2008), Williams (2013), Filby et al. (2016), Dhatt et al. (2017), Shung-King et al. (2018). Dhatt et al. (2017) report that in Kenya, professional hierarchies play an important role in the appointment of health leaders with medical doctors being preferentially appointed into leadership positions. This, in turn, could potentially be gendered, as the medical field in Kenya was historically male dominated; although this has gradually changed over time with equal numbers of men and women entering into medical school and holding entry-level medical positions.

This is an example of how gender and professional cadre can intersect to influence women's participation as leaders in the health system.

In Iran, nurses, a woman-dominant cadre, were reported to avoid being the decision makers in the healthcare team even when they had the knowledge and skills, because their autonomy and authority were undermined by the physician-centered culture of the health systems they worked in (George, 2008). The healthcare culture was found to revolve around physicians. Teamwork with other cadres was less valued, leading to the discouragement and disempowerment of other professional cadres in taking on leadership roles in health teams. This illustrates how professional cadre can intersect with gender and work cultures, limiting the participation of women in leadership spaces, even in woman-dominated professions such as nursing and midwifery as further elaborated below.

Filby et al. (2016) explored the intersectional nature of gender and professional cadre within midwifery leadership in LMICs. They examined the concept of "*gender penalty*" to describe the phenomenon they observed where men assume leadership positions even in professions that are disproportionately comprised of women, such as nursing and midwifery, leaving women to fill the bottom of the occupational hierarchy. This, in part, is due to women's job-related skills in caring professions not being treated as professional skills, but rather as qualities of being a woman.

Another way in which gender intersects with professional cadre is what Williams (2013) describes as the "*glass escalator*". The glass escalator refers to the advantages that men receive even in woman-dominated professions such as nursing, allowing them to climb toward leadership levels more easily and quickly compared to their woman counterparts. This is in contrast to the previously discussed "*glass cliff*" concept, where women are positioned for likely failure (Tominc et al., 2017).

Nonetheless, the "escalator" advantage may not necessarily privilege all men equally, as prior research has shown that behaviors that denote leadership ability in white men are perceived as menacing behavior from black men (Williams, 2013), highlighting the importance of an intersectional approach. As such, gender intersects with race in this case to disadvantage black men and potentially prevent them from exercising their leadership traits (Williams, 2013). In the South African study of health systems managers' experiences, Shung-King et al. (2018) observed a combination of gender, race, and professional hierarchy in influencing leadership experience. To illustrate, they described a black manager recalling that (in addition to the prejudice he experienced as a black man), as a man nurse he had often faced prejudice from his woman nurse colleagues, as well as family members and social circles for doing "a woman's job" (Shung-King et al., 2018). Although his experience did not follow the usual pathways of discrimination, it was drawn upon to show how strongly gender intersects with other social identities in influencing people's experiences. The same study found that black woman managers from a nursing background, experience a "*triple-challenge*" of gender, professional hierarchy and race in their professional life, even post-apartheid. The authors argue that although in theory equal rights now exist for all regardless of race in South Africa, other insidious forms of discrimination still persist, resulting in unique experiences for health professionals based on the intersections of their gender, race, and professional hierarchies.

Another example of the complex effects of the intersection of gender with race is highlighted by George in her 2008 study in the United States. She discusses how government funding assists minority women to be trained for lower levels of nursing, leading to their prominent presence at this level. However, the funding does not apply to baccalaureate training which determines teaching and leadership positions, resulting in an inevitable dearth of minority women in these higher-level and decision-making spaces. This also highlights how well-intentioned policies and interventions—in this case government-assisted education funding—can inadvertently disadvantage intended beneficiaries, "locking" them into particular lower-level categories and limiting their career progression into leadership roles.

Gender, Race, and Ethnicity

Two of the reviewed studies—one in Singapore (Chua et al., 2016), the other in South Africa (van Rensburg, 2014)—examined the intersection of gender and race/ethnicity. The Singapore study focused on the disadvantages men experience, but the intersectional nature of these disadvantages made it important to include in this review. The study examines social capital and the intersection of gender and ethnicity. The authors found that while men of all major ethnicities living in Singapore have an advantage in accessing university education compared to their woman counterparts, there is one exception: Malay men are at a disadvantage compared to Malay women when it comes to critical domains of high-level education and work. This may be due to traditional roles where Malay wives control the household budgets and Malay husbands are responsible for religious practices and rituals. The authors elaborate that this disadvantage in access to university education experienced by Malay men leads to lower social capital over time, for instance, knowing fewer people in high-status jobs. Therefore, while men in general seem to be at an advantage for higher education in Singapore, Malay men experience a unique disadvantage due to the intersection of their ethnicity with their gender (Chua et al., 2016).

In the South African study, van Rensburg (2014) examines the distorted race and gender profiles of the health workforce that persist despite the progress made by affirmative policies in the post-apartheid government. van Rensburg argues that remnants of historical exclusion based on race including in the higher education sector and 'white collar' professions continue to exist to date in South Africa., This is, for example, observed in the number of medical practitioners nationally: 16,936 (whites), 8354 (African blacks), 5314 (Indian) and 927 (colored) (van Rensburg, 2014) (colored in the South African context refers to persons of mixed race ancestry [Index Mundi, 2018]). This is in a country where black Africans make up 80.2% of the population, with colored, white, and Indian/Asian making up 8.8%, 8.4%, and 2.5% of the population respectively (Index Mundi, 2018). The outcomes of this racial exclusion, marked by white privilege and dominance, are further skewed by male dominance (van Rensburg, 2014).

Gender, Religion, and Culture

One of the reviewed studies examined gender and religion (Tlaiss, 2013). Discussing gender and religion in Lebanon's health sector, Tlaiss (2013) noted that 79% of the public health workforce comprises of women, but this is not reflected in the leadership positions. Tlaiss considered socio-cultural factors and Lebanon's society that reinforces traditional gender roles around domestic responsibilities as the key reasons hindering women's upward movement in the hierarchy of the health system. Furthermore, she discusses the role of religion even in this broader context of gendered norms and roles; highlighting that in Lebanon, Muslim communities are generally more conservative and traditional than Christian communities, leading to an under-representation of Muslim women in the workforce as a result of traditional norms and obligations (Tlaiss, 2013).

Gender, Generation, and Culture

One reviewed study conducted in Saudi Arabia with women faculty of medical colleges explored gender and generation (Alwazzan & Rees, 2016). In this study, Alwazzan and Rees (2016) noted that both implicit (e.g., gender stereotyping) and explicit barriers (e.g., lack of research opportunities, lack of mentorship, and difficulty in achieving life-work balance) were identified by participants as hindering their career progression. Some examples of gender stereotypes that were given by the study participants included women lacking the physical strength for some medical specialties, or lacking personality traits that would make them "*fit for leadership positions*". The study discussed the intersecting axes of gender and culture when participants stated that their culture places a higher value on domestic responsibilities for women rather than working professionally and is less encouraging of women to occupy professional spaces. Furthermore, women face generational barriers, in that young professionals are not taken seriously despite being qualified and leadership positions are more readily available to older individuals, even when individuals are equally qualified for a leadership position. While this generational barrier is not exclusive to women, women seem to suffer more prominently due to the intersection of their gender with their generation.

Applying an Intersectional Lens to Analyzing Leadership in the Health Sector

Status Quo: Single-Layered Approaches to Leadership

There has been an upturn of focus on the role of women in health systems, and in particular in leadership positions, such as the WHO Global Strategy on Human Resources for Health: Workforce 2030 (2016), the United Nations High Level Commission on Health Employment and Economic Growth (2016), and the Global Health 50/50 Reports (2018, 2019, 2020), The *Lancet* special theme issue on Advancing Women in Science, Medicine, and Global Health (2019) and The *Lancet* series on Gender Equality, Norms, and Health (2019), and initiatives such as Women in Global Health. However, these reports and initiatives mainly focus on homogenously increasing women's participation in leadership, with little attention paid to other social factors that intersect with gender to inhibit progression to higher-level positions. This linear, single-layered approach does not reflect the complexities of real-world experiences including systems and structures of power that interact to privilege certain women over others.

An intersectionality approach explicitly focuses on the relationships between mutually constructed processes, systems, and structures that lead to social differences and inequities (Hankivsky, 2014). Experiences of power, privilege, disadvantage, and marginalization cannot be reduced to single, distinct factors; rather, they are the outcome of the intersection of different and interlocking social identities and locations (Hankivsky, 2014; Hankivsky & Jordan-Zachery, 2019a). Gender as one aspect of an individual's identity has an immense role in a person's experience of the world, including professional development and career advancement. However, not acknowledging the dynamic interconnectedness of gender with other social identities and locations, especially when considering women who do not fulfill the often portrayed and represented description of women, is a pitfall that hinders adopting solutions that benefit all women. A failure to recognize and analyze diversity among women in leadership experience risks the portrayal of women leaders as primarily white and from/in high-income countries, and of under-representing the visibility and voice of other women leaders. By that very fact, in order to lay a strong, inclusive foundation for change in the gender equity agenda, there have been calls for more visible leadership in global health from LMIC feminist voices (George et al., 2019).

Health systems are often viewed as gender-neutral, technical systems, but in reality, they are complex systems imbued with power relations. They are embedded in, and shaped by, their socio-political contexts, thereby reflecting and reinforcing social norms (Percival et al., 2018). An intersectional approach is essential in understanding health systems and the dynamic and complex human experiences and interactions that make up those health systems (Shung-King et al., 2018).

It is critical to identify a range of interventions and approaches at different levels and across the building blocks of health systems that support moving toward more gender equitable health systems which better serve their staff and the society. Percival et al., in their 2018 study, provide an exemplar and key attributes of a gender equitable health system. This includes provision of care for men and women across the life span; ensuring equitable access that is unrestricted by social, geographic, and financial barriers; operating through evidence-informed policies based on relevant, sex-disaggregated health data; creation of equitable career opportunities for men and women health professionals; and ensuring equitable health outcomes among men and women and across age groups. Additionally, it is essential to advocate for adoption of intersectional approaches that better account for the fluid and interconnected structures of power that affect the dynamic nature of privilege and disadvantage (Larson et al., 2016). This would highlight the importance of identifying how social hierarchies such as professional cadre, race ethnicity, age/generation, religion, and culture intersect with gender to produce unequal outcomes (Weber & Hilfinger Messias, 2012).

Increasing Women's Representation Within Health Systems Leadership: Moving Beyond Gender Parity

The WHO Commission on Social Determinants of Health (CSDH) has clearly stated that social inequities, including gender inequity, are among causes of health disparities and recommends that governments strengthen political and legal systems to acknowledge and support marginalized groups to empower them to represent their needs and claim their rights. The CSDH recommends empowerment of women and marginalized groups at the micro-level of individual people, as well as ensuring their representation at the macro and meso decision-making levels within and beyond health systems to reduce health disadvantages that result from social inequities (Commission on Social Determinants of Health, 2008). Given women's under-representation in leadership, we have focused on this issue in the present chapter, while acknowledging that gender equity goes beyond women's rights.

Increasing women's leadership in health systems at global, national, and subnational levels is a vital step toward addressing women's health challenges, and empowering and recognizing the majority of the health sector's workforce. According to Downs et al. (2014), randomized trials have demonstrated that women in leadership positions of governmental organizations are more likely than men to implement policies that are supportive of women and children. Including diverse groups of women at all levels of health systems leadership is important to ensuring that diverse experiences and perspectives are represented in health systems decision-making and contribute to wider societal transformation (Gronn, 2002; Gilson & Agyepong, 2018). Potential approaches include organizational processes such as equal employment opportunities that acknowledge the impact of different social stratifiers and actively mitigate against barriers that discriminate based on those stratifiers (Shung-King et al., 2018). Newman (2014) argues that the positive effects of equal opportunity and gender equity in the health sector include equal access to professional knowledge and education for the professional development of all health workers, an increased health worker pipeline, an equal chance of being hired, being fairly paid and enjoying advancement opportunities, better work–life balance, and improved health services. Improving women's representation within health systems leadership is, therefore, beneficial to all (Gilson, 2003).

Where Do We Go from Here?

The first step toward identifying and implementing solutions in relation to women's lack of representation within health systems leadership is having a clear, robust understanding of the underlying obstacles to the participation of women, from all types of different social identities. Patriarchal structures manifest in complex, multifaceted, and reinforcing ways. How these processes affect women of color, indigenous women, women from LMICs, transgender and queer women, other groups of women, and even men of color is underexplored and should be a priority (Morgan et al., 2018).

To have more equitable, gender-responsive, and inclusive health systems that reflect these values at all hierarchical levels, gender biases in health systems leadership need to be examined using an intersectional framework. An evidence-based understanding of the key factors that influence gender differences in leadership, and their impact, should contribute to policies and interventions that address drivers of inequity. Some recommendations rising from this study include consciously avoiding gender stereotypes; improving access to family leave and childcare provisions in a gender equitable manner; assuring equitable access to opportunities at different levels and for different professional cadre; creating supportive and enabling environments of success for women and marginalized groups; investment in mentorship of women moving upward in the health systems hierarchy; and finally, increased flexibility to accommodate personal, domestic, and family obligations (George, 2007; Dhatt et al., 2017). It is also imperative to understand how these recommendations should be implemented for different groups. It is worth noting that the positive effects of these changes can be made more sustainable and meaningful by moving beyond gender-specific interventions toward gender-transformative interventions that challenge the status quo of gender norms, address the root causes of gender inequities, and improve current power relationships between women and men (WHO, 2011).

Consistent implementation of the aforementioned key lessons requires a broader policy shift toward the intersectionality paradigm. This shift should be reflected in all steps of the health policy process including agenda setting, policy formulation, policy implementation, and policy assessment. We have laid out a set of recommendations for health policy makers to make this shift, based on the conclusions we have drawn from reviewing the literature (Hankivsky, 2012; Gupta et al., 2019; Hancock, 2019; Hankivsky & Jordan-Zachery, 2019a, 2019b; Hankivsky et al., 2019). The recommendations in Table 13.1 enable policy makers to describe, commit, act, and transform health systems through an intersectional lens to reduce inequities. The line between policies for regular function of health systems and those pertaining to the health workforce has not been defined here, given that adoption of such policies will inevitably affect both aspects of health systems.

Conclusion

Achieving gender equity in health systems leadership at all levels is fundamental to ensuring the diversity of all of the human resources in the global community is being appreciated (Dhatt et al., 2017). If we are to advocate for reforming the workplace and workforce in health systems, and for equal opportunities in leadership positions in health systems across nations and in global health, it is imperative to move beyond gender and be cognizant of the different challenges that women face in their career advancement in different settings, due to the intersection of their gender with other social identities, and not dismiss these differences by oversimplifying gender as the only defining aspect of one's identity. Since using an intersectionality framework in considering women's leadership in health systems in LMICs is virtually absent from the discourse, incorporating an intersectionality lens in addressing their participation in leadership and researching evidence around it can ensure a more holistic approach that does promote advancement of not only the stereotypically portrayed women in leadership, but all women from different nationalities and races, professional cadres, and economic backgrounds. As efforts to reduce gender inequity in health systems are gaining momentum, it is important to look beyond gender as an all-encompassing disadvantage and take into account other social identities that interact with gender and

Table 13.1 Recommendations for health policy makers

	Principles	Recommendations
1	Inclusivity	Be mindful and inclusive of differently positioned population groups and responsive to the needs of diverse populations.
2	Mobilizing power-balancing potential of health systems	Regard health systems as structures with the power to transform unequal social norms, roles, and relations both internally and consequently in the society as a whole.
3	Evidence-informed policy	Capture comprehensive, disaggregated, and intersectional data as part of robust research and other forms of evidence to inform policy.
4	Focus on inequalities	Consider social inequalities and how they affect access to resources (for both health workers and populations).
5	Move beyond intersectionality-aware toward intersectionality-transformative policies	Act to reduce and transform intersecting inequalities by: – Acknowledging the historical roots of inequities for different marginalized groups – Challenging the status quo of power dynamics – Transforming the roles and relations that create exclusive privileges at the root-cause level – Adopting and committing to strategies for fostering progressive change
6	Accountability	Aim to strengthen accountability mechanisms toward patients, health workers, and communities they serve.
7	Reflexivity	Recognize the privilege of being in the decision-making position and reveal harmful biases, assumptions, stereotypes, and exclusions, which will subsequently lead to including a diversity of perspectives.

adopt the shift to an intersectional framework in programs and policies that are collectively amplified by the health sector. The result of this effort is not only more gender equity in HRH, but more equity in general, improving health systems' functioning and downstream health benefits more broadly.

Acknowledgments We would like to acknowledge the support of Research in Gender and Ethics (RinGs): Building Stronger Health Systems, and the RESYST Research Project Consortium (RPC). Both RPCs are funded by the UK Department for International Development (DFID) for the benefit of low- and middle-income countries [Project No PO5683]. Any opinion, finding and conclusion, or recommendation expressed in this material is that of the authors and DFID do not accept any liability in this regard.

References

Advancing women in science, medicine, and global health. (2019). *The Lancet, 393*(10171), 493–610, e6–e28. Retrieved October 13, 2019, from https://www.thelancet.com/journals/lancet/issue/vol393no10171/PIIS0140-6736(19)X0006-9

Alwazzan, L., & Rees, C. E. (2016). Women in medical education: Views and experiences from the Kingdom of Saudi Arabia. *Medical Education, 50*(8), 852–865. https://doi.org/10.1111/medu.12988

Boniol, M., McIsaac, M., Xu, L., Wuliji, T., Diallo, K., & Campbell, J. (2019). WHO | Gender equity in the health workforce: Analysis of 104 countries. *Who,* March. https://apps.who.int/iris/bitstream/handle/10665/311314/WHO-HIS-HWF-Gender-WP1-2019.1-eng.pdf

Chua, V., Mathews, M., & Loh, Y. C. (2016). Social capital in Singapore: Gender differences, ethnic hierarchies, and their intersection. *Social Networks, 47*, 138–150. https://doi.org/10.1016/J.SOCNET.2016.06.004

Commission on Social Determinants of Health. (2008). *Closing the gap in a generation: Health equity through action on the social determinants of health.* Retrieved April 7, 2019, from https://apps.who.int/iris/bitstream/handle/10665/43943/9789241563703_eng.pdf?sequence=1

Dhatt, R., Theobald, S., & Buzuzi, S., et al. (2017). The role of women's leadership and gender equity in leadership and health system strengthening. *Global Health, Epidemiology and Genomics, 2,* e8. https://doi.org/10.1017/gheg.2016.22

Downs, J. A., Reif, L. K., Hokororo, A., & Fitzgerald, D. W. (2014). Increasing women in leadership in global health. *Academic Medicine, 89*(8), 1103–1107. https://doi.org/10.1097/ACM.0000000000000369

Economou, J. S. (2014). Gender bias in biomedical research. *Surgery, 156*(5), 1061–1065. https://doi.org/10.1016/j.surg.2014.07.005

Filby, A., McConville, F., & Portela, A. (2016). What prevents quality midwifery care? A systematic mapping of barriers in low and middle income countries from the provider perspective. *PLoS One, 11*(5), e0153391. https://doi.org/10.1371/ journal.pone.0153391

Gender equality, norms, and health. Series from the Lancet journals. (2019). *The Lancet*. Retrieved October 10, 2019, from https://www.thelancet.com/series/gender-equality-norms-health

George, A. (2007). *Human resources for health: A gender analysis*. Background paper prepared for the Women and Gender Equity Knowledge Network and the Health Systems Knowledge Network of the WHO Commission on Social Determinants of Health Background to the Women and Gender Equity Knowledge Network. Retrieved April 7, 2019, from https://www.who.int/social_determinants/resources/human_resources_for_health_wgkn_2007.pdf

George, A. (2008). Nurses, community health workers, and home carers: gendered human resources compensating for skewed health systems. *Global Public Health, 3*(suppl_1), 75–89. https://doi.org/10.1080/17441690801892240

George, A. S., Amin, A., García-Moreno, C., & Sen, G. (2019). Gender equality and health: Laying the foundations for change. *Lancet, 393*(10189), 2369–2371. https://doi.org/10.1016/S0140-6736(19)30987-0

Gilson, L. (2003). Trust and the development of health care as a social institution. *Social Science & Medicine, 56*(7), 1453–1468. Retrieved May 13, 2019, from http://www.ncbi.nlm.nih.gov/pubmed/12614697

Gilson, L., & Agyepong, I. A. (2018). Strengthening health system leadership for better governance: What does it take? *Health Policy and Planning, 33*(suppl_2), ii1–ii4. https://doi.org/10.1093/heapol/czy052

Global Health 50/50. (2018). *The Global Health 50/50 report 2018*. Global Health 50/50. https://globalhealth5050.org/wp-content/uploads/2018/03/GH5050-Report-2018_Final.pdf

Global Health 50/50. (2020). *The Global Health 50/50 report 2020: Power, privilege and priorities*. Global Health 50/50. https://globalhealth5050.org/wp-content/uploads/2020/03/Power-Privilege-and-Priorities-2020-Global-Health-5050-Report.pdf

Grant, M. J., & Booth, A. (2009). A typology of reviews: An analysis of 14 review types and associated methodologies. *Health Information and Libraries Journal, 26*(2), 91–108. https://doi.org/10.1111/j.1471-1842.2009.00848.x

Gronn, P. (2002). Distributed leadership as a unit of analysis. *The Leadership Quarterly, 13*(4), 423–451. https://doi.org/10.1016/S1048-9843(02)00120-0

Gupta, G. R., Oomman, N., Grown, C., Conn, K., Hawkes, S., Shawar, Y. R., et al. (2019). Gender equality and gender norms: Framing the opportunities for health. *Lancet, 393*(10190), 2550–2562. https://doi.org/10.1016/S0140-6736(19)30651-8

Hancock, A.-M. (2019). Empirical intersectionality: A tale of two approaches. In *The Palgrave handbook of intersectionality in public policy* (pp. 95–132). Springer International Publishing.

Hankivsky, O. (Ed.). (2012). *An intersectionality-based policy analysis framework.* Institute for Intersectionality Research and Policy, Simon Fraser University. Retrieved October 13, 2019, from www.sfu.ca/iirp/ibpa.html

Hankivsky, O. (2014). *Intersectionality 101.* The Institute for Intersectionality Research & Policy, SFU. Retrieved May 16, 2019, from http://vawforum-cwr.ca/sites/default/files/attachments/intersectionallity_101.pdf

Hankivsky, O., Grace, D., Hunting, G., Giesbrecht, M., Fridkin, A., Rudrum, S., et al. (2019). An intersectionality-based policy analysis framework: Critical reflections on a methodology for advancing equity. In *The Palgrave handbook of intersectionality in public policy* (pp. 133–166). Springer International Publishing.

Hankivsky, O., & Jordan-Zachery, J. S. (2019a). Introduction: Bringing intersectionality to public policy. In *The Palgrave handbook of intersectionality in public policy* (pp. 1–28). Springer International Publishing.

Hankivsky, O., & Jordan-Zachery, J. S. (Eds.). (2019b). *The Palgrave handbook of intersectionality in public policy.* Springer International Publishing.

Hay, K., McDougal, L., Percival, V., Henry, S., Klugman, J., Wurie, H., et al. (2019). Disrupting gender norms in health systems: Making the case for change. *Lancet, 393*(10190), 2535–2549. https://doi.org/10.1016/S0140-6736(19)30648-8

Index Mundi. (2018). *South Africa Demographics Profile 2018.* Retrieved May 13, 2019, from https://www.indexmundi.com/south_africa/demographics_profile.html

Kodagoda, T. (2018). Working long hours and its impact on family life: Experiences of women professionals and managers in Sri Lanka. *Indian Journal of Gender Studies, 25*(1), 108–126. https://doi.org/10.1177/0971521517738432

Larson, E., George, A., Morgan, R., & Poteat, T. (2016). 10 Best resources on… intersectionality with an emphasis on low- and middle-income countries.

Health Policy and Planning, 31(8), 964–969. https://doi.org/10.1093/heapol/czw020
Morgan, R., Hawkins, K., & Lundine, J. (2018). The foundation and consequences of gender bias in grant peer review processes. *CMAJ, 190*(16), E487–E488. https://doi.org/10.1503/cmaj.180188
Muraya, K. W., Govender, V., Mbachu, C., Uguru, N. P., & Molyneux, S. (2019). 'Gender is not even a side issue…it's a non-issue': Career trajectories and experiences from the perspective of male and female healthcare managers in Kenya. *Health Policy and Planning, 34*(4), 249–256. https://doi.org/10.1093/heapol/czz019
Newman, C. (2014). Time to address gender discrimination and inequality in the health workforce. *Human Resources for Health, 12,* 25. https://doi.org/10.1186/1478- 4491-12-25
Percival, V., Dusabe-Richards, E., Wurie, H., Namakula, J., Ssali, S., & Theobald, S. (2018). Are health systems interventions gender blind? Examining health system reconstruction in conflict affected states. *Globalization and Health, 14*(1), 90. https://doi.org/10.1186/s12992-018-0401-6
Shung-King, M., Gilson, L., Mbachu, C., Molyneux, S., Muraya, K. W., Uguru, N., & Govender, V. (2018). Leadership experiences and practices of South African health managers: What is the influence of gender? – A qualitative, exploratory study. *International Journal for Equity in Health, 17*(1), 148. https://doi.org/10.1186/s12939-018-0859-0
Thackwell, N., Swartz, L., Dlamini, S., Phahladira, L., Muloiwa, R., & Chiliza, B. (2016). Race trouble: Experiences of Black medical specialist trainees in South Africa. *BMC International Health and Human Rights, 16*(1), 31. https://doi.org/10.1186/s12914- 016-0108-9
Tlaiss, H. A. (2013). Women in healthcare: Barriers and enablers from a developing country perspective. *International Journal of Health Policy and Management, 1*(1), 23–33. https://doi.org/10.15171/ijhpm.2013.05
Tominc, P., Šebjan, U., & Širec, K. (2017). Perceived gender equality in managerial positions in organizations. *Organizacija, 50*(2), 132–149. Retrieved April 7, 2019, from http://organizacija.fov.uni-mb.si/index.php/organizacija/article/viewFile/758/1155
van Rensburg, H. C. (2014). South Africa's protracted struggle for equal distribution and equitable access—still not there. *Human Resources for Health, 12*(1), 26. https://doi.org/10.1186/1478-4491-12-26

Vong, S., Ros, B., Morgan, R., & Theobald, S. (2019). Why are fewer women rising to the top? A life history gender analysis of Cambodia's health workforce. *BMC Health Services Research, 19*(1), 595. https://doi.org/10.1186/s12913-019-4424-3

Weber, L., & Hilfinger Messias, D. K. (2012). Mississippi front-line recovery work after Hurricane Katrina: An analysis of the intersections of gender, race, and class in advocacy, power relations, and health. *Social Science & Medicine, 74*(11), 1833–1841. https://doi.org/10.1016/j.socscimed.2011.08.034

Williams, C. L. (2013). The glass escalator, revisited. *Gender & Society, 27*(5), 609–629. https://doi.org/10.1177/0891243213490232

Women in Global Health. (2019). Tweet from Women in Global Health. Retrieved May 13, 2019, from https://www.womeningh.org/

World Health Organization (WHO). (2011). Gender mainstreaming for health managers: A practical approach. *WHO*. Retrieved October 4, 2019, from http://apps.who.int/iris/bitstream/10665/44516/2/9789241501064_eng.pdf

World Health Organization (WHO). (2016). *Working for health and growth: Investing in the health workforce Growth*. Report of the High-Level Commission on Health Employment and Economic Growth. Retrieved April 7, 2019, from https://apps.who.int/iris/bitstream/handle/10665/250047/9789241511308-eng.pdf?sequence=1

14

Concluding Comments: Voice as a Common Theme Across Studies of Healthcare Management in Challenging Policy Contexts

Kathleen Montgomery, Bjørn Erik Mørk, Diane Burns, and Roman Kislov

Summary and Synthesis: Voice as a Common Theme

The contributions included in this volume offer a picture of the wide-ranging complexities in healthcare policymaking. As we previewed in the introductory chapter, many of the issues presented herein can be arrayed on a continuum, with full integration at one extreme and full

K. Montgomery (✉)
University of California, Riverside, Riverside, CA, USA

University of Sydney, Camperdown, NSW, Australia
e-mail: kmont@ucr.edu

B. E. Mørk
BI Norwegian Business School, Oslo, Norway
e-mail: bjorn.e.mork@bi.no

R. Kislov et al. (eds.), *Managing Healthcare Organisations in Challenging Policy Contexts*, Organizational Behaviour in Healthcare,
https://doi.org/10.1007/978-3-030-81093-1_14

fragmentation at the other. In practice, the process of policymaking and implementation typically falls somewhere along the middle of that continuum, with elements of both integration and fragmentation co-existing. This co-existence can be manifested as productive adaptation, collaboration, and boundary negotiation; but it also can be manifested in conflict, manipulation, and dysfunctional wheel-spinning.

Although the contexts for the papers in this volume vary greatly—from high-level policymaking in the UK National Health Service to provision of older adults' care in Australia to health charities in Africa—a common theme of 'voice' can be discerned. More precisely, the concept of voice and how it is managed can be used as a framework to examine the multiple voices that may (or may not) be heard in the policymaking and implementation process, recognizing that some voices may be prioritized over others. In this framing, we consider voice as the opportunity to express one's views and preferences and to have those views be valued by decision-makers (Burns et al., 2012). See also Satterstrom et al. (2021, p. 380), who offer a similar approach to the concept of voice: 'Upward voice—employees' discretionary offering of constructive ideas for improving organizational or unit functioning to those with authority—is a vital pathway for valuable ideas to reach decision-makers who might otherwise remain in the dark'.

The process of healthcare policymaking and implementation does not take place in a vacuum; rather, the process involves a collection of stakeholders. Moreover, there is substantial variation in the extent to which these stakeholders have a voice in the process, including whether a particular collective stakeholder's voice is internally homogeneous or reflects multiple positions within the same group (Kislov et al., 2021; Rowland

D. Burns
University of Sheffield, Sheffield, UK
e-mail: d.burns@sheffield.ac.uk

R. Kislov
Manchester Metropolitan University, Manchester, UK

The University of Manchester, Manchester, UK
e-mail: r.kislov@mmu.ac.uk

et al., 2021). Attention to this plurality of perspectives is crucial if we are to avoid being trapped by 'monologized' narratives that are dogmatic, one-sided, and inherently exclusive (see also Bakhtin, 2010 [1986]).

Our reading of the chapters in this volume suggests several ways that voice appears as an important feature of the policymaking process—*suppression of voice*, *mobilization of voice*, and *skillful management of voice.* In the next section, we provide examples from the chapters to illustrate this point. By using the lens of voice management, we would argue that there is great potential to advance understanding of how and why some policy implementation efforts fall short, while others succeed.

Suppression of Voice

We have seen evidence of both the explicit effort at voice suppression at the policy formulation level, as well as implicit voice suppression at the formulation and implementation levels. First, Speed and Mannion demonstrate how the voice of a key stakeholder group can be suppressed in a manipulative, explicit way. Their case study reveals how junior doctors were essentially closed out of deliberations to alter their working schedules through a calculated strategy to align the public with the government, against the interests of the medical profession, using questionable data. Although junior doctors attempted to engage in a work stoppage in protest, their voice was ignored, resulting in potential demotivation among this group.

Second, the suppression of voice has long been associated with gender bias in healthcare leadership. This may occur explicitly, when women are not given the opportunity to vie for leadership positions in healthcare. More often, it can occur implicitly through stereotyped assumptions about appropriate role assignments for women and how women should be evaluated. The study by Zeinali et al. expands our understanding of how women's voice is excluded along additional stratifiers such as race, ethnicity, culture, and religion. Whether implicit or explicit, the exclusion of women's voice in healthcare leadership severely limits the potential for improvements in healthcare systems at all levels.

Several chapters illustrate additional ways that suppression of voice leads to a disconnect between those making policy and those implementing it. This is nicely articulated by Pomare et al., who use the concepts of 'work-as-imagined' and 'work-as-done'. These authors demonstrate the negative effects when the voice of key stakeholders responsible for implementing policy, such as staff clinicians, is ignored.

The case study by Ludlow et al. examining elder care policies in Australia and the UK also serves as a compelling example of the implicit suppression of voice. In this study, the authors report that, although family members achieve substantial care coordination for older relatives, their voice about their own needs and observations is absent from policy documents. As a result, there is a loss of valuable input about how best to integrate services provided to this vulnerable patient population.

Churruca et al. offer yet another way to conceptualize the suppression of voice, in this instance by examining how organizational culture is assessed. Using a careful mapping and analysis of survey constructs, these Australian researchers show that instruments designed to measure organizational culture typically are not developed by the actors whose experiences are being studied. Without giving the relevant actors a voice in design, implementation, and analysis, such instruments have limited value.

Mobilization of Voice

Often, this aspect of voice applies at the macro policy formulation level. For example, Ferlie's comparison of two models of policymaking within the NHS demonstrates the potential for mobilizing a broad set of new stakeholders into the process, including non-civil-service actors and the knowledge elite. Ferlie shows how political currents can affect the extent to which the voice of additional stakeholders is successfully mobilized.

Another example of mobilization of voice appears in the chapter by Sachikonye et al. in their study of 'mission drift' in health charities in Africa. These authors identify mechanisms that can be used to mobilize different stakeholder groups in a way that works to advance the mission of the charities and keep it on track.

In both these examples, there is evidence of multiple voices within the same stakeholder groups, requiring decision-makers to determine how best to give voice to the plurality of actors, within an environment that inevitably presents demands for selectivity and deference. This task leads to the third formulation of voice, skillful management of voice.

Skillful Management of Voice

This perspective on voice can be distinguished from system- or organization-level voice mobilization in that it is more focused on the efforts that individuals and groups undertake to move the policy implementation process forward.

At the individual, self-reflective level, Meier and Dopson's examination of context can be reimagined as a call for a critical analysis of one's own assumptions about context and the need to be explicit about assumptions when engaging in collaborative work.

At the group level of reflection, Tazzyman et al. illustrate that when healthcare professionals are able to reiterate and acknowledge their professional identities and boundaries, they can recognize common challenges and threats and work collaboratively to overcome them.

A similar set of findings is reported by Scaratti at el., who examine the experiences of head nurses in Italy. These authors reveal that when head nurses give voice to their own doubts and questions about how best to do their work, they are acknowledging their own reality and hence are better positioned to enhance their performance and that of their staff.

The study by Willocks and Moralee within the context of UK medical education offers similar insights into the need for leaders and educators to skillfully manage the voice of multiple stakeholders with whom they interact.

The skillful management of voice is also evident from the perspective of senior healthcare leaders and how they collaborate with a wide set of stakeholders. In the chapter by Chambers and Exworthy, the focus is on long-serving chief executives in the NHS and reveals how these individuals skillfully balance the interests of their institutions and systems, developing productive relations with a variety of key stakeholders. At the same time, these leaders preserve their own voice, often through self-reflection, 'reinventing' themselves as contexts change.

Implications for Practice

Continuing the theme of voice management in the policymaking process, the volume highlights several implications for practice important in tackling the suppression of voice, enhancing the mobilization of voice, and supporting the skillful management of voice.

Tackling the Suppression of Voice

Across chapters exploring the suppression of voice, authors identify a need for policymakers, leaders, and managers to recognize when, where, and how silence and silencing are present in the process of policymaking and implementation. In combination, these chapters emphasize that in tackling the suppression of voice, renewed consideration must be given to adopting and developing approaches, tools, and techniques to protect and amplify the voices of stakeholders.

At the policy-formulation level, Speed and Mannion call on actors to recognize how populism can be used to generate alliances among disparate groups to create the notion of a 'common enemy'. The authors propose that steps be taken to monitor how data are used to justify policy proposals, in order to protect against any potential data manipulation or misinterpretation.

To address how women's voice is excluded, Zeinali et al. call for interventions to correct imbalances of power in leadership, including increasing women's representation in decision-making positions throughout the healthcare system. They propose a number of interventions, which include investing in mentoring, building equitable access to opportunities, engendering supportive environment- and family-friendly policies, and recognizing and removing gender-based stereotypes from the selection processes for leadership positions.

To ensure that policy reflects what is feasible in the time-restricted, pressured environment of acute care, Pomare et al. call for policy on hospital redevelopment to be realigned with hospital staff experiences of their work during the change process. Moreover, the authors argue that allotted time is essential for staff to participate in consultations on hospital design and that it is scheduled when staff can be covered so that patient care is not disrupted.

Ludlow et al. highlight how the process of policymaking and implementation to integrate services for older adults requires policymakers, managers, leaders, and carers to work cohesively together. The authors argue that future policymaking must consider solutions that involve carers as active agents in coordinating the care of older relatives, with the aim of reducing the burden current practices unduly place upon them.

Assessments of organizational culture are shown by Churruca et al. to offer hospital management important insights in the identification of areas of concern and improvement. In realizing this potential, however, it is necessary to enhance staff voice and participation in these assessments. The authors stress that local hospital management should actively support the process and take steps to ensure that staff experience the exercise as genuinely valuable and worthwhile.

Enhancing the Mobilization of Voice

Some of the chapters highlight opportunities to adapt and develop practices to realize the potential for mobilizing voice in the process.

Focusing on the UK, Ferlie explains how the door is open for non-governmental actors in the four UK nations to have a stronger voice in policy formulation. Consequently, this opportunity will require practitioners to develop skills in working effectively with novel groups from outside the traditional healthcare sector. In addition to greater diversity and power sharing at the national level, Ferlie also emphasizes the possibility of creative policymaking to ensure coordination across the four nations.

To prevent 'mission drift' at the organizational level, Sachikonye and colleagues propose that charity boards adopt several preventive practices and tools. The authors suggest the use of organizational mindfulness as a technique to help members of the board to continuously scrutinize their stakeholder relationships and to adopt strategies most appropriate to specific stakeholder groups. In addition, the authors emphasize the importance of producing measured and corrective responses to any drift as it occurs. The authors also suggest that charity boards operating in African countries invite meaningful stakeholder representation to ensure that knowledge about local cultures, religions, political structures, and operating environments will inform the decision-making process.

Supporting Skillful Management of Voice

In the chapters where the skillful management of voice is a theme, several individual- and group-level practice implications emerge to take policy forward through knowledge building and increased self-reflection and reflexivity, in order to surface implicit assumptions and perspectives.

Meier and Dopson suggest two strategies to explicate whether context is merely the background to a phenomenon under examination or the phenomenon itself. In studies of policy implementation, the authors suggest that scholars attend to their own position by clearly distinguishing 'the change' and 'the context'. The authors also propose that healthcare leaders surface their own assumptions about context and their taken-for-granted perspectives in a given situation, especially in collaborative work.

Tazzyman et al. suggest that recognition and acknowledgment of professional boundaries, and of an associated divergence of voices across stakeholder groups, can be more beneficial for collaboration in the longer term than attempts to break down, blur, or completely ignore differences between them.

Scaratti et al. urge professionals in leadership positions to consider their motivation ('why am I doing this?'), the object and scope of their work ('where shall I direct my intervention?'), and their position in relation to institutional context ('what is my mandate here?'). The authors propose that these questions will help leaders in hybrid roles to reflect upon and enhance inter-professional, inter-organizational, and intersectoral integration.

Willocks and Moralee outline several practical implications for leadership that can be linked to the topic of the skillful management of voice. First, they argue that it is important to reframe and reinvigorate the approach toward leadership development as a dynamic and situated activity. Second, they describe the importance of focusing on collective workplace learning, often taking the form of dialogue, rather than 'correcting' the weaknesses of individual leaders. Third, taking the voice of the patients into account would imply greater emphasis on specific local and national 'problems', rather than merely seeking to be seen to 'do something' through leadership development initiatives.

Chambers and Exworthy advocate that those responsible for nurturing and safeguarding top talent ensure that new (and not-so-new CEOs) develop organizational ambidexterity, personal resilience, and strategic competence to engage in effective system leadership. Drawing together practice-based strategies of long-serving CEOs, the authors identify factors conducive to long service: (1) retaining a focus on patients, staff, and communities; (2) navigating the external system; (3) developing collegial relations with partners and stakeholders; (4) establishing a highly skilled and stable senior leadership team with appropriate delegation to deputies; (5) securing help and support, especially when experiencing levels of stress; and (6) engaging in self-reflection in order to learn from setbacks.

Directions for Future Research

The chapters in this volume suggest several directions for future research that can contribute to our understanding of the management of voice in the policymaking process. We will now take a brief look at each of these streams.

Researching Suppression of Voice

Based on their study of how the voice of junior doctors was suppressed, Speed and Mannion argue that it can be useful to reexamine controversial policy proposals and changes through the lens of the political logics of populism. This can enable us to develop a richer understanding of the role played by particular events and actors.

Both Pomare et al. and Ludlow et al. suggest that future research should further explore the relationship between policies and what actually happens in practice They highlight an analytical potential of using the distinction between 'work-as-imagined' versus 'work-as-done' as a tool for enhancing policy development and ensuring that important voices are being heard.

According to Churruca et al., it is important to reconsider the way measurements of organizational cultures are conducted and used in practice, in order to increase the value of such assessments as part of continuous service improvement in healthcare organizations. This may involve comparing different ways of assessing organizational cultures, developing surveys with items that are better validated and tailored to healthcare contexts, increasing the response rates through enhancing employee engagement, and making cross-country comparisons.

Finally, Zeinali et al. suggest that through gathering more trend data for women's representation, it could be possible to better understand whether and how women's voice might become suppressed.

Examining Mobilization of Voice

In some of the chapters there are also suggestions for how the topic of mobilizing voice can be studied further. Ferlie, for instance, proposes to examine what kinds of policymaking models are used in response to the Covid-19 pandemic and what role different actors play. He also suggests continuing to monitor policy actions to determine whether the shift to a more pluralized model remains, or if there is evidence of a shift back to a more centralized model, depending on the political climate.

Sachikonye et al. argue that further research might theorize and test how mechanisms operating at the socio-institutional level enhance or constrain the agency of organizational boards, as well as explore how these mechanisms become activated.

Exploring Skillful Management of Voice

Tazzyman et al. call for focusing on multiple and inter-related boundaries in the analyses of integration and inter-professional work, for studying similar processes in other countries using a combination of interviews and observations, and for taking service user experiences and views into consideration when examining boundary work.

Scaratti et al., Willocks and Moralee, and Chambers and Exworthy all raise opportunities for more research on healthcare professionals in leading roles. Scaratti et al. highlight the potential of using practice-based approaches to explore ambivalences experienced by hybrid clinical-managerial leaders.

Willocks and Moralee are also interested in leadership-as-practice and call for exploring the subtle yet pervasive ways in which power, context, and history affect collective leadership in healthcare. They also identify the need to examine the inter-relatedness of leadership practices across space and time and to combine different methodological approaches, including observation of leadership-as-practice, when studying collective forms of leadership.

Chambers and Exworthy state that there is a need for a more granular understanding of ambidexterity displayed by CEOs in the healthcare sector, particularly in the context of decentered post-New Public Management forms of governance. They call for developing more detailed insights into the role of the CEO as organization coach and for uncovering the more dysfunctional aspects of being a long-standing CEO, such as a potential association between staying power and hubristic behavior. Another direction for future research emerging from this study is the identification of 'an arc for leadership maturity' by comparing the stories of experienced CEOs with those of new incumbents.

Conclusion

In sum, it is compelling to trace a common thread of voice throughout the otherwise somewhat disparate chapters in this volume. Several chapters herein reveal the dysfunctional effects when voice is suppressed, either explicitly through calculated strategies and discriminatory exclusion, or implicitly through oversight and failure to recognize the importance of various stakeholders. When voices are suppressed or ignored, performance at all levels suffers: Systems and organizations are left to function without the benefit of contributions from all relevant actors, and both groups and individuals are unmotivated to offer their best. This may have negative effects on individual and group performance, extra role behavior, turnover intention, patient safety, quality of healthcare provision, innovation, and learning (Vogus et al., 2010; Lloyd et al., 2015; Edmondson, 2019; Satterstrom et al., 2021).

Yet, voice can be mobilized at a system or organizational level to further policy development and charitable mission programs. Finally, as also noted by Satterstrom et al. (2021), voice management can be used for productive purposes for individuals and groups—allowing for self-growth, enhancing collaborative exchanges, and contributing to leadership efforts. Scholars of healthcare organizations can play their part in supporting these positive developments by truthfully representing the plurality of perspectives in the research accounts they produce, by amplifying those voices that are marginalized, silenced, or ignored, and by facilitating authentic and fruitful dialogues between—and within—multiple stakeholder groups operating in challenging policy contexts.

References

Bakhtin, M. M. (2010 [1986]). *Speech genres and other late essays.* University of Texas Press.

Burns, D., Hyde, P., Killett, A., Poland, F., & Gray, R. (2012). Participatory organizational research: Examining voice in the co-production of knowledge. *British Journal of Management, 25*(1), 133–144. https://doi.org/10.1111/j.1467-8551.2012.00841.x

Edmondson, A. C. (2019). *The fearless organization: Creating psychological safety in the workplace for learning, innovation, and growth*. John Wiley & Sons.

Kislov, R., Harvey, G., & Jones, L. (2021). Boundary organising in healthcare: Theoretical perspectives, empirical insights and future prospects. *Journal of Health Organization and Management, 35*(2), 133–140. https://doi.org/10.1108/JHOM-04-2021-475

Lloyd, K. J., Boer, D., Keller, J. W., & Voelpel, S. (2015). Is my boss really listening to me? The impact of perceived supervisor listening on emotional exhaustion, turnover intention, and organizational citizenship behavior. *Journal of Business Ethics, 130*(3), 509–524. https://doi.org/10.1007/s10551-014-2242-4

Rowland, P., Fancott, C., & Abelson, J. (2021). Metaphors of organisations in patient involvement programs: Connections and contradictions. *Journal of Health Organization and Management, 35*(2), 177–194. https://doi.org/10.1108/JHOM-07-2020-0292

Satterstrom, P., Kerrissey, M., & DiBenigno, J. (2021). The voice cultivation process: How team members can help upward voice live on to implementation. *Administrative Science Quarterly, 66*(2), 380–425. https://doi.org/10.1177/0001839220962795

Vogus, T. J., Sutcliffe, K. M., & Weick, K. E. (2010). Doing no harm: Enabling, enacting, and elaborating a culture of safety in health care. *Academy of Management Perspectives, 24*(4), 60–77. https://doi.org/10.5465/amp.2010.24.4.3652485.a

Index[1]

[1] Note: Page numbers followed by 'n' refer to notes.

R. Kislov et al. (eds.), *Managing Healthcare Organisations in Challenging Policy Contexts*, Organizational Behaviour in Healthcare,
https://doi.org/10.1007/978-3-030-81093-1

The manufacturer's authorised representative in the EU is Springer Nature Customer Service Centre GmbH, Europaplatz 3, 69115 Heidelberg, Germany. If you have any concerns regarding our products, please contact ProductSafety@springernature.com

Printed and bound by CPI Group (UK) Ltd, Croydon, CR0 4YY
30/09/2026
02225455-0015